COOKING

FOR

LIFE

A GUIDE FOR THE WELL-BEING OF MAN

by Michel Abehsera

Swan House

Published by Swan House
P.O. Box 638
Binghamton, New York 13902

Manufactured in the United States of America
Second Printing

TO GEORGES OHSAWA

I AM INFINITELY GRATEFUL

Contents

viii

ACKNOWLEDGMENTS

This book would have never been completed without the help of my wife Claude. Most of the recipes are hers; she cooked, tested and wrote them down, which was not an easy work. Ella Dichter helped her in the kitchen and helped us both in the preliminary correction of our English. Jack Garvy completed the editing of the book and made definite English corrections. My exceptional friend William Dufty gave valuable advice. Finally my brother Charles was very helpful with the proofreading and the art work. To all of them I am very grateful.

COOKING FOR LIFE

Foreword

Ten years ago I was a sick man, struggling to stay alive and to finish a novel. I suspected I might fail in both matters and the doctors of Paris agreed. They abandoned me as a hopeless case.

It was then that I discovered a way of life called Macrobiotics. After a year of eating grains and vegetables, my health restored, I ventured to New York to discover America and to finish my novel.

But my book faltered, and the "New World" seemed in a bad physical and emotional state too, and I found that the force of my will was focused in another direction: I wanted to write, of all things, -a cookbook.

A few years ago, I would have ridiculed such an idea. But now a sense of justice and gratitude compelled me to write about how food-simple, good food- had changed and regenerated my life. In a small way, I hoped, my book might help cure America's multitude of ills.

That first book was called ZEN MACROBIOTIC COOKING. This sequel, COOKING FOR LIFE, has been made necessary by the most common phenomenon of all life: Change. A man changes, his view broadens and deepens, and hopefully he understands more fully the philosophy underlying his recipes. Most important of all, times change. COOKING FOR LIFE contains all I know about the "miraculous" diet and its philosophy.

Recently, with my wife and daughters, I visited my family in France. I met old friends I hadn't seen in years.

- "What happened to the novel?" they wanted to know.

- "I'm not sick enough anymore to finish it," I explained. "I've written a cookbook."

- "A cookbook? Are you serious?"

- "America has plenty of disturbed novelists." I said. "What's needed are some good healthy recipes that will help create better writers and better books."

- "But what about your poetry? Have you given it up?"

- "Absolutely not," I answered. "We try to create our poetry in the kitchen."

Woman in the kitchen

A good wife who can find?
She is far more precious than jewels.
The heart of her husband trusts in her,
and he will have no lack of gain.
She does him good, and not harm,
all the days of her life.
She seeks wool and flax,
and works with willing hands.
She is like the ships of the merchant;
she brings her food from afar.

Proverbs 31, 10-14

Poetry is in the kitchen where pans and pots, warmly colored, hang upon brick walls, waiting to participate in the feast of Man. Flames are the makers of our joys and pains. Wooden spoons are pirouetting dancers that deeply stir the soups and sauces which will satisfy the insatiable guest, Man. Knives cut green leaves for his bloodstream, and boards are for kneading his ancestral bread.

The kitchen is the heart of the home. A happy woman in her kitchen fills everyone in the house with joy. She forgets no one; she is like the old lady in the park who never fails to feed her friends, the birds, even on the coldest and gloomiest days. A woman's happiness is a healing elixir; her presence is a comfort when, as mother and wife, she places a hand upon a feverish brow and softly says, "Everything will be all right." You are cured by that simple touch as if it were her blood she had given. Her love for you comes from far, far away, perhaps just from the memory of you as her natural coach to the heavens. She cooks every day for the promised voyage.

Now she is in the kitchen preparing supper for her husband. She smiles over a vision of him, cold and hungry—how his eyes will open in amazement and delight when she places before him a new and lovely dish! She tells her nearby child that his father will be in a good mood tonight.

"Ask him for the bicycle after supper!" she says confidently to her son.

She washes her hands between cutting the vegetables and kneading the bread, and she sings an old song. Her gestures are as graceful as those of the waltzing flowers of the field. She makes no false and violent movements with the spoon with which she stirs the soup. She turns it one way and keeps with patience and ease the direction of the spiral. The milk she once gave to her child has taken new form; it is now in the pots and pans which she handles with love and care. Utensils are part of her body; that is why she likes to choose herself their volumes and shapes.

Now the man returns home and, while she serves the dinner, he tells her about his day. She sprinkles parsley and croutons on a barley soup, ladles out brown rice along with boiled and broiled cauliflower that sizzles under a white bechamel sauce. Red beans, black seaweeds and carrots sprinkled with toasted sesame seeds provide a colorful complement. Either poetry is in this dish or there is no poetry at all for this food comes as a favor from heaven to man, ennobling his everyday acts.

I judge a man not by what he tells me, but by how he says it. His movements and voice carry him farther than he wishes to go. They betray him each time he rises, moves, sits, eats. The act is the pen of the man of God; the word is the sacred commentary of the movement of life. Those who see a difference are unworthy, ungrateful and ignorant men whose dualistic thinking teaches them to distinguish between verb and flesh.

I judge a man by the happiness of his wife and not by what paradise he promises to the world. If he is a great man, I will eat at his table and then tell you how true are the rumors of his grandeur. If his wife is unhappy, she will cook with a sad face and a bitter heart, and the meal will make of him a false prophet whose scorn of others is actually an indictment of himself. Men blame others because they are not happy with themselves. Their philosophies are always born of defects, not strength. Had they married better women, better cooks, they would be welcomed as poets of the people.

Politics and wars are but symptoms of the hunger of men who have been ill-fed. Struggling all their lives toward a giant feast of conquest and power, they could long ago, in their youths, have been satisfied by a simple bowl of rice. Their mothers were bad cooks and now they suffer under their wives, whose use of devilish spices creates a permanent urge toward dominion.

But now is the time for poets to bring their pens to the kitchen. It is urgent that new recipes founded in love and peace be written.

The cook
is a philosopher

In Chinese, Yin means inertia and darkness, while Yang means dynamism and light.

The process which tends to concentrate energy is called centripetal force. On the contrary, the process that moves an element toward dematerialization, into a loss of its physical cohesion, is called centrifugal force. Yang is centripetal while Yin is centrifugal.

Yin is passive and receptive. It is Space, the moon, cold. It is the water which enters everywhere and assumes all forms. It is the feminine woman whose husband is the master of the house.

Yang is active, creative, energetic. It is the sun, fire. It is Time contracted in consciousness. It is the man whose sentences are short and clear and whose wife listens with respect and obeys with delight.

That which is physically light is Yin, and that which is heavy is Yang. This is the point of view of the man who looks at things of the earth and uses them for practical purposes.

Red, orange and yellow are Yang; they tend to approach us. Blue, purple and green keep their distance, or seem to recede.

A high-pitched sound is Yin. It rises in centrifugal, expansive movement. A low sound is Yang, as is the voice of a deep baritone.

So when the cook-philosopher perceives an apple, he says, "Of all fruits, this one is Yang because it is compact and not so juicy." Then looking at a watermelon, he says, "It is Yin. The apple is round and small, while the watermelon is much bigger and juicier. The former grows in a colder climate than the latter."

Any vegetable that grows deep into the ground is more or less Yang. Carrots, burdock and turnips are more Yang than asparagus, which reaches its full height in only a few days. Above the ground, anything that grows rapidly and upward is often very Yin. That which grows close to the ground and slowly is more Yang. This explains how Time can make things Yang.

Tropical fruits are Yin; their potassium content is very high. Strawberries and apples are more Yang; they have less potassium and more sodium. Knowing that potassium is Yin and sodium is Yang, the balance everyone is looking for is easy to find. It is of course different for every individual, varying with (among other things) climatic conditions and amount of activity.

Balance between Yin and Yang means the best possible health of body and mind. So the choice is easy to make for everyone according to his basic constitution, his daily condition and his purpose—what he may wish to build or create that day, that year, or during his lifetime.

* * *

To understand Yin one must study Yang. We say that a woman is feminine because we know that Man is masculine. The word feminine would have no meaning otherwise.

To understand Yin and Yang, one must not only compare them to one another but must also discover their interrelationships in nature. We know that according to the law of the universe, Yin produces Yang and Yang produces Yin. Many people require coffee in the morning to start the day. Coffee is very Yin—it produces instant Yang. The man who does not understand proper balance and drinks a dozen cups of coffee a day just to keep himself going, is almost a mechanical man. It is the same with athletes who must drink enormous amount of liquid in order to finish a game.

A cerealian, who usually drinks little, cannot produce the activity of a football player. The shape of his body is quite different. That's why the cerealian does not take part in strenuous sports. He practices more subltle games. He does not contain the excess liquid of a basketball player, who is ten pounds lighter after a contest.

Fear, which is Yin, is dramatically accentuated by an uncommon action, Yang—fear of fire, of war, of the enemy, and so on. Any overwhelming action produces pathological phenomena in a Yin and weak person. The activity of people in the south is slowed by the Yang sun. On the contrary, cold brings about a Yang contraction in the body. If a man does not move, he freezes to death. This is the reason why peoples of the north are very active.

* * *

Standing on the deck of a ship, a philosopher says, "The sea is Yin." Then the ship sails northward to where cold has transformed sea-water into immense icebergs. The philosopher views them with wonder and says, "Ice is Yin." The ship again returns to warmer waters and the philosopher, smiling to himself, says, "Ah! water is Yang compared to mountains of ice."

Yes, water is Yin. It is expansive. It flows and fills every form that holds it. But when cold freezes it, it becomes even more Yin. Ice is very Yin, although it appears contracted. If one places a bottleful of water inside a freezer, it will burst within a few hours; the water has expanded and crystallized.

That which is expanding is becoming Yin. That which is contracting is becoming Yang. When one buys a vegetable and cooks it over the fire, one is "Yangizing" it. Fire, being Yang, makes the vegetable shrink by evaporating most of its water. If one compares a vegetable fresh from the market with another that has been cooked, one finds that the former is Yin and the latter is Yang. Fire has made the difference in a matter of a few minutes.

If desirous of reversing the process, changing Yang to Yin, simply add water or any Yin liquid. Soya sauce, for example, is a Yang condiment. For some it is much too strong to take in pure form over tempura or vegetables. To Yinnize it, just add a few drops of water or any other form of Yin—two or three drops of lemon for a salad, tahini for a sauce, etc. One can change anything into Yin or Yang by using only fire or water.

Quantity also makes a difference.

Consider the man who has studied the philosophy of Yin and Yang for several years. Offered a quarter of an apple, he refuses it, but then proceeds to make a fool of himself by stuffing his belly with a bowl of brown rice, a dish of vegetables, a soup, and again more vegetables and soup, then tea with bread and spread. Is this man anything but blind? Hasn't his fear of Yin paralyzed his good sense? The volume of what he has eaten is Yin compared to the so-called Yin fruit. Quantity has changed quality. It *is preferable to eat a small amount of Yin than a great deal of balanced food!*

A cook in the fields

The greatest delight which the fields and woods
minister is the suggestion of an occult relation
between Man and the vegetable.

R. W. Emerson

"Adama" is the Hebrew name for Earth, whose first son and husband
was Adam, the Man. To become Man is to undertake that same long and
adventurous journey from the biological to the spiritual. If you acquaint yourself with the love-stories of Nature, you will come to understand the secret ways of Man; for Nature is his abiding home. With
their four seasons the fields sing the eternal melody of his sunsets
and dawns.

Nature nourishes man and he returns to her the seed she requires for
each new season. She serves him unconditionally throughout his lifetime. He is her legitimate and natural son, and she is the irreplaceable
mother who possesses no favorites among her offspring. She gives
abundantly to whoever wishes to drink and eat. Her table is dressed
with the same cloth for poor and rich alike, for kings as well as serfs. Her
rich gold and silver tableware is displayed in bright and natural settings
amongst waters and soil. Her capital is infinite, her humility never dis-
cussed—she gives without expecting a thing in return.

12

Man is first of all a biological entity. He cannot avoid that stage without becoming inorganic matter. Chlorophyl is transformed into his blood. This transmutation precedes all higher activity.

Everything turns into its opposite—the physical becomes the spiritual. The bread we eat changes into speech and, ultimately, prayer to God. The proverb, "Man does not live by bread alone," implies that what we eat is the counterpart and precondition of our spiritual existence. And truly, Man cannot live by bread alone if what he eats fails to become his blood. Man must be able to transmute his food into his actions and thoughts. Each different dish becomes tomorrow's unique adventure. Man's figure and spirit must reflect his biological heritage.

* * *

Bad soil is like those pink and well-studied mirrors that fancy department stores use to flatter their clientele; they distort more than they reflect a true image. Good soil, however, is free of all foreign matter. It has no need for artificial manure or mixed compost of any sort—even animal excrement. Manure gives good results for the first few years, but afterwards the soil suffers a loss of energy. Its health deteriorates like the health of a man who abuses his body with symptomatic "cures" in an effort to dispel disease.

A simple farmer knows all there is to know about natural agriculture. He realizes that he must have a pure soil and that he must judiciously apply his knowledge of climate. Nothing more is necessary.

Good grains, vegetables and fruits grow in fields free of manure or chemical compost. People who have eaten for years the pale and saddened carrots bought at neon-lighted stands do not realize that *these are not carrots at all.* They possess a character completely foreign to anyone with a good memory for the way they used to taste.

Believe me, the carrot is sick! The cabbage also! And so are all the others who hide their faces in the earth, ashamed of their pestilence! The taste of a good vegetable should awaken and stimulate Man's acutest sense, should tickle his physical and psychological palate. A good taste should resemble a note of music in that it can be raised or lowered

and still please the ear. But today's counterfeiters of the vegetable kingdom have forgotten altogether the quality of the real thing. It is as
though they were producing orange dollar-bills.

Beauty is not only in the form but in the meaning. A beautiful
vegetable is not necessarily as straight as a soldier on parade. It is dis-
concerting to see priced and packaged carrots of the same form and size
lined up like legionnaires in supermarkets. It amounts to a biological
communism, to a brutal indoctrination of the vegetable world. In fact,
it has become so difficult to choose a vegetable (or rather, so easy, since
everything looks the same) that nowadays one has to develop new
techniques when buying food. So be careful of the Table of Food, the
classification from Yang to Yin, given later in this book. It is purely
academic. In the modern marketplace one must be continually alert to
the changes wrought in carrots and cauliflowers, pumpkins and peas, by
the chemical industry and the farmer it has so successfully duped.

The cerealian's dictionary

> All religions have lost their authority
> because they have neglected by ignorance
> to maintain and teach their dietetic rules.
>
> Georges Ohsawa

Nothing is more inspiring and beautiful on a kitchen shelf than a bag of grain. It is a true companion whose promise is to impart life and understanding to the body and spirit. One partakes of its simplicity and is rendered safe from the complexities of the world.

Brown Rice is the staple of the cerealian who does not wish to involve himself in the difficult process of balancing food. Brown rice assures him of proper nourishment. It is the most balanced cereal, the only grain which contains nearly all of the ingredients our body needs, either directly or through the process of transmutation.

For nine years now I have eaten brown rice every single day. Long ago, for a period of one month, I substituted other grains. However, we all come back to brown rice sooner or later, for its taste and practicality —and for a thousand other reasons. I am grateful to the Japanese and Chinese who made it known to the Occident, thus providing me with a cure for my diseases.

There are a number of varieties of brown rice—the short, the long and the very long. Short-grain rice is the most suitable for cold climates and the most satisfying for those who have given up meat.

Wheat is the grain of my native country, Morocco, where people prepare it in different ways. Sentimentally, I am more attracted to it than any other grain. My childhood is bound up with it. I remember its aroma floating in the air at Jam El Fna in Marrakech, mingling with the fine strong spices of the street-merchants. You eat couscous at Hassan's Restaurant and memories of exotic nights surround you like a bouquet. That is how foreign adventurers, especially American writers, are seduced by the romance of North Africa.

Bulghur and Cracked Wheat are the dishes of the poor. They do not catch the eye like couscous, but appeal to a more elemental level. They are the most nourishing and faithful companions of Oriental travellers, who cook them during brief stopovers, for they are quickly prepared and require no seasoning.

In taste and form, *Barley* is the young prince, son of its king, Father Wheat. In digestibility it is a cousin to rice. Although not often used, it should be, for it is perhaps the noblest of the grains. In Morocco it is a common alternative to wheat, and in Korea and Japan monks mix it with white rice when the brown variety is unavailable.

Buckwheat is to Russians what rice is to Japanese. Called "kasha" by American Jews, it is still cooked in hot knishes sold on the lower East Side of New York City. True kasha knish is now rare. Its buckwheat flavor is perhaps too strong for the conditioned tongues of uptown ladies, who prefer it mixed with potato and flavored with black pepper.

Millet is an underrated grain whose light bitterness makes it as masculine as a cerealian could wish. It has been used in almost every civilization in history, from China to Africa, where it is cooked with onions and other vegetables. Some people prepare it with scallions and flavor it with dill. A multi-purpose grain, millet is very alkaline and makes deliciously sweet croquettes.

The word *Rye* has a magical sound. It has made me dream more than once of the bread my mother used to make in Morocco. On the road, or at home in the kitchen, chatting with friends, there is nothing humbler and simply satisfying than warm rye bread accompanied by black olives. I have eaten all kinds of rye bread in the U.S.A., but none matches the

Moroccan, whose grain grows in old and flavorful grounds and whose mills still grind with ancestral stones.

Corn is the sacred grain whose kernels satisfied stomach, eye and spirit of the American Indian. It was used all year round in the form of flour or bread, shelled or "on the cob." Meanwhile, the French fed it to pigs, fattening them for the fair. In Paris I have seen it being sold in fine stores in the chic Sixteenth Arrondissement, between Metro Passy and Ranelagh. Exquisite ladies buy it with the same expression of discernment on their faces that snobs evince when tasting a rare dish at a *café louche*, downtown.

Corn is the grain that accompanies a smaller amount of rice during the hottest months of the year.

Oats are eaten by horses as well as by the Scotch, who find it better to draw nigh the stable than to neigh in the freezing cold. Oats can be served as creams or soups for breakfast, lunch or dinner, in breads and cookies, or in anything that needs a little something to make it fluffy and crisp. A Scotchman might say of oats that they are "the hot dame of the bellies."

A grain-eater is like a jeweler who artfully prepares and displays a rare diamond. Although grains may not be as varied as gems, they have dazzled just as many eyes in history. The stone-lover uses platinum, silver and gold for showing off his rarities; the man of rice, wheat and corn possesses an equal cast. He sets grains off with condiments, vegetables and black and green seaweeds from the bottom of the Japanese seas. He has numerous teas, fine oils and salted plums for vinegar. He is an artisan not only of flowers, but also of roots. Nor are sauces forgotten in his craft.

Natural-food stores all over the U.S.A. now carry cerealian staples. Below, classified according to family (i.e., beans, seaweeds, etc.), are the more important products. Please do not use them rigidly. Creativity, as well as practicality, should be a byword of cooking and eating.

Beans

Aduki Beans are small red beans imported from Japan. In ancient China old men, a few years prior to dying, subsisted almost exclusively on them because experience had taught that, when their bodies were exhumed two years after death, they would not emit a foul smell. Although we use Adukis quite often at home, it is not for the aforegoing reason—I have other aspirations than to preserve my remains uncorrupted.

Adukis are appropriate anywhere, anytime, cooked with brown rice or any other grain. They enhance a dish with their earthly red color, and make excellent soups and pies.

Black Beans, twin brothers of the red aduki in size, are sold in Chinese, Japanese and natural-food stores. They are the milk and honey of the bean family, and their flavor and texture impart a delightful sweetness and richness to any soup or vegetable dish.

Chick-peas, or Garbanzo Beans, are the bread of the "pulse" -eater. I have a great-uncle, eighty-five years old, whose sole food consists of dried chick-peas and lentils. Additionally, he eats couscous on Friday nights, with nothing but chick-peas and vegetables on the side. He has been doing that for seventy years! And believe me, he is as healthy as a man can be. Some scientists have recently reported that whole-wheat and chick-peas are sufficient to fulfill a man's dietary requirements. Combined, they equal the properties of brown rice. If those same scientists would like living proof, I'll be happy to introduce them to my great-uncle.

The chick-pea is the Middle-Eastern aduki. It adapts perfectly well to couscous and vegetables. "Humus Tahina," and more recently the "Falafel" (an Israeli sandwich made of Syrian bread filled with salad and chick-pea croquettes) have popularized it. The unhappy and frustrated vegetarian, who craves a bit of meat, should try it as a beef-substitute.

Noodles

Soba is the noodle Marco Polo presumably brought with him from China, later Italianized and called "macaroni." It is made with buckwheat. A similar noodle, made with whole wheat and lighter in color, is called *Udon.* Both are prepared from whole grains in the traditional manner.

Soba is served burning hot in Tokyo, where people are in too great a hurry to chew rice. They swallow it, as it were, between thoughts, standing or sitting at one of the thousands of noodle-shops. Soba is a handy and delightful meal when friends drop in, best served with hot bouillon and sprinkled with nori and scallions.

Somen are long thin noodles, practical for soups and special dishes. They are not a complete food and are used in our home mainly for appearance and flavor.

Seaweeds

Seaweeds everyone remembers, having been alarmed by the unpleasantness of their touch while swimming. As children, we thought they might be sea-monsters.

Hijiki resembles thick black hair and tastes like noodles soaked in sea-water. A grain without hijiki on the side is like a pie-dough without filling. It is excellent for the heavy meat-eater who needs a cleansing.

Kombu looks like dark green ribbons. We often use it in soups, dishes and as a condiment. It is a delight when deep-fried in oil or toasted in a very hot oven. It has a taste unlike anything you've ever had before.

Wakame is a very tender seaweed especially good when cooked with onions or scallions. We use it in Miso soup, which we enjoy almost every day. Excellent for a healthy growth of hair.

Nori has the advantage of being in many ways the most practical. It comes in pressed, paper-thin sheets with which the Japanese prepare their famous Nori Maki. The sheet is dark brown, but when passed rapidly over a flame it turns a crisp, toasted green. We use it for rice balls or simply, when reduced to crumbs, over rice and noodles.

Dulse looks like chopped nori. It has such a strong taste and is so naturally spicy, that serving it to a friend runs the risk of alienating him.

Agar Agar makes a firm jelly for desserts. Its uses are unlimited. When diluted in water, heated, mixed with vegetables or fish and cooled, it provides an amateur cook with what he has previously seen only in photographs—a true aquarium-like aspic with carrots, parsley and striped bass all caught in dramatic stop-action.

The Wild Vegetables

Japanese stores and some natural-food stores and vegetable stands sell the following roots. Be sure to learn their uses.

Burdock grows wild in fields and gardens and is very difficult to unearth, so deep is its root. It is a cousin of the dandelion, whose struggle for survival in the spring is nonetheless legendary despite its ill fate. Gardeners dislike them both. Burdock, however, receives special attention from root-eaters, who prize it for its tasts and food value.

Ginger Root: A tiny bit of ginger, grated and boiled with bancha tea and soya sauce, is an excellent diaphoretic in cases of cold. Sometimes we add a tablespoon of grated daikon to make the remedy more palatable.

There is nothing more appropriate for a slice of halibut or swordfish than, before broiling, to pre-soak it in soya sauce flavored with ginger.

Daikon is a Japanese radish which looks like a gigantic white carrot. Heavy eaters find it helpful after an exaggerated intake of liquid and food. It is a great aid to digestion. Besides its medicinal values, it has a subtle taste akin to the radish, nevertheless retaining its own unique quality. It is excellent raw, pickled or cooked. Japanese stores also sell it shredded and dried.

Lotus Root is sold in Chinatown in New York City and San Francisco. It is available fresh or dried. Fritters can be made by soaking and deep-frying it. Kohren tea is the name given to its powdered form, used mostly to fortify weak lungs.

Jinenjo must be growing somewhere in the mountains of the U.S.A. However, if you live on the plains it can be obtained at Japanese stores. A long and heavy root the size of a policeman's club, it tastes like potato when sliced and deep-fried in oil. For the cerealian, jinenjo is a very strengthening food. When grated raw and mixed with soya sauce, it is excellent for anemia.

Condiments

Sesame Salt, or Gomasio, is a combination of toasted sesame seeds and genuine sea salt, ground together. It is a balanced table condiment, good for people who tend to drink too much. One uses it sprinkled on grains and vegetables.

Soya Sauce is also called Tamari or Shoyu in Japan. Good-quality Tamari is twice as expensive as the chemicalized, quickly-processed variety. Made from wheat, soya beans and water, it is fermented over a period of two years. We always have some in our home. It is used in sauteed vegetables, soups, sauces, fish, etc.

Miso is a soya-bean paste made from the same ingredients as soya sauce. It is used in the famous Miso Soup, enhances the taste of a pâté, and makes good spreads and sauces. Unique in value, its richness has no limit and plays a most important role in body metabolism. It is a great energy-source for those wishing to accomplish hard work.

Seitan: Your guests will almost certainly mistake this for meat. Teeth find it pleasant to chew. A combination of wheat gluten, wheat soya beans, water and salt, it comes in handy when mixed with vegetables, sauces and soups.

Salted Plums, or Umeboshi, are Japanese plums pickled in salt for three years. For centuries the Japanese have been using them to make the best-tasting and most harmless vinegar. They have hundreds of practical and successful medicinal uses.

Sesame Butter, in Arabic countries, is known as Tahini or Tahina. Its uses are unlimited—if your imagination is! It makes a delicious spread when mixed with miso, and is excellent in sauces, creams, cookies and custards.

Tofu is another name for soya-bean curd. In Chinatown, you'll see it in wooden barrels. It looks like Feta Greek Cheese and some people would swear it tastes like chicken. It is excellent served with sauteed vegetables, sauces, fried or cooked in Miso Soup.

Kuzu can be bought in any natural-food store. It is a twin brother of arrow-root. While kuzu is most often used for colds and digestive troubles, arrow-root is used for thickening sauces and pie fillings. The former grows in the mountains, so it is very Yang. The latter grows in hotter climates and is therefore more Yin.

Bonita (or Bonito) and *Chirimen Iriko* are sold in Japanese markets and in Chinatown. Chirimen Iriko is a tiny fish, the size and shape of a vermicelli noodle. Bonita comes in a hard stone-like form or shredded and packaged. Both are excellent for flavoring soup stocks.

Sea Salt is not the conditioned, sparkling salt usually sold in grocery stores. The true one comes from the ocean, while the other comes from laboratories. There is a gray, unwashed kind which we use in our home, and there is a lighter one which has been previously washed in sea-water. Both of these contain many natural mineral salts. Some cerealians roast their salt before using it to liberate excess chlorine gas.

The Yin and Yang story

There was a time when Yin and Yang worked
harmoniously and the spirits of men and beasts
did not interfere with the life of the people,
when the four seasons were in order and all
creation was unharmed and the people did not
die young.

Chuang-Tzu

Harmony is the word that perfectly sums up all that can be said
about Yin and Yang.

When Yin Meets Yang anywhere in this world, they produce an illuminating spark that brightens the spirit. Of this union is born the true
miracle of life.

The Law of this visible universe is the continual vacillation of all
things between these two activities and their innumerable tribulations.
The man of antiquity guided himself by these laws and thus governed
his world. Days were spent hunting or working in the fields, while at
night he found rest. The clarity of day and opaqueness of night created
his equilibrium.

Man knew something of primordial importance — the metamorphoses of the night were different from those of the day. The effect of light upon plants did not resemble the effect of darkness — neither did action of Time resemble action of Space. Night could only give birth to day.

Woman and Man are as different from each other as Yin is from Yang, yet they form one body when they meet. The instant of their ultimate encounter, lovers become one and are transported into invisible realms.

Dawn is the gray instant in which night and day momentarily observe one another. However, everything is in a flux of perpetual change, and dawn, which unites darkness and light, also separates them. In this universe, all that seems stable is only ephemeral.

Yin and Yang attract one another mutually as air is drawn to a burning flame. Woman attracts Man; if she fails to do so, she loses her feminine qualities and dies alone, exiled from her source of harmony.

No relative thing is absolute, be it passive (Yin) or active (Yang), and everything is meaningfully characterized only when it is compared to that which is already existing. Ice is passive while water is active. But the philosopher who has sailed the ocean will say that the river is passive and calm.

The wise man knows that there is no being or object in this visible universe that is not active. Everything is perpetually changing. Nothing rests, not even the silent night which is the diurnal mother of light.

Opposites attract. Their forces of attraction are augmented proportionally to the degree of their antagonistic activity. A particular activity does not attract that which resembles it; their forces of repulsion increase gradually in proportion to the degree of their resemblance. A man of angry temperament seeks peace with a woman of sweet manner and voice.

All that is internally active is externally passive. The pregnant passive woman quietly guards and cherishes within her the energy of life itself.

* * *

Philosophers have too often preoccupied themselves with their own ideas and not with the laws of the universe, from which they should learn the first of all truths — the one that every philosopher worth his salt should know — namely, that an idea has a destiny only if it can help a simple man toward health or happiness, starting tomorrow morning. However magnificent their concepts, few philosophers lived them through to the end with conviction, first of all because they were impractical, and second, because they had no foundation.

The truth of an idea is judged by its realization in practice, and at the utmost in its material metamorphosis. As the word *work* implies a precise and practical form, so any idea should realize itself in some degree every day — otherwise, it is only the whisper of an illusion.

It is not philosophy that determines life but the very opposite, life determines philosophy. If one seeks consciousness, it should be Absolute Consciousness or none at all. Hence, those who desire only a relative knowledge of the world are misguided by their senses, because even a relative consciousness is as difficult to apprehend as one that is absolute. That which seems relative is but one phase of the Infinite. If you want the elephant alive, take him whole.

This universe is a unity and we can only understand it through knowledge of its Law. One may try to know it by touch, sight or smell; but these are only sense perceptions which do not suffice. One can seek it through sentiment, intellect, social awareness or ideologies, but these means also are relative and will end in nothing but anxiety and loneliness.

When one wants knowledge, it is necessary to apply oneself to the study of not only the laws of the senses, but to those that assemble this universe. The man who knows does not often insert himself into the intellectual debates of his time. In his eyes such debates are symptomatic of chaotic, fragmentary knowledge. For him, the infinite alphabet, all that is knowable in philosophy or science, can only be apprehended through the profound study of Yin and Yang.

* * *

When in the beginning of September the last summer days are mellowed by a soft moist breeze, and the migratory birds fly southward on tireless wings, when autumn is no longer far away and only a few tender nights remain to be enjoyed, then the great Yang is but a memory.

And when gray December days bring snow, and cold forces people indoors so that the streets seem desolate and naked, the great Yin makes its appearance. Thus goes the world, from summer to winter, from Yang to Yin and Yin to Yang, eternally.

Plant, animal and Man — all living beings — follow this Law. If they refuse to, they condemn themselves to misery, sickness and death.

Man adapts himself to nature by necessity. He also does so for his freedom, because all that conforms to Yin and Yang is free.

To be a man is to be free of all exaggerated desires as well as their opposite, asceticism. To be a man is to take that middle course which makes of two extremes an equilibrium.

When a man refuses to conform to the Law he allows himself to be swayed by the indicator on a scale that is continually thumbed to a false reading by some diabolical merchant. Such a man's life is spent in compulsion and disorder.

He who conforms to the Law is gratified by it; he who refuses is destroyed.

Yin produces Yang by instinct and desire to create. A man who does not create is a Yang not far from involuntary suicide. Creation is the mother of Harmony. He who frustrates his deep desire to create precipitates imbalance.

The barren woman in her forties seeks equilibrium in sexuality or in the study of esoteric philosophies. Thousands of such women wander into the world of spiritualism, hoping to conceive an internal life that a child could have provided in an instant. Through sexuality — with a child for sign — they might have created the Spirit itself.

* * *

The deep root in the damp, unfathomable night brings forth from its abode luminous leaves. Darkness gives birth to light.

Dry earth gives forth mellow fruits; humid earth develops firm fruits, as rice grows upon water. That which is Yin produces that which is Yang.

Hot African earth furthers the growth of tall plants that are heavy with big, juicy fruits. The cold earth of North America, however, produces shorter plants with smaller, drier fruit. That which grows in a hot climate cannot tolerate the cold. For Yin can only produce Yang, and vice versa.

Yin fundamentally differs from Yang as night differs from day. But they have need of each other in order to survive and procreate, together producing their offspring. They are opposed to one another by structure, but are complimentary in their function.

Time is subjective. It passes quickly. It is active in consciousness and memory. Conversely, Space is objective and passive, with neither past nor future.

The sun and moon, objects in Space, give us on earth our sense of Time. Thus Space produces Time. Both produce all things on earth, in measurements of hour and volume.

Eternity seems to be simultaneously the mother and daughter of this pendular movement which fluctuates between Space and Time, Yin and Yang, in an unceasing and regular flow.

* * *

Yin is ephemeral. Yang is ephemeral. They produce the realities of life, which at times seem only illusory. Everything depends on the position of the observer.

He who lacks equilibrium changes his opinion every day. At times he sees a nightmare, at times a dream. He who has found harmony is conscious of the ephemerality of things and consequently acts intelligently, making of illusion his own reality, his own dream, everyday.

The promised land

Those who like and perpetually eat much fruit become with time suspicious, jealous, fearful, hesitant and chilly beings who often end in heart disease.

Georges Ohsawa

There is nothing in this chapter that you cannot eat, be it Yin or Yang. Everything is permitted. "Know thyself," and then choose from this table whatever you like.

Understand an important point—that Yang is no better than Yin, in food or in any other form. If I have, like many people, developed a preference for a limited number of vegetables, it is only for practical reasons. It is, for example, easier to balance a Yang vegetable than a Yin one. That which is very Yin I seldom eat. Some people can drink more alcohol, while others get dizzy with the first glass. In like measure, for the time being I eat and drink what my body and mind can assimilate. Perhaps in the future, if I happen to live in a hot climate, I will include more Yin vegetables in my diet.

All cereals, vegetables, fruits, etc., classified below from Yang to Yin, are to be chosen according to your own particular desires and condition. I will tell you what my own habits are, then you must choose for yourself. If you are living in a climate where it is cold six months of the year, as it is here in upper New York State, perhaps it would be safer to follow my "habits" as closely as you can. On the contrary, if you happen to live in a warmer climate, such as Southern California, it may be wiser for you to increase your intake of vegetables and fruits. In any event, as your judgment improves, your body will tell you what you should eat, and you will be better equipped to take care of yourself. See the chapter entitled "The Traveller's Pack—" for some advice for the summertime.

All this must seem to you like the start of a great adventure. It is, and most interesting of all, it is also the beginning of the sacred transmutation of Man. If you feel dizzy, it's a good sign! It's from exhilaration at the prospect of your *grand voyage!*

CEREALS

Buckwheat

Millet

Rice

Couscous*

Cracked wheat*

Bulghur*

Whole wheat

Rye

Oats

Barley

Corn

Buckwheat is more Yang than all other cereals. Next comes millet, then rice, which is more balanced. Those marked with an asterisk are made from processed wheat; we use them once or twice a week. They are as Yang as wheat. Rye, oats and barley are less Yang. Corn is the most Yin of all cereals.

VEGETABLES

Those we often use		Those we very seldom eat
Jinenjo	Turnip	Garlic
Burdock	Parsnip	Green pea
Dandelion Root	Kale	Mushroom
Salsify	Escarole	Bamboo shoot
Watercress	Endive	Artichoke
Coltsfoot	Lettuce	Spinach
Carrot	Dandelion leaves	Asparagus
Aduki beans	White cabbage	Cucumber
Acorn squash	Chinese cabbage	Beans (all kinds)
Butternut squash	Broccoli	Green and red pepper
Pumpkin	Cauliflower	Potato
Chick-peas	Brussel sprouts	Yam
Parsley	Lentils	Sweet potato
Onions	Small black beans	Tomato
Leeks	Beets	Eggplant
Scallions	Celery	
Radish	String beans	
Daikon	Swiss chard	
(white Japanese radish)		

Burdock is the most Yang of all available vegetables. Dandelion root runs a close second, with salsify not far behind. I overlook jinenjo, which is too difficult to find. Burdock is readily available in season, while salsify is rare. Once in a while we dig up a dandelion root from our garden. But all in all, these roots are only occasionally used in our home. What we enjoy most often are aduki beans, butternut and acorn squash, carrots, onions, leeks, scallions, turnips, cabbage, broccoli, and all others, when we can get them or when needed in a special recipe. I like beets sauteed or in salad; celery with or without fish; deep-fried or sauteed parsnip; radish in salad, chick-peas in soup, and so on. We seldom eat those vegetables listed in the right-hand column. In summer, we may use cucumber for a pickled salad; we may enjoy boiled asparagus accompanied by the juice of a salted plum; a piece of green pepper on a fish kebbab; or a spinach pie when friends come calling. We don't reject the others rigidly. However, we believe that some of them, such as potato, eggplant and tomato, are poisonous and unfit for human consumption. Still, perhaps for the fun of it or out of curiosity, I wouldn't refuse to taste them if they were offered to me.

In season

Apple
Strawberry
Chestnut
Cherry
Blackberry
Blueberry
Raspberry
Apricot
Peach
Hazel nut
Cashew
Peanut
Almond
Pecan
Walnut
Pear
Watermelon
Canteloupe
Orange
Tangerine
Grapefruit
Grapes
Prunes
Banana
Rhubarb
Mango
Avocado
Papaya
Dates
Pineapple
Coconut
Lime
Fig

FRUITS

"In season" means that we mostly eat what is locally grown. And there are no bananas or coconuts in upper New York State! In summer, of course, things change. We enjoy many of the fruits listed here—sparingly, though. We make blackberry, strawberry or cherry pies, which we sometimes sprinkle with crushed almonds. Occasionally, we have one or two slices of watermelon or canteloupe. But we have never eaten anything like papaya or avocado although, two or three times in the past three years, I have run to the fruit market to buy an orange, which I have devoured with great joy!

FISH

Caviar
Red snapper
Herring
Sardine
Mackerel
Shrimp
Tuna fish
Sword fish
Striped bass
Salmon
Sole
Flounder
Trout
Halibut
Mussel
Carp
Eel
Octopus
Clam
Oyster

We consider Caviar to be the most Yang and oyster to be the most Yin. We buy what is available and then try to cook something delicious and well-balanced. Red snapper is one of my favorites, but I have a strong liking, too, for sardines—perhaps because of good memories associated with them. I eat all the others, except shellfish. In our home, however, fish is rarely seen, especially now that we live in the country. It has been 3 months since we had our last bite of fish. For a time we ate it frequently —when we needed that lift animal food gives you. This happens to everyone who takes the trip from meat to cereals and vegetables. But we don't need that kind of drug anymore; we eat fish for enjoyment.

A friend once came to see me. He was literally green! "What have you done to yourself?" I asked. "Nothing at all, " he answered uneasily. "But you must have been eating a lot of fish." "Yes," he replied, "at least twice a day. Why? Is it wrong to eat it with some vegetables?" "Yes," I answered emphatically, astonished at his foolish conception of balanced food, "it is wrong to eat fish twice a day! How did you get into that? Who told you to do it?" "I've just been doing what the book says. Fish is okay, isn't it?" "Yes, it's okay," I said this time. "Continue on your present course and your face will soon turn black."

BEVERAGES

Ginseng*
Mu tea*
Yannoh*
Dandelion coffee
Bancha*
Sage
Mugwort
Camomile
Jasmin
Thyme
Mint
Water
Soda
Mineral water
Beer
Sake
Wine
Champagne
Whiskey
Soft drinks
Fruit juice
Regular coffee
Dyed tea

*See Chapter "How About A Drink?"

Ginseng is very Yang. It is more of a medicine than a beverage. It is better to avoid it. Mu tea—once in a while. Bancha, every day if you wish. Mugwort, camomile, jasmin and thyme are included to please the herbalist. In addition, they are quite beneficial for minor ailments. Water is water. In summer we drink it right from the spring to quench great thirst. Beer is a long story. The cerealian likes it because it is made of cereals. Ten years ago, I had never known the taste of it. Now, in summer, I enjoy it once in a while—an imported brand, of course! Sake? When offered. Whiskey? If at a gathering, I drink a drop of it and am immediately ready to sing "Madame Butterfly." As for coffee, last year I had two or three cups—and they were wonderful!

ANIMAL FOODS

Pheasant
Egg
Turkey
Duck
Partridge
Pigeon
Chicken
Hare
Horse
Beef
Pork
Frog
Snail

Eskimos live in a very cold climate. They eat seal in order to survive and accomplish their hard work.

While it is essential for icebound man to eat animal meat, people who live in warm and temperate climates generally fare better without eating flesh.

However, in special cases, pheasant or duck may provide the required swift shock to a languid man. And on occasion, fertile eggs and chicken are used sparingly to dress up a gala buffet.

DAIRY FOOD

Goat cheese
Sheep cheese
Goat milk
Dutch cheese
Roquefort
Gruyere
Camembert
Blue cheese
Milk
Margarine

Dairy food brought me directly to grains. Today I have forgotten how it once made me sick, so, every so often such as when I visit France, I have Camembert accompanied by an old red wine. The older the wine, the more expensive and better it is. Goat cheese is so Yang that one is compelled to balance it with something Yin, such as an imported beer. But truly, everything is fine when happiness reigns at the host's table.

MISCELLANEOUS

Black sesame oil
Corn germ oil
Corn oil
White sesame oil
Sunflower seed oil
Olive oil
Peanut oil
Soy oil
Safflower oil
Coconut oil
Margarine
Mayonnaise
Ketchup
Lard
Jams and jellies
Molasses
Syrups
Honey

The most Yang of oils is that which is made from sesame seeds. We use it for all sorts of things—for cookies, sauteing vegetables, etc. The oil we use most is corn oil. Corn germ oil is a new product which we are using quite often, for pastries and other delicacies. Olive oil is good for fish casseroles. Sunflower is more Yang and we sometimes prefer it in cookies, tempura, etc. We never use anything from peanut oil down to the bottom of the list, except honey, which we have enjoyed a few times in the past eight years.

* * *

About this Table of Food many people may say, "Why all the fuss over eating this in preference to that? What's there to worry about? What's so special about grains?"

I asked the same questions myself until the day I began choosing my food with care. I would have perhaps laughed at people eating only cereals, vegetables and a little fish, if I hadn't known what they were up to. It may seem strange to some, but the fact is that I actually feel no limitations at all upon myself. Using simple food sharpens the imagination and enables one to create true miracles.

We use little animal food, and avoid a few other things, but is this much to "give up" in comparison to those who, by refusing to eat simply, suffer the syndromes and traumas associated with meat, fruits and creams? What comes to our table is so rich in appearance and taste that I often wonder if I have actually lost anything at all "sensorially."

A few years ago a woman said to my wife, "You have no right to deprive your child "of chocolate". Her utterance indicated how sentimentally and deliberately she had obstructed the expansion of her mind. My daughter does not eat chocolate and can get along perfectly well without it. In fact, she is much better off without it.

This Table of Food has been prepared for sensitive people, for those who are willing to lose a few pounds as well as their fears, frustrations and sicknesses. It is not written for fools who believe that a full belly is to be desired, no matter with what it is stuffed.

Yin and Yang are necessary guides along the trail of philosophy who gradually show you how to balance your food. Don't make of them rigid and abstract concepts that spoil all your fun and pleasure. Look and listen carefully in order to develop better intuition.

Utensils

Not long ago I bought my wife a gift that astonished and pleased her more than a pearl necklace: a dozen cast-iron enameled pots imported from Europe. I spent more than I had spent on our kitchen in eight years of marriage. At the same time I also bought another dozen assorted heavy-ceramic French pots, oven-proof, of the sort she had always dreamed about. To this day, whenever she cooks in one of these pans or serves a vegetable or a casserole in one of the ceramic pots, she talks about how handy and beautiful they are.

And that is how I got her to improve her cooking!

The right utensils in a kitchen are necessary tools for good-quality cooking. Aluminum pots, apart from the fact that they produce poison when food is allowed to stand in them for any appreciable length of time, do not provide the fine taste that results from use of an earthenware or heavy enameled cast-iron pot.

Everyone should own a large wooden or enameled iron pan in which to knead bread. Here is a list of what we use most. I hope it inspires you to improve your cooking.

We always prepare rice, as well as most other grains, in a stainless steel *pressure-cooker,* thereby retaining all the nutritious elements which would normally evaporate in a standard pot—except for those with extremely heavy lids, which are practically impossible to find these days.

The only pot of this sort I have ever seen was in Gloria Swanson's kitchen. She got it from Sweden twenty years ago. It was so heavy I wondered how a woman as small as Gloria could possibly lift it. In ancient China pots had lids so heavy, two men were required to shift them into place.

A Japanese *steamer* is most important for heating rice or preparing couscous. It has many other uses, too. My wife finds it so practical that she continually invents excuses for employing it in the creation of dozens of breathtaking specialties. We used to make couscous in an aluminum steamer but now, since discovering this Japanese marvel, we depend exclusively on its practical size and safer material.

For cutting vegetables, my wife uses a *Japanese knife*, wide and square at its end. It is accompanied by a multi-purpose wooden *cutting board.* Before cutting the vegetables, she uses a special *brush* (Tawashi) that can be purchased in any Japanese store, with which she scrubs off dirt and mud under running water. We seldom peel vegetables—in fact, we do so only when they have been waxed by the farmer to protect them from spoiling in the cold.

For stirring soups and sauteing vegetables we have a set of *wooden spoons* of different sizes. For toasting flours and seeds, we use wooden *flat spatulas* or rice paddles, which are also very practical for serving grain. For delicate preparations my wife prefers *giant chopsticks* for stirring and turning vegetables.

To prepare sesame salt we have a special bowl a *suribachi,* and a wooden pestle. To make instant pickles we use a *salad press,* which is quite practical for spring and summer.

A *colander,* a must in every kitchen, comes in handy for rinsing noodles and washing fruits such as cherries or strawberries.

A metal or porcelain *grater* is definitely indispensable to the proper grating of ginger, garlic, etc. An *asbestos pad* is very practical to prevent creamy soups and sauces from burning.

And I shouldn't forget a *pot for deep frying*. We use one quite often. Japanese stores sell a good stainless-steel variety which includes a small moon-shaped *rack* that holds the deep-fried pieces in the top of the pot when they are removed from the oil. It also includes a *skimmer* for retrieving the fried food. My wife uses chopsticks now, having lost the skimmer somewhere during our move to the country.

A *grain mill* is as important as the stove in your kitchen. Freshly ground flours make better bread, and cereal creams ground at home retain qualities of wholesomeness and superior taste, missing in ordinary packaged flours.

Fried Rice

2 cups brown rice
4 cups water
¼ tsp sea salt
2 TBS oil
6 scallions, sliced thinly
1 stalk celery,
  sliced thinly
1 carrot, cut into
  matchsticks
2 or more TBS soy sauce

Wash rice thoroughly in cold water. Add water and salt and bring to a boil. Allow to boil for a few minutes, then reduce heat and simmer, covered, for 1 hour. OR, cook in a pressure cooker with 3 cups water for 45 minutes. Either way, an asbestos pad placed under the pot while cooking will prevent scorching. This is a basic recipe for plain brown rice.

Curried Rice

1½ cups brown rice
4 cups water
1 tsp sea salt
2 TBS oil
1 clove garlic, slivered
½ cup chopped onion
½ cup chopped green pepper
½ cup sunflower seeds
½ cup raisins
¼ tsp curry powder
  (or to taste)

Wash rice, then bring to a boil with 3 cups water and salt. Let boil for a minute, then reduce heat and simmer, covered, about 1 hour. Meanwhile place frying pan on medium heat and add oil. When oil is hot add garlic; stir for a moment until brown, add onion and stir a minute more. Add green pepper, seeds, and a pinch of salt and stir another minute or two;

(over)

Cooking brown rice

A man who cannot cure himself and cannot realize his own freedom, his own happiness and absolute justice, by himself, without the help of the others and of any mechanical instrument, is created to be exploited and devoured by the others, to feed worms and microbes. He has no need to go to hell after death for he is living in hell.

Georges Ohsawa

Before cooking rice you should learn the ritual of selection and preparation. First, determine if the rice you have is of good quality. To be sure, buy it at a natural-food store. Second, choose a rice that is short-grained, especially if you live in a cold climate. The shorter it is, the better. Make certain it is not too old, discolored or scratched.

There are many ways to cook it. In our house we have found a pressure-cooker, most practical. It is faster, minerals are more efficiently retained, and the rice is tastier. For people who eat rice only occasionally and therefore have more time to watch over it, cooking in an earthenware pot might be more appropriate and pleasurable. For us it is another story; by employing a pressure-cooker we can still take care of the many other side-dishes that accompany our principal food.

Wash the pressure-cooker well and fill with the desired amount of rice. Try not to use more than half the cooker or the rice may go overboard and fail to cook well. It may also burn because of insufficient water. (Try 1 cup rice for 1¼ or 1½ cups water.)

Cover with lid and set over high flame. When the pressure-regulator begins jiggling, lower flame to simmering point. Let cook for 45 minutes or so. It should then be done. If it has burned, the cause may be a flame kept too high during the simmering-period. Lower it a bit next time. If the rice is too wet, or even uncooked, it may be that the flame was too low. If it is mushy, too much water was used.

When you have turned off the gas, wait approximately 5 minutes, or until there is no more pressure. Remove the regulator. Open when you can see no more steam escaping.

If you do not have a pressure-cooker, use an enameled cast-iron pot or something equally as practical, such as fire-proof glassware or a stainless-steel pot.

Cooking rice in a pot.

Wash rice. This time use 3 cups of water for 1 cup rice. Add salt and cover. The lighter the lid, the more evaporation you can expect. When water starts boiling, lower the flame and let it simmer for 45 minutes to 1 hour. It might even take longer to cook, depending on the quality of the pot.

I have friends who like their morning rice to have a softer consistency. For 1 cup of rice they use 3 cups of water in a pressure-cooker; they keep it on the flame for 1 hour. Allow 2 hours in a pot.

When rice is cold, you can either serve it as is or heat it. There are three practical methods of heating rice: (1) steam in a Japanese steamer; (2) bake in the oven in an earthenware pot; or (3) saute in a little oil. Most of the time we either steam or bake it—both are excellent and practical methods. Once you've put rice in a French earthenware pot, cover it and place in the oven for 30 to 45 minutes, you'll have a hard time convincing your guests you haven't added butter to it. We were surprised, too, the first time we tried this method.

Steaming is the second-best method. Buy yourself a steamer at any Japanese store. You'll find it has many other uses. Pour 1 inch water in the bottom half of the steamer. Put cooked rice in the upper perforated section. Cover with lid. Set over a high flame for 10 minutes or more, until rice is very hot.

We seldom have fried rice anymore; however, it is enjoyable and easy to prepare for those just starting the diet. There are two methods of frying rice, a simple one which takes longer, and a more decorative one which uses ingredients such as oil, scallions and soya sauce.

Fried Rice.

For two or three people, put a teaspoon of oil in a pan or skillet. Heat the oil and add the proper amount of rice. Use a very low flame, as the rice might easily burn. Cover and allow to fry for 15 minutes, stirring from time to time.

Fried Rice with Scallions.

Chop 4-5 scallions finely and saute in oil. Use a large skillet. Stir constantly with a wooden spoon for 2 minutes or so; add 2 to 3 cups cooked rice. Keep stirring, breaking sticky pieces into the smallest possible particles. While stirring, add a mixture of 1 tablespoon soya sauce and 1 tablespoon water, immediately raising the flame so that the liquid you have added combines rapidly with the rice and then evaporates. Stir for a minute and serve hot in small bowls.

Aduki Rice.

Add 10% Aduki beans to rice and allow to cook together as if cooking rice alone. This gives rice a sweet taste and a pink color. Serve in small bowls for a more attractive appearance.

Soft Rice.

Cook rice in five times its volume of water. Japanese eat it for breakfast during cold weather. After the initial boiling, allow to cook 1 hour over a low flame. Excellent for children who are too young to chew properly.

Nori Sandwich.

Very practical if you're taking a trip.

Gently toast a sheet of Nori over the fire, holding four inches above the flame. Cut into pieces 2 inches square. Wet your hands with slightly salt-ed water and shape rice into balls about 2 inches in diameter. Poke a hole in the rice ball, 1 inch deep, and put half a salted plum or less in the hollow. Close by pressing a few times with your palm and fingers. Take a square of Nori, wet slightly with your hands and stick it to the rice (a bowl of water must be handy for this purpose). Repeat the operation until the rice ball is completely covered with Nori. You can now put all the handsome greenish-black sandwiches in a bag for your trip.

* * *

There are hundreds of other ways to prepare rice. I have given only basic methods. From here on use your imagination and creativity.

In the chapter entitled, "Special Dishes," you'll find recipes to which you may always add rice as an accompaniment.

No matter what, you'll have a different kind of rice every day. Because of a higher or a lower flame, more or less water, variables of time, temperature, humidity and you'll never be able to taste rice identical to what you had the day before. Your daily meal is always a new adventure.

Rice Cream.

This is a breakfast favorite with those who have just started the diet. The rice cream is available in natural-food stores, but I advise you to grind it yourself in a special flour mill. Wash rice, rinse and toast over a medium-high flame in a large cast-iron skillet, stirring rapidly in order to prevent burning. It should not take more than 10 minutes for 1 cup of rice. Grind in the mill when cool.

For 2-3 people

5 tablespoons rice cream
4 cups water
¼ teaspoon salt

Mix rice cream with cold water. Keep stirring over high flame until it boils. Add salt. Cover and simmer 30 minutes. Come back to it two or three times to stir in order to prevent burning. Serve in bowls with sesame salt on the side.

About salt

Three things are good in a little
measure and evil in large: yeast,
salt and hesitation.

Gemara

Much has been said and written about salt. Some are for it and some
are against it. Those who are against it claim it is responsible for many
illnesses. Colds are often attributed to it, and weak kidneys are said to
be caused by it. It has been judged so severely by modern-day nutritionists that our sea-mother now wonders if she should have gone to all the
trouble of producing offspring so rife with ingratitude.

Man's blood is composed of that same ocean from whence he came.
Salt is the catalyst of his actions. His thoughts move like waves through
his salt-sea blood, creating the foam of his intelligence.

But Man, eating fruits and sweets, expands his mind, inhibiting his ability to concentrate on earthly matters. Salt is his balance for that expansion; it contracts his mind to the limits of his potential understanding. Salt is the natural and physiological judge of our spiritual actions. We cannot think more than the salt in our blood permits us to think. There is a Russian proverb which says, "Eat bread and salt and speak the truth." Sodium and potassium in our cells determine the contraction and expansion of our imagination. The true state of Manhood should taste as salty as the shores of its beginning and yearn for the sweetness of its unseen end.

We make our food delicious with salt. Should we exaggerate by a grain, the taste becomes too strong. Similarly, that which sweetens a dish, in excessive amounts makes it bitter. A strawberry with a grain of salt is sweeter than a raw strawberry. A second grain, though, makes it taste like vinegar. The appropriate quantity is discernible by intuition. If there is no intuition, use your reason. If there is even less reason, go then to the fields and woods, sow and plow, hammer and saw; and when you return to your home, the amount of salt you take will be correct.

Yes, the greater our activity, the greater should be our intake of salt. Sedentary people, officeworkers, should take less. Bedridden sick people should take none at all. In this respect I agree with those who are against salt.

And perhaps, after all, they are right in a larger sense. For Man has become so inactive since the appearance of computers and slave-machines, that he now relegates salt to an undistinguished position in his wife's fancy herb-cabinet, just another spice among many. It is a strange story indeed. Man, before discovering fire and salt, was a slow paced being unworthy of his present aspirations. After those great discoveries, he climbed high and higher, but now descends the other side of the hill. He is a slave of his own slave-machines, a captive of his own inventions, living again an inactive life. How ironic! Yes, activity is the sacred movement that creates Man. From the greatest activity of the heavens he was made. Through activity he grows to infinite dimensions. When we work, the oxygen we inhale combines with sodium in our cells, creating potassium. The more salt we take, the more active we should be; then the more oxygen we breathe, the more potassium we produce.

Remaining inactive, we inhale less oxygen, upsetting the sodium-potassium balance and making the maintenance of a normal metabolism extremely difficult.

In conclusion, let me make it clear that the intake of salt is a matter for individual discretion. If you have an active child, give him what he needs to grow and play; if a new-born baby, salt should be administered with care. My wife gave hardly any salt to our children until they could stand and run.

Salt-balance is a serious matter, of course—but not so serious as to make a happy and healthy man tremble at the table as he reaches for the gomasio. Develop your intuition. Yes, develop your intuition, and leave to others the scales and petty limits of scientific definition.

Cooking
other grains

And when you eat, have above you the angel
of air, and below you the angel of water.
Breathe long and deeply at all your meals,
that the angel of air may bless your repasts.
And chew well your food with your teeth,
that it become water, and that the angel
of water turn it into blood into your body.
And eat slowly, as it were a prayer you
make to the lord.

Jesus, from the Essene
Gospel of John

Buckwheat.

We cook Buckwheat (Kasha) when the weather is cold. It is a typical
winter cereal which we never eat on a warm day. We always cook it in a
pot, never in a pressure-cooker, as it cooks much more quickly than rice.
Definite advantages derive from being able to lift off the pot-lid once or
twice to see if the buckwheat is still watery or might be about to burn.

You can buy raw groats and toast them yourself until brown in a cast-
iron skillet. This requires 10 minutes or more. To avoid burning, stir
rapidly with a wooden spatula or spoon.

Fluffy kasha.

> 1 cup groats
>
> 2 cups water
>
> ¼ teaspoon salt

Boil water; add buckwheat groats. When water again comes to a boil, lower flame. Add salt, cover with lid and simmer for 20 minutes.

This is the kind of kasha you would serve with vegetables as the cereal of the day. Softer and less chewy buckwheat is for other occasions. A delicious method of serving this fluffy kasha is to mix it with sauteed scallions. Proceed as if preparing fried rice, using 1 teaspoon oil in which to saute the scallions.

Soft kasha.

Toast 1 cup buckwheat groats, cool and put into 5 cups boiling water. Add ¼ teaspoon salt. Bring again to a boil, lower flame and simmer 25 minutes.

This kind of kasha can be eaten as is for breakfast, or used for croquettes and loaves.

To make buckwheat cream for breakfast in winter, use 2 tablespoons buckwheat flour toasted in 1 teaspoon oil. Mix with 2 cups cold water and heat while stirring. Simmer 15-20 minutes. Add salt before the end.

Millet.

Some people prefer millet rather dry, others like it moist. The dry variety is often mixed with sauteed scallions, onions or some other vegetable very finely chopped. The soft millet is perfect for tiny croquettes (Millestones; see recipe, page 199).

> To cook millet grains use:
>
> 1 teaspoon oil
>
> 1 cup millet
>
> 3 cups water
>
> ¼ teaspoon salt

Toast millet in cast-iron skillet until golden (approximately 15 minutes). Stir rapidly to achieve even toasting. Add water, millet and salt to pot. Cover and place over high flame. When it boils, lower flame and simmer covered 30 minutes.

Soft millet.

> 1 teaspoon oil
>
> 1 cup millet
>
> 4 cups water
>
> ¼ teaspoon salt

Toast millet as usual and put in pot with water. After boiling, simmer covered for 35-40 minutes.

Whole wheat berries.

> 1 cup wheat berries
>
> 3 ½ cups water
>
> ¼ teaspoon salt

Soak wheat berries overnight. Put in pressure-cooker with water and salt. Place over high flame until regulator starts jiggling. Lower flame and simmer 2 hours. Instead of plain water, you may use a stock made of sauteed onions, prepared in oil and water, which will give a succulent taste to the berries.

Bulghur.

There are two kinds of bulghur, the dark and the light.

You need:

> 1 cup dark bulghur for 2 cups water or
>
> (1 cup light bulghur for 3 cups water)
>
> ¼ teaspoon salt
>
> ¼ bay leaf (optional)

Boil water and add bulghur, salt and bay leaf at the same time. Cover and place over high flame. When it boils, lower flame and simmer for 25 minutes. Serve plain or covered with bechamel.

Cracked wheat.

Cook cracked wheat as if cooking dark bulghur.

Couscous.

For cooking directions, see chapter entitled "The International Chef."

Barley.

>1 cup barley
>
>3 cups water
>
>¼ teaspoon salt

Boil water in pot and put in barley. Cover. Bring to a boil again, add salt, lower flame and simmer for 25 minutes or so.

You will find another excellent method of cooking barley in the chapter entitled, "Special Dishes." See recipe for Oden, page 229.

Rye.

>3 cups water, or onion stock
>
>1 cup whole grain rye
>
>1 tablespoon oil
>
>¼ teaspoon salt

Bring water or soup stock to a boil. Add rye, oil and salt. Cover. Bring to a boil again, lower flame and simmer covered 35-40 minutes. Serve plain or with bechamel sauce. Sprinkle with chopped parsley.

Oats.

We have oats for breakfast when we awaken very early. Some people prefer it almost "solid," but we like it creamy—a bit more liquid than the Scottish porridge.

>1 cup oats, rolled or steel cut
>
>4 cups water
>
>¼ teaspoon salt

Boil water, add oats (which may be pre-toasted for 10 minutes). When water boils again, lower flame, add salt and simmer covered for 30 minutes. If you are not using an asbestos pad, it is better to stir from time to time to prevent burning. Serve hot and in bowls.

Corn.

Corn can be served in many different ways, on the cob, in polenta, in soups, etc.

Corn on the Cob.

Put corn into 1 ½ inches of water. Add salt, cover and place cooking pot over a high flame. When it comes to a boil, lower flame a bit and let simmer 15-20 minutes. Serve hot.

Polenta.

Polenta is used in several recipes. This method is a basic preparation for white or yellow polenta, from which you can advance in many delicious directions. Try serving it with different kinds of vegetables, or pouring hot into molds. Polenta can be fried or served with raisins and nuts as a dessert.

> Recipe for plain polenta:
>
> 1 cup polenta
>
> 3 cups water
>
> ¼ teaspoon salt

Boil water and gently pour in polenta. Stir while pouring. When water comes to a boil again, add salt, cover and let simmer for 30 to 40 minutes. Stir from time to time.

Corn meal.

Cook it the same way as polenta, only pre-toast it in 1 teaspoon corn oil for 10 minutes before pouring into boiling water. It is an excellent base for soups, desserts and other delicious dishes.

Nutritionists versus nutrition

The little lady in black called her nutritionist. She wanted to know how many vitamin pills she should be taking every day. The nutritionist, who didn't quite remember who the hell she was, said seventeen.

"Seventeen what?" asked the little lady in black.

"A, B, C, D, E, Iron, Calcium, Magnesium, and so on," an impatient voice replied.

So the little lady in black hurried to the health-food store, where she bought herself pills of all sorts. Home again, she poured herself a glass of water, arranged the seventeen pills in orderly fashion, then hesitated. Hurrying to the phone, she dialed her nutritionist again.

"When should I take them?" she asked

"Who is this?"

"It's the little lady in black with the seventeen pills."

"Seventeen pills? Ah, yes! What do you want to know?"

"How many times a day should I take them and for how long?"

"Twice a day. For a month or two. Then come see me."

* * *

There are seventeen million seventeen-pill ladies in the United States who call or regularly see a nutritionist, as though consulting an account-tant about his specialty—numbers. These days nutritionists have to have a good head for figures. Vitamins are in fashion. Health-food stores look like pharmacies, while pharmacies are becoming bazaars. Merchants have assumed control of people's health. Manufacturers and salesmen point to statistics as though to a court of last resort. No mention is made of sound principles of health. And the great success experienced by such interests is due almost exclusively to fear—fear inspired by modern nutritionists.

One such unthinking nutritionist writes that vitamin C, taken in ex-cess, is not harmful, he claims that the body keeps what it needs and excretes the rest through the urinary canal. He advises everybody to take more than less, just to be on the "safe side." His fellow pill-pushers agree; they teach their ignorant patients how to be machines. This theory of an automatic excretion of excess fuel is witless and dangerous.

In grains there are enough vitamins to make a man think, work and faithfully resemble the being God designed him to be. But nowadays Man is in a hurry. He drinks what he does not have time to chew. By doing so he destroys most of the precious vitamins he has taken with his food. The more one drinks, the more vitamins one should ingest. Vita-min B is fragile; it can be "washed out" of the system. Because people drink and eat more, creating deficiencies, the "B-complex" has become quite famous. Certain physicians have clinically established the fact that schizophrenia is often due to a B-vitamin lack. Why have they failed to note that schizophrenics, because of their extremes of behavior, also drink more and eat more foolishly than anybody else?

A cerealian should drink little. The amount of vitamin B contained in grains is only just sufficient to supply his needs. If he drinks one cup of water or tea after a meal, this will not harm him; but if he swallows cup after cup, he will endanger his balance.

So it is with vitamin C, which is as fragile as the B-complex vitamins, although in different ways. Drugs, alcohol, heat and overactivity re-move it from the body.

It is overeating, too much drinking and myriad of other excesses that are responsible for the current massive intake of vitamins. Man has for-gotten that he is first of all a physiological being, not a machine to be pumped up or over stimulated. His faulty memory induces him to try to cure bleeding gums symptomatically with vitamin C, like a repairman patching a hole in a tire without first removing the nail that caused it. Yes, mechanically speaking, bleeding gums are due to a lack of vitamin C. But why has the metabolism failed to maintain sufficient levels? What about the improper eating habits, the cooking, the chewing? I have seen bleeding gums cured in a few brief days, or simply by good eating over a month or two.

If man continues to behave this way, counting out his daily ration of vitamins before making a move, all his life long he is going to be at the mercy of some nutritionist-accountant. He will be only a junky, as dependent and luckless as a heroin-addict, indistinguishable from a "mainliner" except for the fact that his life is less dramatic and he has fewer police to bother him.

An equally disturbing thing to see is people who worry about protein. Following a lecture given to a group of students at Cornell University, a concerned young girl came to see me and asked, for what seemed the thousandth time, an all-too-familiar question: "Can you tell me the best food to take? I've been eating grains and vegetables since June and I'm worried—actually it's my parents—about proteins.

We all know now that grains are rich sources of protein—beans too, especially Adukis*. Nori seaweed is the richest source of all, even richer than animal products. The condiments, Miso* and Tamari*, which are used daily, are also a fairly good source of supply. For those who are interested, here is a little table* comparing animal products with what we ordinarily eat:

Vegetable	Protein		Animal Food	
Brown Rice	7.5%		Beef	20.0%
Barley	10.8%		Pork	21.4%
Wheat	19.0%		Ham	22.7%
Buckwheat Flour	13.0%		Chicken	21.0%
Sesame Seeds	16.7%		Eggs	12.7%
Soya Beans	34.3%		Milk	3.0%
Aduki Beans	20.9%		Cheese	25.2%
Miso	12.6%		Fish	17 to 25 %
Tamari	6.0%			

* See chapter "The cerealian's dictionary"

A few biochemists* claim that we don't even need to take protein in order to keep our body properly supplied. They explain (and prove) that by combination and transmutation, protein is synthesized out of nitrogen from the air and hydrogen from the intestines.

I believe them. But we won't go so far as to talk about transmutation and chemistry in this cookbook. Instead of entertaining you with intricate formulas and tables of comparison, let me give you what I believe to be the best answer: *We are Man and, as such, have no need to analyze everything we eat.*

Lack of intuition and faith has made modern man more of a scientist than a poet. He disbelieves in the miracles of nature and, even more so, in those of God. He is suspicious of his body and mind as one is suspicious of an unfamiliar machine. Man, as Man, must be able to change a miserable condition into a better one; he must be able to transmute biologically any element into another within his body.

And is not that, truly, the beginning of freedom?

* Dr. C. Evans

Cooking beans, chick-peas and lentils

In general, the best way to cook beans is in a pressure-cooker. It saves time and water and the beans emerge softer. This goes for aduki beans, richest of all and the least harmful, as well as for navy, pinto, kidney, soya and black beans, and for chick-peas, black-eyed peas and lentils.

To cook beans in a regular pot requires several hours. If you do, here is a classic warning: always add salt at the *end* of the cooking. If you put it in at the beginning, beans will take much more time to soften. A good procedure is to cook beans with a piece of kombu (seaweed) added, one inch wide and three inches long. To keep them firm and unbroken, limit stirring to a minimum and cook gently over a low flame.

Prepare a goodly amount of beans each time you cook them; leftovers can be combined in a variety of dishes. Soak overnight.

Soya beans need to be kept in a cool place or refrigerated in their soaking water to prevent fermentation. Lentils, pinto beans and black-eyed peas do not have to be soaked.

Cooking beans in a pressure-cooker

This way of cooking does not require pre-soaking. Rinse beans in a strainer. It takes 2 ½ cups of water to cook 1 cup of beans, which will yield 6 to 8 servings.

Bring up pressure, then lower flame and allow to cook 1 hour. Chick-peas require 1 ½ hour. Lentils only 12 minutes. To bring the pressure down, quickly place the cooker in the sink under running cold water. Open the cooker and add a small amount of water, just enough to cover the beans; then add ¼ teaspoon salt per cup of water (for 2 ½ cups, as in our case, add a total of ½ teaspoon plus a pinch). In place of salt, you can add 1 tablespoon soya sauce per cup of water. Cook uncovered 20 minutes more until water boils away.

When cooking aduki beans, you can use more water, then reserve the liquid to be served as a drink or to be combined into soups or sauces.

Do not pressure-cook black beans. Their skins may come off and clog the pressure-cooker spout. It's quite dangerous!

Cooking beans in a pot

Wash beans in a strainer; soak for 2 or 3 hours before cooking. Soya beans and chick-peas must soak overnight. Don't throw away the water in which the beans have been soaked; it is always good in soup. For 1 cup of beans use 4 cups of cold water. Bring water and beans to a boil, lower flame, leaving the lid slightly open. Two hours are required for cooking. Add ½ tablespoon salt near the end, while there is still some liquid in the pot. Add more water if necessary. Lentils in a pot need 35 minutes to cook.

As an example of what you can create, here are some recipes with beans, chick-peas and lentils that may help you find more simple or complicated ones:

Sweet-beans Casserole.

Cook 1 ½ cup aduki beans in pressure-cooker. Have already prepared:

1 apple, cut into thin slices

2 medium-size onions, chopped

¼ green pepper, chopped

1 bay leaf

1 tablespoon oil

1 teaspoon salt

and the cooked adukis.

Saute the onions in oil, add green pepper, then apple. Mix everything with cooked adukis; add salt. Put in a casserole pan, add bay leaf on top. Bake ½ hour covered (with aluminum foil if your casserole has no lid). Cook uncovered ½ hour more.

Soft Adukis.

Cook 1 cup adukis in pressure-cooker. Put in earthenware pot with their own juice. Add 2 tablespoons miso previously diluted in ½ cup water. Cover and bake in 350-degree oven for 2 or 3 hours.

Chick-pea Stew.

> 1 ½ cup chick-peas, already cooked
>
> 2 onions, diced
>
> 4 stalks celery, finely chopped
>
> 2 tablespoons sesame butter
>
> 2 tablespoons soya sauce
>
> 1 tablespoon corn oil

Heat oil in heavy stew-pot. Saute onions for 2 minutes and add celery. Two minutes later add cooked chick-peas with their juice. Mix soya sauce and sesame butter together and put into pot. Cover tightly and allow to simmer 1 hour. Check every once in a while to prevent burning.

Variation: Instead of chick-peas, you can use aduki beans or lentils.

Black-Bean Stew.

> 2 cups black beans, soaked 3 hours
>
> 1 cup parsnip, diced
>
> 1 cup onions, diced
>
> ½ cup burdock, slivered
>
> 3 by 6 inch piece of kombu, soaked in water, then sliced into thin strips
>
> ¼ fresh lotus root, sliced, or 6 dried pieces of lotus root, soaked overnight and diced
>
> 1 tablespoon sesame oil
>
> ½ teaspoon salt
>
> 3 tablespoons miso, diluted in 2 cups water

Cook black beans in heavy pot for 2 hours in 8 cups of water. Heat oil in a deep saucepan and saute onions. Two minutes later add parsnip, then lotus and burdock. Simmer uncovered 5 minutes; add kombu. Add cooked beans, salt and miso. Simmer covered for 1 hour. If there is too much liquid, simmer a few more minutes, uncovered, to obtain the desired consistency.

Soja Jardiniere.

> 1 cup cooked soya beans
>
> 5 carrots, cubed
>
> 5 turnips, cubed
>
> 5 small onions, quartered
>
> 3 leaves of lettuce, cut into thin strips
>
> 2 tablespoons miso
>
> 2 tablespoons corn oil
>
> 3 tablespoons parsley, chopped
>
> 1 cup water
>
> ½ teaspoon salt (if soya beans are not pre-salted)

Saute onions in oil. Add turnips, carrots, lettuce and parsley. When vegetables start turning golden, add water and salt. Cook for 15 minutes, then add cooked soya beans. Mix well, cover and simmer for 15 minutes more. Dilute miso in ½ cup of water and pour into pot. Allow to simmer 10 more minutes, covered. Serves 8 to 12.

Lentil Casserole.

      3 cups lentils, cooked and pureed

      1 cup turnips, diced

      1 cup squash, diced

      2 onions, diced

      1 egg (optional)

      2 tablespoons oil

      ½ teaspoon salt

      1 cup umeboshi juice (see recipe, page 183)

      2 tablespoons soya sauce

      ½ cup water

Saute onions, turnips and squash in pressure-cooker for 10 minutes. Add ½ cup water, cover and pressure-cook for 20 minutes. Once cooked, mash with fork and combine with remaining ingredients in a casserole pot. Bake in 350-degree oven for 30 minutes. Will serve 6 to 10.

Pinto-Bean Stew.

> 4 cups pinto beans, pressure-cooked for 2 hours
>
> 1 cup carrots, diced
>
> 1 cup parsnips, diced
>
> 1 cup onions, chopped
>
> 1 cup bechamel sauce (see recipe, page 177)
>
> 2 tablespoons seitan
>
> 2 tablespoons corn oil
>
> ½ teaspoon salt

In a heavy pot, saute all vegetables, beginning with onions. Add beans and their juice to sauteed vegetables. Cover and simmer 1 hour. Add remaining ingredients. Cover and simmer for 30 more minutes. Serve on the side or over grains as a sauce.

Variation: Use adukis instead of pinto beans.

For other bean recipes, refer to chapters on soups, salads, spreads, pâtés and other special dishes.

Doctor M is cooking at my brother's restaurant tonight

The Physician has to be skilled in Nature and must
strive to know what Man is in relation to food, drink,
occupation, and which effect each of these has on the other.

Hippocrates.

"And the old lady—how is she?"

"She won't take Aspirin. She says if that's all there is to it, coming to the hospital for some pills she could buy at any drugstore, she'd be better off staying at home! What'll I do?"

"Give her three Phenafens a day for the next three days—no more!"

"Of course, Doctor."

76

A nurse from another room calls, "Doctor an outside call."

Doctor Robert M, cool and impressive in white uniform and black-rimmed glasses, walks with confidence and composure to the telephone.

"Hello?"

"Hello, Bob, it's Georges!"

"Hey, Georgie, what's up? You're *cooking* tonight! I'm taking my girl to the movies, remember?"

"Is it my turn tonight? I'd completely forgot! I'll be there in forty-five minutes. Just three or four more patients to see, O.K.?

"Everythin's ready and waiting for the chef."

"O.K., Georgie, I'm practically on my way!"

Doctor M has been eating grains and vegetables for six months. Once a week he cooks at my brother's restaurant. Everybody in the East Village knows him simply as "Bob".

At the outset he worked for three weeks as a dishwasher. For another week or two he helped cut vegetables. After further apprenticeship as an assistant, he now assumes complete responsibility for the entire preparation and cooking. He is delighted with his job, although the pay is less than a dollar an hour.

"Here," he explains, "I create life."

Everyone agrees that his cooking is delicious and health-giving.

"You know, Bob," he is often told, "you actually make me *high* with your food!"

Robert M comes regularly to lectures and listens attentively—more attentively than most—to discussions of philosophy, Chinese medicine and food. Six months ago he was still using medical terms few could understand; now he has simplified his vocabulary. He speaks continually of Yin and Yang, which is a normal reaction for a beginner.

"What causes constipation—Yin or Yang?" he used to ask me on the phone. "And what causes fever?"

I found it hard to believe that a practicing M.D. didn't know the answers. He began macrobiotics when he saw how it benefitted his younger brother Richard, a dying drug-addict. So grateful was he at the improvement that he felt compelled to involve himself in Richard's new way of life. There had been no hope for his brother, whose only future had seemed to be suicide; but like thousands of other ex-hippies, Richard had "straightened-up" had begun to lead a normal life.

The alternatives are extreme for all who find themselves in Richard's condition—simply, diet or die. But is it so difficult to choose? For who can fail to prefer a simple way of eating that is joined to a universal philosophy? The youth of America, having been drawn toward mind-expanding drugs, find it natural to gravitate toward mind-expanding food. Enlightened and robust, freed of dependence on drugs, they can stand independent of their degenerate surroundings. Having returned to good food and a simpler life, they could reject with confidence the pat answers of doctors and psychoanalysts whose very statements seemed symptomatic of the society's illnesses.

After one of my lectures, a hippie who had recently abandoned drugs in favor of grains and vegetables said to me, "It's great to eat this way. I'm high, man, but I'm *here*!" And that's what cereals were intended to do: to place you firmly and solidly on earth but with your antennae tuned to the heavens.

Really, the Hippie Movement died the day cereals were "discovered," because the true hippie was no junky. He was simply a young man revolted by the condition of his times, in search of himself. Drugs provided a dramatic and practical means of escaping an America that was going blind. Drugs opened up his mind's eye and bared the country's tragedy while simultaneously creating an urge to be separate from that tragedy.

The true hippie of today is taking care of himself and his family by eating and living well. He is aware of the importance of what is on his table. He is now on his way toward a more realistic and even grander trip.

A mother should breastfeed her child for emotional and physical sustenance. When the child's early hungers are not satisfied, he later develops a psychological frailty and susceptibility to disease. From his teens on he unconsciously searches for the source of life that was unjustly denied him.

Denied the warmth from his parents, he later develops peculiar attitudes toward friends and problems. When his physiological needs remain unfulfilled, psychological disturbances arise. His frustrated heart becomes a cunning mind which tries in vain to solve his deep-rooted problems. With the passage of years he increases the intellectuality and coldness of his point of view and loses the reality of the whole.

When desire is inhibited, it cuts back upon the self and opens in the deepest part of the being a wound most difficult to close. If desire points out a path, better to follow it; otherwise we become separated from ourselves—flesh, mind and bones. Desire is what gives us life. Kill it and there is nothing left but a comedian without lines. Master desire as a man and the rewards are immeasurable.

When we stand still between a change—between the physiological and the spiritual, between what we are in our bones and flesh and what the will yearns to be—we are stricken and exhausted by the effort necessary to resist the natural inclination; and we die a little. Change is the Law—in Man as in Nature. One must help and even "activate" its course. Our refusal to do this stems only from cowardice, ignorance and stupidity. No man is a dam sturdy enough to deflect the running waters of Creation. Rather he is but a stone animated by them. He is part of the change that runs past, turning and spinning him until at last he regains his feet and his equilibrium, only to be turned again.

No man can declare, "I am master of myself," until he has experienced seven-thousand-times-seventy-thousand changes of body and mind. And no man can ever find his great desire if he has not mastered his smaller ones. Man must awaken, must literally come to his senses. But for the time being he must not trust his ailing brain, which has been evertaxed. He must learn to trust his heart.

Consider the psychologically disturbed youth of today. Has he not unclogged, although in sometimes reckless ways, the rivers of wonder and change? Are not now ships, freighted and beautiful with the staff of life, sailing south of the mind toward a new and happier age?

For three months now, Dr. M has been unsuccessfully trying to convince his psychoanalyst friend that physiology is the mother of psychology. Dr. T's office is on Fifth Avenue. He is one of the new breed of experimentalists who are eager to try all manner and means of curing patients. Dr. T's latest "discovery" is to require a patient to disrobe during analysis, or further still, if female, to perform the act of sexual intercourse with him before the very eyes of her husband (endeavoring, to satisfy or cure whose senses or difficulties?) Perhaps Dr. T will succeed in convincing husband and wife that all disturbances are traceable to sex—if that is what is meant by "success."

Psychology, although it seeks to delve deeply into the mechanisms of personality, is actually as symptomatic as modern medicine. It merely unveils problems hidden behind our present recollections of childhood. But what is to happen when we are unexpectedly faced with a different side of the prism of ourselves? Sometimes we reach "normality," but have no idea how to maintain the balance. This is because psychology teaches us how to rearrange past thoughts but not how to direct them creatively toward the future. We are taught techniques of survival, whereas it is a common tenet of Man's universal understanding that a time inevitably comes when we must pass from the behavior of survival to that of transcendence.

Symptomatic treatments have transformed Man from a giving into a demanding being. He has lost his self-respect and, more than once, has sheepishly dropped his trousers before a serious-looking man purporting to understand the causes and effects of disease. Are the mechanical "miracles" and dextrous sleights-of-hand of modern medicine so impressive that we must sign away our existences and our judgments, and sentence ourselves to go blind?

Young doctors and cooks ought to learn in the same lecture-halls, for customers and patients have much in common. Both, for example, suspend their instincts and judgments in favor of little shows of taste and miracle.

Doctors should not take advantage of a patient's "moment of ruin" in order to exaggerate their own importance or impose their drugs. On the other hand cooks, who have always been the only doctors working without license, (never interfered with by the A.M.A.), should cease to emphasize only the sensorial in their menus. Food does not always have to be as exciting as a St. Pauli woman at her inviting window. A good dish does not speak only to the lascivious tongue; it has other missions—at the level of Man's innermost desire. Food should satisfy *all* senses, not merely one.

While symptomatic hunger can be satisfied by mechanically prepared food, true hunger is poetry inspired by the Muses themselves. A man's voice is profound and clear in proportion to the enormity of his hunger for food and life. The bigger his longing, the more sublime his poetry. A great secret of philosophy is the message of emptiness. Always be hungry, let every cell be deeply seeking food and fulfillment.

A good doctor should be a good cook. His spare time should be spent puttering with pots and pans, which will teach him unsuspected secrets. A good chef, in like manner, should study the rudiments of physiology. Then at last we, as patients and gourmets, will live gratefully and confidently in a world of delights.

The symptom of a sickness should not be confused with its cause. If you indiscriminately extinguish a symptom, you will find yourself devoid of a guiding light in the darkness of indecision.

All sicknesses have their causes and cures far from their symptoms. That which is close to a symptom and seems to be its cause is in reality but the tray that presents it. The farther you go toward the cause, the better—even if you appear to be heading toward immaterial ends.

Most people mistakenly believe they can cure themselves by extinguishing only the symptoms of their profound ignorance. They turn to mechanical lesson-learning in modern-day pseudo-sciences. But even if these "sciences" bear the highest philosophical credentials, they cannot cure the root-causes of ignorance.

A man who is a shadow of himself is also a symptom of his diseased being. To cure himself he must go deep down within himself to the very doors to the heavens. To be cured both physiologically and metaphysically is not a matter of mere intellectual decision or commitment. It is more a matter of faith and understanding.

Soups

We have perhaps a thousand and one soup-recipes. They are not in written form, but exist in our imaginations and in our wills to create. Soups give us special inspirations throughout the four seasons. When it is cold, imagination harkens to inner need and we cook what will produce warmth and health. My wife, for example, is sensitive to weather-moods and the dispositions of friends coming for the evening—and creates new soups accordingly.

The soup-recipes given in this chapter will hopefully inspire you to develop your own variations. I could have given you more, it is not my wish to leave you in a state of dependency.

I begin with miso soup, which we have almost every day. There is no better way to introduce this renowned soup than to quote a famous Japanese physician, Dr. Tatsuichiro Akizuki, M.D.:

"One day as I lay in bed, ill with tuberculosis, I decided to change my constitution. I knew I could cure my sickness, but how could I change my constitution? The answer was that I had to change my diet.

"Although my parents did not farm, they lived in the country. Grain and miso soup were staples of their diet. To the best of my knowledge, they never experienced any serious illnesses. If they caught a cold, they cured it simply by taking a diaphoretic (a drug which induces sweating). To stop diarrhea they took salt-plum tea. Compared to them I had very serious sicknesses: for example, whooping cough, diphtheria, pneumonia, lung tuberculosis.

When I was twenty, we moved from the countryside to Nagasaki. Fish was abundant in that seaside city and vegetables were scarce, so my family stopped taking miso soup for breakfast. Even when my mother did cook miso soup for breakfast, my brothers and sisters would eat fish or fish cakes. My mother finally stopped making miso soup altogether.

"Another reason for the change was that my parents did not have an understanding of the importance of miso soup in the Japanese diet. Nutritional authorities recommended eggs, milk or meat rather than miso soup. It was from the latter diet that I became sick.

"Of course, in the beginning I did not have much faith in miso soup. I was completely disappointed by occidental medicine because no remedy had ever cured my sickness entirely. Then I decided to change my diet to brown rice, vegetables and miso soup.

"On August 9, 1945, the atomic bomb was dropped on Nagasaki. It killed many thousands of people. The hospital I was in charge of at the time was located only one mile from the center of the blast. It was destroyed completely. My assistants and I helped many victims who suffered from the effects of the bomb. In my hospital there was a large stock of miso and tamari. We also kept plenty of brown rice and wakame. So I fed my co-workers brown rice and miso soup. I remember that none of them suffered from the atomic radiation. I believe this is because they had been eating miso soup. How could miso soup prevent sickness from radiation? I contend that science will answer that question conclusively if people are allowed to provide data for experiments. I, myself, would like to do such an experiment.

"At that time occidental medicine had introduced many drugs for tuberculosis. Streptomycin, PAS (para-amino-salicylic acid); these drugs were introduced and proven to remedy many tuberculosis cases. Many improved surgical methods were also introduced. I applied these new drugs and new techniques of occidental medicine to my patients. I do not deny their effectiveness. But even while applying these new medicines I never forgot that if man does not change his constitution, his sickness will never be cured completely. Whether the sickness is easily cured or not is dependent upon the patient's constitution. Some improve quickly, others find it difficult to improve, even while taking the same drugs.

"I think that miso soup is the most important part of one's diet. Modern medicine recommends milk, eggs, tomato juice etc. Miso soup, on the other hand, awaits evaluation. Few have considered studying the importance of authentic Japanese food. Whenever I see a patient, I ask whether he eats miso soup or not. It is very interesting; most people answer that they do sometimes. Mothers complaining about their children's illnesses, when asked whether or not they give their family miso soup, invariably say no. They are most interested in giving them eggs, etc.—occidental food. On the other hand, the family that is rarely sick always takes miso soup every day, without exception. However, miso soup is not a drug such as a cortical hormone or an antibiotic. It does not cure sickness right away. If you are taking it daily your constitution improves and you acquire resistance to sickness.

"People call miso a condiment; but miso is an agent which brings out the value of all food. And it more easily allows the body to assimilate its food.

"The diet of a child is difficult. His tendency with regard to food is to go to extremes. If the diet is too strict he becomes nervous. Therefore, in my family I suggested that every morning the children eat a soup which contains wakame, age (fried tofu) and vegetables. The rest of the diet I left up to their choice. The result was favorable. I recommend to parents at PTA meetings that they should give their children some miso soup every morning."

Doctor Akiduki then goes on to give precise details about the food value of miso soup:

"As a source of protein miso is excellent. Soy beans, which are the basic ingredient of miso, are called "vegetable meat." Soy beans contain 36% protein and 17% fats. Soy beans are very hard to digest, even when they are cooked, roasted or boiled. In miso, natto and tofu (soy beans) they are biologically transformed and the protein and fat can be digested and assimilated by humans. One cup of miso soup contains four grams of protein.

"Every morning, then, when one eats miso one gets four grams of protein. Some people say that vegetable protein is inferior to animal protein. Protein from soy beans lacks certain amino acids. However, this deficiency can be corrected by adding bonita flakes or small fishes and scallions to the miso soup.

"Animal protein is not always good. Physiologically speaking, animal protein overworks the kidneys. In other words, the residue left by meat results in such overwork. Fermentation in the intestines produces poison and damages the heart, arteries and the nervous system. Animal protein also produces allergies as well as causing acidosis.

"Miso soup never produces these effects. Moreover, miso soup removes the fermentation caused by animal protein. Therefore, miso soup is the best source of protein for our body.

FAT.

"For the Japanese people miso is a very important source of fat. One cup of miso soup containing approximately ½ gram. If you take one cup of miso soup every day, this is quite a sufficient amount of fat. Fat should be taken regularly, not in too large a quantity at one time. Excess fat is rather poisonous, if not a waste.

"Once Dr. Kumagai, who was internationally recognized as an expert on tuberculosis, said: 'The reason why Japanese have many tuberculosis cases is because the Japanese intake of fat is much less than the occidental intake.' The Japanese diet lacks fat, compared with the occidental diet; therefore, miso soup with age (fried tofu) is very important. Fish contains much fat; however, fat found in fish oxidizes easily, especially in summer; the same as butter and cheese do. Foods such as these are not recommended in Japan between April and October; however, miso is recommended all year long. The older the miso, the better the taste."

MINERALS.

"Miso contains many bacteria such as lactobacilli. Our large intestine contains many of these bacteria. They decompose carbohydrates and protein in our large intestine. Cellulose, especially, can be digested by this bacteria in the large intestine. Japanese food contains much cellulose. It is found in brown rice, barley, vegetables such as burdock, pickles, radishes and carrots. Such cellulose is digested by bacteria. Therefore, if we do not have bacteria in our intestine, even good food will not be digested and cannot be consequently assimilated by the body. From this standpoint, miso soup is superior when compared to chicken, eggs or butter, because miso soup aids digestion. Miso soup supplements animal food if a person does not have enough. And for those who have too much animal food miso soup neutralizes poisons produced by their excess.

"As medicine miso soup produces an alkaline condition of the body. Many diseases today are caused by infection from bacteria. Such an underlying condition leads to infection (acidosis). An alkaline condition withstands infection. This kind of constitution can be built with our diet. Miso is a food that produces an alkaline constitution.

"Parasites cannot live if our food contains many minerals and fats. Salt is especially an important factor in preventing parasites. Miso soup contains much fat, minerals and salt; therefore, whoever takes it every morning hardly ever suffers from parasites.

"A frail constitution is caused by a lack of minerals and by acidosis. We lack minerals in our daily food because of eating too much animal food and too many sweets. I was once a frail child. I tried many different ways to strengthen my body. For example, I took cold showers and tried other activities. However, these are not recommended for a frail child. One cup of miso soup each morning seems to be the best way to give strength.

"Dr. Mechinicoff, a Russian physician, said that the most effective way to promote longevity is to prevent the poisoning of the intestines. He recommended lactic acid every day. Miso contains substantial amounts of it.

"From ancient times the Zen monks ate brown rice and miso as their main food. Many of them were very strong and kept their vitality until a ripe age. This kind of vitality and longevity came from or was based on their diet. It is a fact that meditation will be fruitless unless one's daily food provides the proper nutrition for the body."

Here is the recipe for miso soup!

Miso Soup.

> 2 onions, minced
>
> 2 carrots, sliced
>
> ¼ small cabbage
>
> 1 tablespoon oil
>
> 4 cups water
>
> 6 rounded teaspoons miso paste
>
> 1 or 2 scallions, finely chopped and kept uncooked in a small
> bowl

Saute vegetables in oil, starting with onions. Simmer 10-15 minutes. Boil water and pour it in the deep pot in which vegetables have just been sauteed. Cover and simmer for 30 minutes. Dilute miso in 1 cup of simmering soup and add mixture 5 minutes before end of cooking. Try not to bring soup to a boil after adding miso. It will spoil the delicateness of the soup. Serve in bowls with finely chopped scallions on top. You might occasionally add a square of fried tofu.

Miso Soup

1 tsp sesame oil
1 onion, sliced
1 pinch sea salt
5 cups water
1 cup chopped greens
1 carrot, sliced
1 cup miso
¼ cup soybean paste

Place soup pot on medium heat and add oil. When oil is hot add onions; stir for 2–5 minutes until slightly transparent and strong smell goes away. Add salt, water and remaining vegetables and bring to a boil. Reduce he and simmer, covered, for 20–30 utes or until vegetables are just to Remove from heat. (over)

Brown Islands. (Barley soup)

>   1 onion, minced
>
>   3 celery stalks, chopped
>
>   1 cup whole barley grain
>
>   ½ cup lentils
>
>   1 tablespoon oil
>
>   6 cups water
>
>   1 teaspoon salt

Saute onions in oil for a few minutes, add celery, and simmer 10 minutes. Add water, bring to a boil, then add lentils and barley. Bring to a boil again and simmer 1 hour. Add salt 15 minutes before end. Can also be cooked in a pressure-cooker in ½ hour.

Barley in Green.

>   1/3 cup cracked barley
>
>   3 cups water
>
>   1 bunch watercress cut into ½-inch strips
>
>   ¼ teaspoon salt
>
>   1 tablespoon olive oil

Saute watercress in oil, add water, bring to a boil, add barley and simmer 30 minutes. Serve with bread croutons.

Scotch Barley Soup.

　　4 carrots, grated

　　3 onions, chopped

　　2 parsnips, diced

　　2 tablespoons oil

　　2 quarts water

　　1 cup pearl barley

　　1/3 teaspoon fresh ginger, grated

　　2 tablespoons parsley, chopped

　　1 ½ teaspoon salt

Saute onions, carrots, parsnips in oil. Add water, bring to a boil and stir in the barley, salt and ginger. Simmer 1 ½ hours. Serve sprinkled with parsley.

Rice and Vegetable Soup.

    1 large butternut squash, cubed

    2 onions, diced

    2 turnips, cubed

    1 carrot, thinly sliced

    3 cabbage leaves cut into strips ½-inch long

    5 tablespoons toasted rice

    1 tablespoon oil

    1 ½ quarts water

    1 tablespoon chopped parsley

    2 tablespoons sesame butter

    1 bay leaf

Heat oil, saute onions, add cabbage and turnips. After 3 or 4 minutes add carrots and squash. Cover with water and add rice. When it comes to a boil, add rest of water and salt. Bring to a boil again and simmer 40 minutes. Stir from time to time. Add sesame butter and parsley 5 minutes before end.

Millet Soup.

>   2 onions, finely chopped
>
>   2 carrots, grated
>
>   1 burdock root, shaved
>
>   1 cup millet, toasted
>
>   1 tablespoon oil
>
>   1 ½ teaspoon salt
>
>   2 quarts water

Saute onions, carrots and burdock, in that order. Add millet, then water. Bring to a boil and simmer 35 minutes. Add salt before end. Serve with chopped parsley on top for a dash of color.

Celery Velouté.

>   5 stalks celery, diced
>
>   1 onion, minced
>
>   3 tablespoons whole-wheat flour, lightly toasted
>
>   ¼ teaspoon oil
>
>   2 tablespoons sesame butter
>
>   6 cups water

Saute onions and celery in oil. Add water, bring to a boil, simmer 20 minutes. Dilute flour in ½ cup water and pour into soup. Add sesame butter and salt, stir and simmer 15 minutes. Serve with croutons.

Cauliflower Field.

>1 small cauliflower, separated into flowerettes
>
>1 onion, minced
>
>1 bunch scallions, finely chopped
>
>1 teaspoon oil
>
>2 tablespoons soya sauce
>
>¼ teaspoon salt
>
>6 cups water
>
>3 tablespoons rice flour

Saute onions, scallions and cauliflower. Add water, bring to a boil and simmer 30 minutes. Dilute rice flour in ½ cup water and add to soup. Add salt and soya sauce and simmer 20 minutes more. Serve with chopped parsley on top.

Cabbage Soup.

>1 medium-size cabbage, shredded
>
>2 onions, chopped
>
>1 carrot, finely sliced
>
>2 tablespoons oil
>
>2 tablespoons w.w. flour or rice flour, lightly toasted
>
>5 cups water
>
>½ cup buckwheat groats, toasted
>
>3 tablespoons soya sauce
>
>½ teaspoon salt

Saute onions, cabbage and carrot, in that order. Add water and bring to a boil. Add buckwheat groats, flour diluted in 1/3 cup water, salt, and soya sauce, then simmer 1 hour. Sauerkraut can be used instead of fresh cabbage. The taste will be more exotic.

Le Verger.

    2 onions, diced

    2 carrots, finely sliced

    1 cup shredded cabbage

    1 cup string beans, diced

    1 cup lima beans, soaked and precooked

    1 cup butternut squash, diced

    2 quarts water

    1 ½ teaspoon salt

    1 tablespoon oil

Saute onions, carrots, cabbage, string beans and squash. Add water and cooked beans; salt. Bring to a boil and simmer for 35 minutes. Serve topped with chopped parsley.

Black-Bean Soup.

    1 cup dried beans, soaked overnight

    2 onions, minced

    3 teaspoons oil

    4 tablespoons w.w. flour, toasted and diluted in ½ cup water

    1 bay leaf

    1 celery stalk with leaves, chopped

    7 cups water

    1 small teaspoon salt

Saute onions with bay leaf, add water and beans, then bring to a boil. Simmer 2 hours. Add toasted flour, diluted in water, and salt. Simmer another hour. Serve topped with chopped parsley.

Panade.

    2 onions, chopped

    2 leeks, cut into ½-inch pieces

    2 carrots, finely sliced

    2 tablespoons bonito flakes

    2 tablespoons soya sauce

    6 cups water

    1 teaspoon salt

    Pieces of left-over bread

    6 slices toasted bread (one per person)

Saute onions, leeks, carrots. Add water and bring to a boil. Add bread, bonito flakes, salt and soya sauce. Simmer 30 minutes. Serve with 1 toasted slice of bread and chopped parsley atop each portion. To give a "gourmet" taste, rub some fresh garlic into the toasted slices of bread.

Kreplach Soup.

    3 onions, chopped

    1 bunch scallions, chopped

    2 ears corn

    3 tablespoons soya sauce

    2 teaspoons oil

    6 cups water

    1 teaspoon salt

Saute onions, scallions, kernels of corn. Add water and bring to a boil. Put kreplach into soup and simmer 25 minutes.

Dough for Kreplach:

2 cups pastry or white unbleached flour

¾ cup water

½ teaspoon salt

Place flour in a bowl, add salt, then water. Work well with one hand and knead until smooth and elastic. Roll and stretch dough as thin as possible. The thinner, the better. Cut into pieces 3 inches square or into circles 3 inches in diameter. Place 1 tablespoon of the filling described below on each square of dough. Fold over dough into triangles. Press edges with a fork and put into soup for 25 minutes or until they float to the top.

Fillings for kreplach: To sauteed onions you can add one of these ingredients:

Pieces of seitan

Cabbage, shredded

Buckwheat groats, cooked (1 cup onion for 1 ½ cup kasha)

The Rising Sun.

>   4 carrots, sliced into ½-inch pieces
>
>   1 medium butter-nut squash, cut into 1-inch square pieces
>
>   3 onions, minced
>
>   ½ medium-size cabbage, shredded
>
>   2 cups cooked chick-peas (pressure-cooked)
>
>   1 tablespoon corn oil
>
>   2 quarts water (juice of chick-peas)
>
>   1 ½ teaspoon salt

Saute onions first, then add cabbage, carrots and squash. Simmer 10 minutes. Add chick-peas and water. Bring to a boil, add salt and simmer 1 hour. It can be served as is or thickened with 1 cup oat flakes presoaked in 1 cup water. Add oats 10 minutes before end of cooking.

This soup can also be served creamy if you blend it in a vegetable mill. Serve with croutons and chopped parsley.

Beet Soup.

>   2 onions, minced
>
>   4 medium beets with their greens. Heads are cut into matchsticks (Julienne) and greens are chopped
>
>   2 cups cooked rice
>
>   7 cups water
>
>   1 teaspoon salt
>
>   1 teaspoon oil
>
>   3 tablespoons soya sauce

Saute onions first, add greens of beets, then heads. Simmer 10 minutes. Add water, rice and salt. Bring to a boil and simmer 1 hour. Add soya sauce before end of cooking.

Sweet Leeks.

> 6 leeks, finely chopped
>
> 1 onion, minced
>
> 1 tablespoon oil
>
> 7 cups water
>
> 1 teaspoon salt
>
> 1 tablespoon soya sauce
>
> 1 tablespoon tahini
>
> ¾ cup oat flakes, presoaked in 1 cup water

Saute onions in oil for 5 minutes, add leeks and then water and salt. Bring to a boil and simmer 20 minutes. Add oat flakes and simmer 15 minutes more. A few minutes before end, add soya sauce and tahini.

Soupe de Vermicelles.

This soup is easy and fast to make. Serve it hot to your husband or a guest who has just arrived from a long journey.

> 2 onions, chopped
>
> 1 cup vermicelli
>
> ½ bay leaf
>
> 3 tablespoons soya sauce
>
> 1 teaspoon oil
>
> ½ teaspoon salt
>
> 1 cup fresh corn kernels
>
> 6 cups water

Saute onions and bay leaf in oil. Add water and bring to a boil. Add vermicelli, salt and corn kernels, then simmer 10-15 minutes. Add soya sauce before end. Instead of vermicelli, wheat semolina, couscous or noodles can be used. They also cook very quickly.

Bulghur Valley.

>   2 leeks, chopped
>
>   2 leaves lettuce, chopped
>
>   Few leaves radish
>
>   1 tablespoon oil
>
>   5 cups water
>
>   4 tablespoons bulghur
>
>   1 teaspoon salt

Saute all greens, add water and bring to a boil. Simmer 10 minutes. Remove from fire and pass through a food mill or blender. Pour back in cooking pot with bulghur and salt. Bring to a boil again and simmer 1 ½ hours. Garnish with croutons and parsley.

Aduki-beans and Company.

>   1 ½ cups aduki beans, already cooked
>
>   1 cup carrots, diced
>
>   1 cup onions, diced
>
>   1 cup celery, diced
>
>   ½ cup scallions, chopped
>
>   8 cups water (juice from cooked adukis can be used)
>
>   1 teaspoon salt
>
>   1 teaspoon miso
>
>   1 tablespoon oil
>
>   ½ cup oat flakes, presoaked in ½ cup water

Saute onions first, then scallions, celery and carrots in oil. Add water, aduki beans, salt and bring to a boil. Simmer 35 minutes. Add flakes and simmer 10 minutes more.

Wakame seaweed or kombu can be added to sauteed vegetables. It is an excellent soup for winter.

Yellow Pool. (Corn soup)

> ½ cup onions, minced
>
> 3 tablespoons tahini
>
> ½ cup oat flakes, soaked in ½ cup water
>
> 6 cobs of corn (use kernels only)
>
> ¼ teaspoon fresh ginger, grated
>
> 1 teaspoon salt
>
> 1 tablespoon oil
>
> 6 cups water

Saute onions in oil; 5 minutes later, add kernels, then water and bring to a boil. Simmer 15 minutes. Add oats, tahini and ginger, then simmer 15 minutes more.

Swiss Chard Velouté.

> 1 pound swiss chard, chopped
>
> 1 onion, minced
>
> 8 tablespoons oat flakes, presoaked in 1 cup water
>
> 5 cups boiling water
>
> 2 tablespoons oil
>
> ¾ teaspoon salt
>
> 1 pinch ground cumin

Saute onions first, then add swiss chard. Add boiling water after 5 minutes. Maintain a low flame and add oats and salt. Cover and simmer 30 to 40 minutes. Stir from time to time, even if you are using an asbestos pad. Add cumin 15 minutes before end. Garnish with parsley.

Celery Fou.

    1 ½ cups lentils

    2 celery stalks with leaves, chopped

    1 onion, sliced

    2 small carrots, diced

    1 ½ quarts water

    1 tablespoon oil

    ¾ teaspoon salt

Cook lentils in water. Cover, bring to a boil and simmer until they are tender (approximately 30 minutes). Add celery, onions and carrots which have been sauteed in oil for 10-15 minutes. Cover and simmer for another 15 minutes. Add salt before end.

Carrot in Thyme.

Although we very seldom put spices in our soups, it helps to have them at home to use on special occasions. You will discover that unsprayed vegetables have such a fine flavor that no cover-ups are needed.

    1 quart water

    2 carrots, diced

    3 onions, minced

    ½ teaspoon salt

    3 tablespoons of any flour, slightly toasted in 1 teaspoon oil

    1 tablespoon oil

    1 pinch thyme

    1 bay leaf

Saute onions and carrots in oil for 10 minutes. Put into boiling water. Add flour gently while stirring. Add bay leaf and thyme, cover and simmer for 25 minutes. Add salt 5 minutes before end.

Amber Stones in Opaque Waters.

To prepare this soup you will have to cook the polenta or corn meal one day in advance. Let it cool, unmold it and later cut it into 1-inch cubes. (See recipe for polenta and corn meal, page 60).

  1 quart water

  3 tablespoons polenta

  2 onions, diced

  1 tablespoon oil

  1 teaspoon salt

Saute onions in oil. Put into boiling water. Pour polenta slowly while stirring. Cover and simmer for 20 minutes. While this is being cooked, oil bottom of a skillet and saute cubes of polenta. Turn gently in order not to break them. It should not take more than 10 minutes to form a surface crust. One tablespoon soya sauce mixed to another of water can be poured over cubes while they are frying in the skillet. Do this just before end. Put 2 or 3 cubes in soup bowls and pour soup on top. Garnish with chopped parsley.

Garden Chick-Pea.

  1 ½ quarts water

  1 cup chick-peas, soaked overnight in warm water

  2 cups celery, chopped

  1 onion, minced

  2 tablespoons tahini

  1 tablespoon oil

  2 tablespoons parsley, chopped

  ½ teaspoon salt

Boil water. Saute onions in oil and put into boiling water. Add soaked chick-peas and cover. Bring to a boil over high flame and simmer for 35 minutes. Add celery, tahini (sesame butter) and parsley. Cover and simmer another 25 minutes.

Velouté de Pois Chiches. (Chick-pea soup)

This is one of the simplest soups, but one of the best. You may use it as a sauce on cereals such as bulghur, cracked wheat, etc.

1 ½ quarts water

1 ½ cups chick-peas, soaked overnight in warm water

2 onions, diced

1 garlic clove, minced

1 tablespoon sesame oil

½ to ¾ teaspoon salt

1 tablespoon parsley, minced

Boil water. Saute garlic in oil over a low flame. When golden, add onions and simmer 10 minutes. Put into boiling water with chick-peas. Cover and bring to a boil over a high flame. Let cook over a medium-high flame for 45 minutes. Add salt 5 minutes before end. Whip mixture in a blender, putting in half the liquid and half the solid matter each time. Serve hot with minced parsley on top.

Fish in the Pond.

This soup is perfect for holidays. It is very easy to prepare, although it looks complicated.

> 2 pounds fresh fish, ground (striped bass or flounder)
>
> 1 egg
>
> 2 tablespoons corn meal or matzo meal
>
> 1 handful parsley, minced
>
> ¼ teaspoon salt

That's for the balls. For the soup prepare:

> 2 garlic cloves, finely chopped
>
> 1 quart water
>
> 2 onions, diced
>
> ¼ teaspoon salt
>
> 2 tablespoons oil
>
> 1 tablespoon parsley, chopped

Saute garlic in oil over a low flame. After 3-4 minutes add onions and parsley. Simmer 10 minutes. In the meantime bring water to a boil and put in onions and parsley.

To make balls, mix well ground fish with egg, corn meal, salt and parsley. Shape into balls 1 inch in diameter, then drop gently into soup. Cover and simmer for 10-15 minutes.

Gazpacho. (Cold soup for summertime)

>2 cups chick-peas cooked in 8 cups water (reserve liquid, which should approximate 4 cups)
>
>2 cups water boiled with 2 umeboshi plums
>
>2 tablespoons tahini
>
>1 onion, minced and sauteed in 1 teaspoon olive oil
>
>¾ teaspoon salt

Put in blender: chick-peas, onion, salt, tahini and 6 cups water.

Then prepare:

>1 grated carrot
>
>1 cucumber, peeled and diced
>
>¼ green pepper, finely chopped and sauteed in 1 teaspoon olive oil
>
>1 fresh garlic clove, grated
>
>3 scallions, finely chopped
>
>4 tablespoons soya sauce

Mix together and serve raw atop blended mixture. Sauteed bread-croutons on top lend a gourmet touch.

Borscht. (For winter)

    3 large onions, chopped

    5 beets, heads grated

    2 carrots, chopped

    1 medium cabbage, shredded

    ½ teaspoon salt

    1 sprig dill

    2 teaspoons oil

    1 tablespoon w.w. flour, toasted

    3 tablespoons soya sauce

    Water to cover

[Handwritten annotations:]
1 Beef soup bone or ribs
1-2 large onions grated
5 beets skinned, grated raw
2 carrotts, grated
1 large potatoe grated
1 teaspoon salt
2 TBS white vinegar   } add right away so beets keep color
1-2 TBS. sugar
Water to cover
Cool a plateful of soup add
3-4 TBS. sour cream & return to pot

Saute the vegetables in oil, first onions, then cabbage, beets and carrots. Pour enough water to cover up the vegetables. Cover, bring to a boil and simmer until vegetables are tender—approximately 25 minutes. Add salt, dill, soya sauce and flour. Simmer 10 more minutes. Garnish with chopped parsley.

Tamari Broth (Soup stock)

    3 inch piece Kombu

    1 tablespoon Bonita flakes or Chirimen Iriko

    3 cups water

    6 tablespoons soya sauce

Bring water to a boil. Add kombu. When water starts boiling again, add dried fish. Simmer 10 minutes. Strain. Then add soya sauce and allow to simmer 10 more minutes.

A Few Things To Remember

Here are the different ingredients you can add to a broth:

Sauteed vegetables

Noodles

Seaweeds

Leftovers of grains or beans

Dumplings

Creamy soups can be made with the following cereals:

Barley flour, toasted

Oat flakes

Buckwheat flour, toasted

Semolina, toasted in oil

Corn meal, toasted in oil

Vegetables

When shopping in a vegetable store, most of us instinctively pick up what is most generous in size for one of two reasons. Either we are attracted by the form itself, which seems beautiful (Americans are fascinated by "bigness" for its own sake), or we discriminate on a practical basis: the larger size is easier to handle, wash and cut.

We find it faster to undress a large onion than four small ones. The same applies, for example, to small, round turnips—in the beginning, unskilled and hurried, our attempts to handle them result in sudden slips and unexpected wounds. Actually, the smaller a vegetable the better, for nutritional and inspirational reasons. A small vegetable forces us to slow down while cooking, thus enhancing the taste and quality of our food: there is nothing worse than fast cooking. It is what produces acidity. The slower the handling and longer the cooking, the more alkaline the food. By looking at a cook at work I can tell if he produces acid or alkaline food. Small vegetables, then, will help you cook better by teaching you patience.

Buy your vegetables fresh. Try to find a source of chemically unsprayed greens. In our home we have been eating vegetables bought at
the local market for years, for it was all we could get. Now, a few miles
from us a natural-food store has opened. Carrots, onions, celery, squash
and a few other vegetables are available—quite enough for the winter.
In spring again, our variety will be larger.

Once home, prior to cooking by means of sauteeing, stewing, steaming or baking, we enact a complete ritual of preparation involving selection, washing and cutting. Always wash vegetables under cold water,
scrubbing off dirt with a special brush. Avoid soaking or peeling. For
cutting, use a Japanese knife with a square end. The most practical method, preferred by chefs, is to place the square end of the knife (at the
tip) against the cutting board. Without lifting the tip, raise and lower
the handle-end of the knife. Be careful not to cut yourself—this kind of
knife is very sharp!

Each kind of cooking has a different method of cutting. For sauteeing
alone there are more than two or three dozen shapes. Let us examine a
few of them and from there you can follow your own inclinations.

Grating means to scrape with any mechanical device, machine or
grater in order to obtain shavings the size of which never exceeds the
volume and shape of a half-inch vermicelli.

Slicing means to cut a vegetable finely into thin flat and round (or
oval) pieces. A slice of carrot may be so thin that it curls up. To prepare
Fish Kebab, slicing would be the required method to provide sufficient
time for cooking in oil. A sliced zucchini, on the other hand, should be
a bit thicker to prevent its falling apart while being cooked.

Chopping means to cut vegetables rapidly into small pieces ranging
in size from a grain of rice to a green pea. Typical vegetables for chopping would be parsley and onions, which would be used in a sauce more
for the taste they could add to the preparation than for their looks.

Dicing means to cut in small cubes slightly smaller than one-quarter
-inch square. The cubes should have a definite outline and should be as
geometrically perfect as possible.

Cubing is identical to dicing except that the cut forms should have a
shape approximately half-an-inch square.

Shredding means to cut vegetables into very thin, long strips. To facilitate such cutting in the case of cabbage, lettuce, etc., trim a few leaves, place them atop each other, roll tightly together into a spiral and cut through every eighth of an inch.

Slivering is like sharpening a pencil with a knife. Slivered burdock, for example, is cut in this manner so that it will more quickly saute or cook in soups. You know that the smaller the size of a vegetable, the less time it takes to cook.

Julienne is the name the French apply to vegetables cut in the form of matchsticks. Length can be one to three inches, thickness an eighth of an inch or so, depending on the consistency of the vegetable and on the way you plan to cook it.

Chunks are large pieces. Volume varies from 1 inch in width to 2 inches in length.

There are other shapes such as triangles (when, for instance, a cross-section of carrot is cut into four equal parts), moons, circles, squares, and dozens of others which I leave to your creative imagination. We are now ready to take the big step that will bring us right down to our pots and pans and preparations.

* * *

Sauteing Vegetables

We saute our vegetables more than we steam, pressure-cook, bake or boil them. We boil them in soups, of course, and cook them in many other ways during a typical week. But we prefer sauteing because we believe it to be the most nutritious form of preparation, apart from the fact that it is very practical and tasty. If you prefer your vegetables steamed or baked; however, be assured that there is nothing wrong with these methods as long as you are using the right cooking utensils.

Speaking of pots, it is advisable to use the heaviest you can find, be they enameled, cast iron, stainless steel, glassware or earthenware. The thicker they are, the less acid your food will be.

The different methods.

Some vegetables have a better taste and are more practical to cook when finely cut and sauteed in a relatively short time, in a skillet or Chinese wok. The fast method is most helpful when you have unexpected and hungry guests waiting in your livingroom. Either cook your vegetables one at a time in separate pans, or prepare in combination. First let us learn how to saute a vegetable by itself according to the fast method.

The fast method.

Cut a carrot or any other member of this family into matchsticks (Julienne). For two carrots use 1 teaspoon oil which has been previously heated in a skillet. Keep flame high while stirring constantly and rapidly for 5 minutes. Now you may either cover and let cook over a medium-high flame for another 10 minutes, stirring from time to time, or remain near the fire for another 8 minutes or so, stirring constantly with a wooden instrument over a high flame. The later method produces crispier vegetables. They are softer with the former method because of being covered.

In both cases, add salt or soya sauce a minute or two before the end. Serve hot with rice or any other cereal. You can use this method in combining different vegetables together. Do not forget that only chopped, shredded, diced and finely sliced vegetables can cook in a relatively fast time. Try together:

> Onions, carrots, cabbage
>
> Watercress and carrots
>
> Turnips and beets
>
> Lettuce, scallions and slivered burdock
>
> Other combinations recommended elsewhere.

The long method.

In this longer method there are two variations, one with water and one without.

Sauteing vegetables without water.

This is the way we cook vegetables most of the time in our home. It is easy and takes 30 to 45 minutes, depending on how big and tough the vegetables are.

Use a heavy pot with a lid instead of a skillet. In this way you can cook a larger volume of vegetables.

Cut vegetables into cubes or chunks—you may even dice them—and place in a pan covered with pre-heated oil. Use 1 tablespoon of oil for 1 pound of vegetables. To avoid burned oil, which will give a bad taste to your cooking, maintain a low flame. Hold the covered pan by its handles and shake it in a counter-clockwise circle. This will cause the oil to spread and will prevent the vegetables from burning. Cover with a heavy lid and simmer for 30 to 45 minutes. Every now and then shake the pot with the same counter-clockwise movement. While some people use wooden spoons to stir instead of shaking, I prefer not to break the food with any instrument. However, if you find the shaking too tiresome, use a wooden spoon or three extra-large chopsticks. Add salt 5 minutes before the end.

Sauteing vegetables with water.

Most people find it too difficult to cook without water. Because of a high flame or the wrong kind of pot they burn their vegetables. Here is a practical method for them.

Heat oil in pan and put in vegetables. Use 1 tablespoon oil for 1 pound of vegetables. Cover and let cook over high flame for 5 minutes. Uncover and pour in half a glass of water. Cover again and bring to a boil, then lower the flame and simmer 30 to 45 minutes. Check from time to time to see if water has evaporated. Add a few drops if necessary. Salt before the end.

A few combinations.

There are some vegetables that can be satisfactorily combined in cooking, and others that can only be prepared separately because of certain hazards arising from incompatible textures or flavors. Here are some examples of those you can mix together:

Onions-carrots-cabbage

Do not forget to cook onions first whenever you cook other vegetables with them. Saute onions over medium flame until they change color (3-5 minutes), then add others.

Scallions-carrots-watercress

If you use this combination you should saute scallions first, wait 2 minutes and then add carrots (diced). Add watercress at the end.

Scallions-carrots-boiled chick-peas

This combination is excellent, especially when you mix it with cooked rice. Saute the scallions first; 2 minutes later add diced carrots, then chick-peas. Be careful not to use chick-peas that are too soft. They could disintegrate and make the dish unattractive. To avoid, add them 10 minutes before the end.

Try:

Onions-carrots-boiled chick-peas

Scallions-zucchini-celery

Onions-string beans-carrots

Onions-brussel sprouts-carrots

Scallions-lettuce-slivered burdock

Onions-cauliflower-carrots

Onions-scallions-dandelion

Onions-beets

Parsley-carrots

Beets-turnips

Here are a few combinations I advise you to cook and present separately:

Broccoli-carrots-turnips

Onions-squash-broccoli

Burdock-carrots-beets

Swiss chard-carrots-cauliflower

Lotus root-scallions-carrots

Cabbage-onions-broccoli

Zuchini-lotus root-onions

Onions-celery-fresh corn kernels

Parsnips-carrots-burdock

Some vegetables such as lettuce, celery, swiss chard, etc. need little water in cooking. Others such as carrots and turnips need more oil to keep from burning. Burdock, which takes a great while to cook when cut into big chunks, needs much more water than any other vegetable. Cover it with water and pressure-cook for 30 minutes. Some people add 1 or 2 salted plums instead of salt. It's excellent!

If you use soya sauce instead of salt, always add it toward the end, especially when vegetables are not cooked with water. When soya sauce mixed with water (1/3 water to 2/3 tamari) hits the bottom of the pan, it splashes and penetrates because of the heat and quickly flavors the vegetables. Always stir following addition of tamari.

Some vegetables require special treatment before being put in the pot. Broccoli, for example, should be shorn of its large leaves and harder portions. Use flowerettes and stalks only. Hard portions can be used in soups, or chopped or diced for faster cooking. If broccoli flowerettes do not appear fresh, revive them in salted water. They will turn a surprisingly crisp green. The same is true of cauliflower. Broccoli has a succulent taste when cooked with salted plums and sesame seeds; instead of salt or soya sauce add 2 or 3 plums for 1 pound of broccoli. Always cook broccoli and cauliflower in more water than other vegetables. For 1 pound use ½ cup water. Don't forget to cover with a lid.

Saute Specials.

Here are other special combinations which you should try. They are easy to make and very delicious.

Radishes in miso.

Saute 2 dozen red radishes in 1 tablespoon oil. Add ¼ cup water and simmer 10 minutes. Later add chopped leaves and simmer another 10 minutes, covered. Dilute 1 round teaspoon miso in 3 tablespoons water and add to radish. Simmer 5 minutes more.

In a similar vein, try:

> Beets "Julienne," with their leaves chopped
>
> Turnips "Julienne," with their leaves chopped
>
> Watercress with sesame seeds. Saute watercress and add slightly toasted sesame seeds before the end. Watercress should not take more than 10 minutes to cook. Chop it into small pieces.

Sauerkraut Express.

Another excellent and fast dish! It tastes like sauerkraut, but is a bit finer.

> 1 small cabbage, shredded
>
> 2 onions, minced
>
> 3 pits of salted plums (use pulp for instant vinegar)
>
> 1 pinch salt
>
> 1/8 cup water
>
> 1 tablespoon oil

Saute onions in oil for 2 minutes. Add cabbage and pits. Cover and simmer 15 minutes. Add water and simmer another 15 minutes.

String beans in umeboshi juice.

> 2 pounds string beans, cut into pieces half an inch in length (slice ends diagonally)
>
> 1 tablespoon oil
>
> 1 pinch salt
>
> 1 cup umeboshi juice (see recipe, page 183)

Saute string beans in oil over a medium-high flame for 5 minutes. Keep stirring and add umeboshi juice. Cover and simmer until beans are tender. It takes approximately 20 minutes. Add pinch of salt before the end.

Endives a la francaise.

> 10 small endives (Belgian)
>
> 1 garlic clove, minced
>
> 1 tablespoon olive oil
>
> 2 tablespoons soya sauce
>
> 3 tablespoons water
>
> 1 tablespoon sesame butter

Saute garlic in oil over low flame for 1 minute. Place endives on top, cover and simmer 10 minutes. Add water mixed with sesame butter and soya sauce. Cover and simmer again 10 minutes more. Instead of endives, you can use kale.

Onion-apple dialogue, with salt as a witness.

> 4 apples, including peel, cut into 8 slices
>
> 4 onions, cut into quarters
>
> 1 tablespoon raisins
>
> 1 pinch salt
>
> 1 tablespoon sesame oil

Saute onions in oil for 5 minutes. Add apples and raisins. Cover and simmer for 15 minutes. Serve with a sweet cereal such as barley or polenta in summertime. Most excellent!

Rutabaga Madame.

> 1 large rutabaga, cut "Julienne"
>
> 2 onions, minced
>
> 1 tablespoon oil
>
> 1 umeboshi pit
>
> 1 tablespoon soya sauce
>
> 1 pinch salt

Saute onions in oil for 5 minutes. Add rutabaga and umeboshi pit. Cover and simmer 10 minutes. Add salt and soya sauce; cover and simmer 10 minutes more. Use a low flame to avoid having to add water.

Zucchini in dill.

　　1 pound zucchini, cut "Julienne"

　　1 tablespoon oil

　　1 pinch salt

　　1 tablespoon sesame butter

　　1 teaspoon fresh dill

　　1 tablespoon soya sauce

Saute zucchini in oil for 5 minutes. Add salt and mixture of sesame butter and soya sauce. Add dill, cover and simmer 10 minutes.

Carrot in ginger.

　　4 cups carrots, cubed

　　¼ teaspoon ginger, grated

　　½ teaspoon arrow-root, diluted in 3 tablespoons water

　　2 tablespoons sesame oil

　　¼ cup water

　　½ teaspoon salt

Saute carrots in oil for 5 minutes. Add ginger. Cover and simmer until tender. Add diluted arrow-root. Simmer another minute or two.

Carrot panee (for holidays).

　　6 medium-size carrots

　　1 egg

　　½ cup bread-crumbs or corn-meal

Roll in beaten egg, then cornmeal, then saute in oiled skillet. Remove when golden. Serve hot with soya sauce.

CREAMED VEGETABLES

If you wish, vegetables prepared this way can be served as a sauce poured over grains. Because of their excellent appearance and taste, they can also be served separately, as an accompaniment to grains. They do not take long to cook.

Creamed onions.

> 12-16 small onions, whole
>
> 1 teaspoon salt
>
> 1 teaspoon oil
>
> 1 teaspoon bonito flakes
>
> 1 piece of kombu, 2 by 2 inches square
>
> 1 cup bechamel sauce (see recipe, page 177)

Saute onions in oil, add kombu and ¼ cup water. Pressure-cook for 3 minutes, open lid and remove kombu. Add a thick bechamel sauce and allow to mix with juices of cooked kombu and whole onions. Use as a stuffing for squash or pour over bulghur. Leek and endives can be substituted for onions.

Chou-Fleur Mondain.

> 1 small cauliflower
>
> 3 carrots, cut into ½-inch slices
>
> 3 medium-size onions, cut into quarters
>
> ½ teaspoon salt
>
> 1 teaspoon oil
>
> 2 cups bechamel sauce (see recipe, page 177)

Separate cauliflower-head into flowerettes. Saute onions in oil, add cauliflower, then carrots for 5 minutes. Add 1 cup water, salt and pressure-cook for 8 minutes. Open lid, add bechamel sauce, and pour over any cereal.

Swiss Chard Rue de Seine.

> 1 bunch swiss chard, hard part diced, leaves chopped
>
> 1 teaspoon oil
>
> 1 pinch salt
>
> ½ cup water
>
> 1 cup bechamel sauce (see recipe, page 177)

Saute hard parts in oil for 1 minute, then add leaves and saute together for 5 minutes. Add ½ cup water, salt and cook for ½ hour until tender. Add bechamel.

Variation: Yellow summer squash or broccoli.

BAKED VEGETABLES

Once in a while as a change-of-pace, try this method of cooking your vegetables. The advantage it has is that you don't have to take much care of it. Vegetables come out "unbroken" and with a softer texture. It is perfect when you're entertaining many guests. Just serve in the platter in which the vegetables have been cooked and let everyone help himself!

A few vegetables can be baked just as they are on a baking sheet; simply oil their surfaces:

> Whole squash, unpeeled. Bake in oven 45 minutes, uncovered
>
> Whole beets baked in a dish, unpeeled and covered with aluminum foil. Leave in oven 40 minutes.
>
> Carrots, cut into halves or whole. Bake 40 minutes

The silent spring.

> 3 carrots, cut into chunks
>
> 2 tablespoons oil
>
> 1 butternut squash, cut into chunks and peeled
>
> ½ cup water
>
> 2 tablespoons tamari

Saute carrots and butternut squash in oil for 5-10 minutes, put in a casserole dish, add water and tamari (soya sauce). Cover with aluminum foil and bake 40 minutes in a 350-degree oven. Uncover and bake another 15-20 minutes more.

Variations:

> Carrot-cauliflower. Use the same method as in the preceding recipe except that cauliflower should be boiled for 10 minutes in salted water before baking.
>
> Carrots-small turnips.

Stuffed turnips.

Saute whole turnips after cutting holes in tops. Boil in a small amount of water to soften (2 cups for 6-8 turnips). Place in casserole dish and fill with puree of squash and onions. Use water in which turnips have been boiled and add 2 tablespoons tamari. Cover and bake 40 minutes.

Potiron en fleur.

Oil yellow surface of squash cut in half. Acorn or buttercup squash is preferable. Bake in a 400-degree oven for 40 minutes or so until tender. Take out seeds. Stuff with *creamed onions* (see recipe, page 118) and place under broiler for 5 minutes before serving.

VEGETABLES AU GRATIN

This method of cooking is very French, although many countries have adopted it. Vegetables are always baked in earthenware pots or heavy glassware. They arrive steaming hot from the oven to grace the table. Sometimes, to give added color and a richer taste, we take them out of the oven and place them in a broiler for 5-10 minutes, time enough for the top to scorch to a golden brown.

To gratine, top with the following:

½ cup toasted oats (also try other kinds of flakes)

or

½ cup raw rice cream combined with 2 tablespoons oil

or

½ cup bread crumbs

or

½ cup "wheatena"

In general, bake in a 350-degree oven and then broil to brown the top.

Chou fleur gratinee.

1 cauliflower head, cut into flowerettes

1 tablespoon oil

1 cup water

1 cup bechamel sauce (see recipe, page 177)

½ cup topping

Saute flowerettes in oil for 5 minutes. Add 1 cup water and simmer until tender but crispy. Put in a casserole dish, cover with bechamel sauce, sprinkle with a topping of your choice and bake for 20 minutes until top is brown. You may put it in a broiler for 5 minutes or so.

Instead of cauliflower broccoli can be used.

Parsnip gratinee.

> 1 pound parsnip, sliced
>
> 1 tablespoon oil
>
> 1 cup water
>
> 1 pinch salt
>
> 1 cup bechamel sauce
>
> ½ cup topping of your choice

Saute parsnip in oil, add water, pinch of salt and cook until soft. Mash with a fork and put into a casserole pan. Cover with bechamel sauce and sprinkle with topping. Bake for 20 minutes until a brown top is obtained.

Variations:

> Endives au gratin
>
> Leeks au gratin

Always saute vegetables until soft and then bake.

Chopped toasted almonds can be used as a topping for these fine vegetables.

VEGETABLE CASSEROLE

Casserole cookery is another French method of preparing food layered in heavy pots and cooked in the oven. Here is a combination of vegetables baked one on top of the other.

Squash asleep, with onions and watercress for blankets.

> 2 butternut squash, cut into chunks, sauteed in 1 tablespoon oil
>
> 3 onions, minced and sauteed in 1 tablespoon oil
>
> 1 bunch watercress, sauteed in 1 tablespoon oil
>
> ½ cup water
>
> 2 tablespoons tamari
>
> ½ cup bread crumbs mixed with 2 tablespoons oil

Place ½ the squash in the bottom of casserole dish; then in succeeding layers add onions, the other half of the squash and, on top, watercress. Pour on tamari-water solution. Sprinkle mixture with bread crumbs and bake in a 350-degree oven. Watercress can be substituted with swiss chard, and bread crumbs with raw rice cream.

124

Cabbage and apple embrace.

> 3 cups red cabbage, shredded and sauteed in
>
> 1 teaspoon oil
>
> 1 cup apples, peeled, thinly sliced and sauteed in
>
> 1 teaspoon oil
>
> 1 pinch salt
>
> ¼ cup water
>
> 1 tablespoon tahini
>
> ½ cup bread crumbs mixed with 2 tablespoons oil

In an oiled casserole dish, make four layers by alternating the following: ½ the sauteed cabbage followed by ½ the sauteed apples, then the remaining cabbage and, finally, the rest of the apples. Pour over the layers ¼ cup water mixed with tahini and containing a pinch of salt. Top with crumb mixture and bake in a 350-degree oven for 20 minutes covered, then for 10 additional minutes, uncovered.

Variations:

> 1 pound sauteed and steamed brussel sprouts covered with
>
> 1 cup pureed squash or carrot, covered again with
>
> 2 sauteed onions.
>
> Top with a mixture of 1 cup toasted oats and 1/3 cup chopped almonds.

VEGETABLE STEW

A stew is a dish which looks almost like a soup. You set the pot on the table and everyone helps himself with a wooden spoon. It also makes a nice side dish.

Chestnut Scaphandrier.

> 1 pound chestnuts, pressure-cooked for 30 minutes and peeled
>
> 2 carrots, diced
>
> 2 parsnips, diced
>
> 1 onion, diced
>
> 2 cabbage leaves, shredded
>
> ¼ teaspoon salt
>
> 1 tablespoon sesame oil
>
> 1 dash marjoram

In a heavy pot saute onions, cabbage, parsnips and carrots. Ten minutes later add chestnuts, salt and cover with water. Boil, then simmer for 45 minutes until vegetables are well-cooked. The longer it cooks, the better it tastes. Try to cook for 1 ½ hours.

Three sailors after three mermaids.

>   3 carrots, cut into diagonal slices of ½ inch thickness
>
>   3 burdock roots, cut into diagonal slices of ½ inch thickness
>
>   2 onions, chopped
>
>   1 Chinese cabbage, sliced into ½-inch pieces
>
>   2 tablespoons oil
>
>   2 tablespoons arrow-root diluted in ½ cup water
>
>   2 tablespoons miso diluted in ¼ cup lukewarm water
>
>   ¼ teaspoon salt
>
>   1 piece kombu cut into ½-inch squares

Saute onions until golden and add cabbage; carrot, kombu and burdock are added together at the end. Cover with water, bring to a boil, add salt and simmer until vegetables are tender. Add miso and arrow-root diluted in water, mix, then simmer 20 minutes.

Sweet and sour stew.

>   1 cup onions, chopped
>
>   1 cup cabbage, shredded
>
>   ½ cup parsnips, diced
>
>   ½ cup carrots, diced
>
>   1 teaspoon sesame oil
>
>   1/3 cup raisins
>
>   ½ teaspoon salt
>
>   1 tablespoon tahini
>
>   2 pits of umeboshi plums

Saute cabbage in oil, then parsnip and carrots. Add raisins and pits, then tahini and salt and cover with water. Bring to a boil and simmer approximately 1 hour.

You can also cook vegetables by boiling, pressure-cooking or steaming them.

For steaming, pour 3 or 4 cups of water in the lower part of the steamer. Place vegetables in the upper, perforated part and cover. Bring to a boil and simmer 30 minutes or so—depending on the size of the vegetable. Add salt to taste just before the end.

Vegetables can also be boiled, especially leafy varities such as swiss chard, lettuce, etc. Retain their juices for soups or cold salads during summertime.

The pressure-cooking of vegetables should be saved for days when you find yourself at a loss for time. Only a few minutes are necessary; in fact, most vegetables take no more than 2 or 3 minutes, once the pressure-regulator starts jiggling. Cabbage and squash, however, require 6 to 8 minutes. Just remember, the smaller the vegetable, the faster it cooks.

The first meal

Eating one's first cerealian meal is the solemn moment of transition between the world of dependency and the world of freedom. To switch from one to the other requires an act of faith. Meat eating keeps man thinking within the enveloping star formed by the five senses. While his sixth sense, his "impossible dream" remains undeveloped. He draws its fantasies in his mind, but never dares to act or sail upon its waves. The heavy meat eater is a slave whose burden is as great as his ignorance.

When I was in France, however, I frankly enjoyed meat balls. I ate meat balls when I was in France. My mother made them for my father, who is accustomed to having them on Saturdays. I took one, and even two. They were delicious! I have no fear of meat when it is presented in moderation. I am sensitive to quality, be it meat or grain.

I know personally hundreds of meat-eaters who have switched to cereals. They change so much that I always find myself astonished to see them two or three months after the day of their "conversion." Some commit themselves immediately, completely abandoning meat in favor of cereals. Others proceed more slowly, introducing a modicum of grains and vegetables into their meat-based diets. Both ways are satisfactory. Everyone should advance at his own pace. For those who decide to follow the more leisurely path I recommend a three-stage approach.

Stage one: Avoid soft drinks or sugar in any form, and reduce the a-mount of liquid taken in. Eat widely, including many varieties of cer-eals and vegetables. Instead of meat twice a day, have it only once. You can satisfactorily remain at this stage for a month or two or even longer.

Generally speaking, for dinner, have a vegetable soup and a main course including two-fifths meat, one-fifth cereal, and two-fifths salad and vegetables. With time try to increase the proportion of cereals, preferably brown rice; gradually decrease the amount of meat. For dessert, try to avoid all sweet products containing sugar. If possible, a-void drinking during meals, and afterwards replace coffee with hot Bancha tea.

Stage two: Continue serving soup, preferably made with miso. In place of meat begin eating fish; on occasion fowl is acceptable. Other evenings focus exclusively on grains and vegetables. Generally, balance of the meals should be two-fifths cereals, one-fifth vegetables, one-fifth salad and one-fifth soup. With time increase the percentage of grains. As a variant to rice, try buckwheat or millet.

For dessert, emphasize unsweetened varieties such as baked or boiled fruits or pies. Afterwards, serve hot bancha tea or grain coffee.

Stage three: This is less difficult, especially if stage two has been going smoothly. Meals will become simpler. Fish should be eaten only occasionally. After soup, the main dish will include half grains and half vegetables which have been sauteed or baked. This is a safe stage from which you can proceed downward or upward. When visiting, eat in moderation what is offered—if you are healthy. If your condition is not so good, it is wiser to avoid eating outside your home.

Those who wish to involve themselves with the diet quickly should begin with the third stage, which is still sufficiently flexible. Every so often it is possible to suspend or resume this stage without difficulty, if desired.

Both the "fast" and the "slow" beginners should of course attempt to maintain good balance in their meals. It is essential to learn to respect the four seasons and to eat accordingly. The chapter entitled "What We Ate Last Week" is a good example of how my family and I have managed for nine years, without once being drawn into bingeing.

Sea vegetables

If you are unfamiliar with seaweeds, you will discover, after cooking them for only a short while, that it is no fiction, fashion or fad, and it is not because of food shortages due to overpopulation on earth, that we come to eat them. Seaweed has a fine taste, elegant enough for the most discriminating palate. Besides, it is good for the nervous system and hair. Beneficial effects which I have experienced myself!

Generally, all seaweeds must be soaked and washed before being cooked. As a rule we leave them in water between 5 to 15 minutes until they soften.

Hijiki.

We use this seaweed more than any other, perhaps because it is the most practical to cook and serve. It can be eaten warm or cold, in salads, mixed with vegetables, or served as a side dish.

>3 ounces hijiki
>
>2 tablespoons oil
>
>10 tablespoons soya sauce
>
>Water to cover

Rinse hijiki with cold water in a strainer. Allow to soak 10 minutes. Rinse again. Do not discard water, which will be used later for the cooking. Chop or cut hijiki into 1 to 2 inch lengths. Heat oil in a large skillet, then saute hijiki on a medium-high flame for 10 minutes. Remove from fire and put aside for a few minutes. Add water in which it has been presoaked. Bring to a boil, add soya sauce and simmer uncovered for 45 minutes to an hour, until most of the liquid has evaporated.

Hijiki-carrot-onion.

>2 ounces hijiki
>
>2 carrots, diced
>
>2 onions, diced
>
>1 tablespoon oil for hijiki
>
>1 tablespoon oil for vegetables
>
>10 tablespoons soya sauce

Wash and soak hijiki. Saute onions and carrots; after 5 minutes add hijiki with its water. Bring to a boil and simmer uncovered for 30 minutes. Add soya sauce, cover and simmer again for 30 minutes. Stir from time to time.

Hijiki, Lotus-Root.

> 3 ounces hijiki
>
> 8 ounces lotus-root
>
> 2 tablespoons sesame oil
>
> 12 tablespoons soya sauce
>
> 1 tablespoon toasted sesame seeds

If you are using dried lotus-root, soak it overnight. Wash and soak hijiki, then saute it. Dice lotus-root and saute. Put hijiki and lotus-root in a saucepan or a large skillet with water in which hijiki has been soaked. Bring to a boil, cover and simmer 45 minutes. Uncover for the final 15 minutes. Add soya sauce and sesame seeds once you have uncovered the saucepan. Serve with chopped parsley on top.

Kombu.

> 1 sheet kombu
>
> 4 cups water
>
> 1 teaspoon salt
>
> 12 tablespoons soya sauce

Break a sheet of kombu into 4 or 5 pieces and soak in water for 10 minutes. Kombu sheets are now tender. Cut into 1-inch squares. Boil water in which kombu has been soaked. Add kombu and another 6 cups of water, then simmer 45 minutes. Add salt and soya sauce and simmer 15 to 20 minutes more. Serve as is or in soups. Keeps in a jar for weeks.

Deep-fried kombu.

To soften, clean a big sheet of kombu with a wet cloth. Cut into 1 by 4 inch pieces and form each piece into a knot.

Rolled Kombu.

> 1 piece kombu, 6" by 2"
>
> 1 carrot, sliced into ¼-inch pieces
>
> 1 burdock root, sliced
>
> 2 tablespoons soya sauce
>
> 3 cups water
>
> 8 gourd strips, 6 inches long (sold in Japanese stores)
>
> 1 teaspoon oil

Saute carrot and burdock in oil for 15 minutes over medium-high flame. Place lengthwise in center of kombu sheet and tie sheet tight with gourd strips. Place in a pressure-cooker with the 3 cups of water in which kombu has been soaked. Close and pressure-cook for 30 minutes. Open pressure-cooker, add soya sauce and cook covered without pressure for another 10 minutes. Cut roll into 4 equal pieces and serve hot or cooled.

Nori.

Toasted nori is sprinkled over noodles, rice, soups, vegetables, etc. To toast it, hold it over a high flame, waving constantly with a quick motion to prevent burning. It takes no more than 15-20 seconds. Some people cook nori for 10 minutes in a bit of water.

Nori-Sesame Seeds.

> 5 sheets nori
>
> 1 teaspoon sesame seeds
>
> 1 teaspoon sesame oil
>
> 2 tablespoons soya sauce

Cut each sheet into 4 equal pieces. Soak in water and saute in oil. Simmer 10 minutes in ¼ cup water in which it has been soaked. Add soya sauce and simmer another 5 minutes. Serve sprinkled with sesame seeds or pieces of fried tofu (bean curds).

Wakame.

There are many ways to cook this seaweed. Miso soup without it is not miso soup. It can be baked in the oven, deep-fried or toasted over a flame like nori.

For cooking, soak it in water 5 or 10 minutes, then cut into ¼-inch pieces and bring to a boil the water in which it has been soaked. Add soya sauce before end of cooking. Use same proportions as for hijiki but with less water.

Wakame-Burdock-Onion.

> 3 ounces wakame
>
> 2 burdock roots, slivered
>
> 2 onions, diced
>
> 1 tablespoon oil
>
> 6 tablespoons soya sauce

Soak wakame and cut into ½-inch pieces. Saute onions in oil; after 5 minutes add burdock, then wakame. Add 1 cup water in which wakame has been soaked. Cover and bring to a boil. Simmer 20 minutes. Add a few drops of soaking water if necessary. Add soya sauce and simmer 10 minutes more.

Variation: Wakame-carrot-onion

Dulse.

Prepare and cook dulse like wakame. It takes less water and time to cook. Soak, then saute in oil. Add ½ cup water in which it has been soaked and simmer 15 minutes. Add soya sauce and simmer 5 minutes more.

Agar-Agar.

Soak 1 sponge bar in 2 3/4 cups of water for 30 minutes. Bring to a boil and allow to simmer covered for 10 minutes. It will thicken when cooled. It is an important ingredient for desserts and aspics.

Fruits, meat, grains and man

Health or freedom given by others is your debt. You must pay your debt sooner or later, otherwise you are a slave or a thief.

Georges Ohsawa

The sleek, bald, pale and ascetic fruitarian lives next to the health-food store in midtown Manhattan, drinks a quart of orange juice, and forces down another quart of carrot juice mixed with celery and parlsey every day. He is looking for a way out. Florida, where he hopes the sun will warm his flesh and simmer the chill out of his bones, beckons irresistibly.

For twenty winters, he has been unable to cope with the biting cold. He has had to be hyperactive in order to compensate for his sedentary job and the energy lacking in his food. In quest of energy he has eaten, every two hours or so, almonds, wheat germ, honey and other mock meats. On the other hand he has had to fast two or three times a month for a few days to prevent coming down with a cold and to dispel mucus.

He appears healthy and alert—but his alertness derives from fear of the lunatic moods of New York City weather.

I met him not long ago, just two weeks prior to his anticipated departure for the south. He complained of not having enough money to stay away longer than three or four months. He said he liked his job in the city and wondered if he could find a similar position in Florida.

I made him a proposition. "Why do you want to go to Florida? Why not let Florida come to you?"

"That's easy to say," he replied, "but slightly impractical."

"It's the food you eat that makes you cold. Change it and you'll save all the trouble of a trip."

And he did. I last saw him at my brother's restaurant.

"I have burning charcoal in here!" he exclaimed, slapping his belly.

Franz Kafka wrote melancholy literature and died from tuberculosis at forty-two. He lived in the cold city of Prague, where he followed a strict vegetarian diet. The Yellow Emperor's Classic of Internal Medicine, 5,000 years old, proclaims, "Bad lungs, melancholia." Such was Kafka's condition.

Vegetarians possess a laudable human wish to return to nature. Unfortunately, the method of attaining their goal counters the very laws of that same nature. Any such return should not be childish but should be that of a man who chooses his way in full understanding.

At times nature produces excessive heat, and at other times, through cold and rough winds, she stimulates philosophical thought. In turn, we are grateful to her for her magnanimous teachings, even though they be hard-learned.

But this the vegetarian does not know. He is a child who refuses to grow, so overwhelmed is he by nature's wonders. He runs and hides under her wing like a feathery chick.

Man should not bow to nature. On the contrary, she has been created his unconditional servant. When Man's sentiments run high, unity with nature is accomplished.

Vegetarianism is a satisfactory intermediate stage for the meat-eater who requires cleansing. Meat-produced energy "stays" for a while in the body. But when raw food can no longer satisfy, a new diet must be adopted which balanced the extremes of fruit and meat.

* * *

There is nothing wrong with eating fruit. However, within the last few decades, *overeating* it has become a source of innumerable sicknesses. It is easy to see that the number of children stricken with poliomyelitis increases during times of excess consumption of fruit. In America, there is no such thing as the "fruit season." Summer or winter, a large variety of fruit is displayed on the stands. There is no season for sickness in a place where sickness is sold at any time by the bushel. A bouquet of taste and color enters by the front door and shamefully exits through the back door as a crippled child.

Fruit is certainly not bad. He who believes so is a fool. Fruit is another of Man's companions, and, as a dear friend, should not be abused. Freedom is measure for measure and proper proportion—not pathological inundation of the senses. I eat of fruit what is appropriate for myself. Each moment has its measure. Infinity, and infinite actions and thoughts, are my self-determined scale. I am what I eat and I know that the garden of Eden is nothing but a replica of my freedom. So, while I will have no part of restricted action, neither will I forget that my desire is the true desire to become Man. Any smaller desire, such as the craving for fruit, must be measured against that higher purpose.

The ultra-sensitive vegetarian or fruitarian who is repelled by meat is like a disturbed young man who does not include in his love for the world the love of his father and mother. Love is universal and excludes no one. It is not a matter of choice. It comes free and returns free to its source.

I am eternally grateful to the birds and fowl whose flesh satisfied the hunger of my brothers lost in the wilderness. I am grateful to any meal that makes Man happy.

Food is food and Man is Man. The choice that converts one to the other should be a matter of understanding and not of prejudice. If a man asks you for food, give him what he wants—not what your ignorance prefers to feed him. Everyone is his own master and is free to determine at each moment the direction of his growth.

There is no shame in eating meat and no law that forbids it. He who prefers not to consume it must not proclaim its condemnation. If he finds fault in it, let him speak in sound understanding alone, not out of affectation or extreme weakness of the senses.

A daily ration of meat, of course, is not for the man who wishes to study philosophy. For that he must eat what is biologically farther removed in history. God created food in this order: water, the vegetal, grains, fruits, fish, birds and animals. Eating what is farther back on the evolutionary trail takes us to the origins of body and mind; it enlightens the far-distant past, stimulating memory so that we recall life's infinite depths.

Without doubt, a vegetarian has a far better memory than a meat-eater. It is a biological fact, and it is justice. We are what we eat.

The meaning of a phenomenon is found in its physical or metaphysical counterpart—everything depends on point of view. True similarities are never symmetrical; one is flesh and the other spirit. Consider two brothers who do not look alike physically but have a similar "air" and are often mistaken for one another. So with Man's food—it is not by physical resemblance that he chooses, but rather by seeking that same familiar air that betokens recognition, as though he were meeting a long-lost friend in a far country.

We eat flesh to be more of this earth, and eat vegetables to acquaint ourselves with heaven. The vegetarian is a pious man and the meat-eater a man of sensorial actions.

Scientifically speaking, meat is not suitable for man's daily consumption for many reasons. After an excessive intake, it decomposes in the intestines, creating poisons such as uric acid, which accumulates in the tissues and blood. (This happens more often when meat is not accompanied by salad or fruit.) In time a generally acid condition results, bringing the person thus afflicted to the continual use of alkaline "anti-acids." Everyone knows how widespread their use is today.

Meat has another extraordinary side-effect. It quickens activity in the organs, thus causing deleterious changes in the entire system, insufficient time being left for the body to perfect its natural transmutations.

Flesh-eating has been found by many biochemists to be one of the most significant factors in producing heart disease and high blood pressure. Consuming flesh almost immediately accelerates the heart-beat. Paradoxically, even though this may seem beneficial, it is the rapid decay of flesh that creates this reaction. Poisons accumulate in the intestines. In order to expel them, the body accelerates its functions. People mistake this activity with true strength because of the false (and short-lived) vigor deriving from it. Two or three hours after their meals, most meat-eaters experience a feeling of lassitude, which they correct by again eating meat.

Besides, vegetable and grain protein are superior to animal protein. They contain no saturated fats, which cause cholesterol to accumulate in the system, creating a toxic condition.

As we can see, meat is an incomplete food for man—for physical as well as metaphysical reasons. Although acceptable occasionally, let us have *bread* for our daily bread.

* * *

Man's dreams come true when his realities equal his profoundest aspirations. We are what we dream and dream what we are. When a wish fails to realize itself, we blame the heavens or society. We lose our temper and take short-cuts to bring about quick changes in our situation. Things get worse and we are doomed by our own stupidity.

Extreme ways are for adventurers. The middle way is the path of health and wisdom. The right woman is worth ten thousand, for in her is the balance man has always sought. He recognizes her at first glance and stays with her, faithful and undisturbed.

In the same way that there is a middle road in our attitude toward philosophy, there is as well a middle course in relationship to food. Some people choose for an entire lifetime to eat meat as a staple; others choose fruits; and others still, vegetables. Some exaggerate to the point of eating every morning two pounds of grapes (or some other kind of fruit)—simply because somebody told them to.

There is no ideal diet that prescribes one specific food. No individual and no climate are the same. Extreme ways formulated by men who apply their peculiar ideas and needs to others are dangerous. The ideal food for a particular moment is the one that applies to a single individual, according to the weather, his constitution, and his present condition of health. The ideal diet is flexible to such an extent that its critics, the nutritionists, are incapable of attacking it because it is neither here nor there, neither this nor that, but is always changing.

To get Man on his two feet, one must know what causes him to walk—his will. This is the first cause. His nervous system, organ-activities, thought processes—everything—are all only physiological results of his will. Will is the arrow which points toward Manhood. One follows it and, at once, desires and thirsts are quenched.

Grains, which are the middle way between vegetables and meat, and stand in history between God and Man, possess a sacred role. Through their natural balance they unite Man with his soul again. Willing one's self to choose grains is to draw a path toward God.

Believing only in fruits or meat, or both, without knowing a proper way to balance them, is hazardous—a dangerous voyage which often leads to fear and confusion. Eating primarily cereals, along with some vegetables and fruits, is a simple course which avoids excessive risk.

The food we choose should be determined by the work that has to be done. The laborer, the writer, the philosopher and the merchant should eat accordingly. *A different food for each different purpose.*

Moses, Lao Tzu, *Christ and, not long ago, Georges Ohsawa* did not prescribe dietary laws for the sole purpose of making Man healthy, for the sake of physical fitness. They taught that foods are paths to God. Such great men would not have spent their lifetimes teaching these verities had they not intended to impress upon Man the fact that food is his key to the highest form of existence.

The condiments
on your table

Most of us who have abandoned ketchup-splashing (along with other assorted bad habits) in favor of healthier relishes more suited to the human digestive system, realize that the purpose of a condiment is not to tame and calm the wild cravings of peculiar hungers and thirsts, but to accompany and highlight a meal. A flavoring that performs its function well, serves a particular dish the way a guitar accompanies a fine singer. Listening (or chewing), we cannot tell whether it is the music or the poetry we are intended to hear! Or is it both?

Sesame Salt.

Sesame salt, or Gomasio, is the daily "seasoner." It is made from sesame seeds and salt and has a fine flavor. Used in place of salt alone, it is more balanced, the combination creating a perfect "stabilizer." Sesame seeds, which are oily, coat the salt, helping to prevent thirst.

There are different proportions in which it can be prepared. The French, for example, use 1 teaspoon of salt for every 5 teaspoons of sesame seeds. Here in America, most people I know use much more sesame. One to eight, or even one to twelve, are not uncommon proportions. We will use here the 1 to 8 ratio, but please remember that you may change it if necessary for reasons of climate or individual preference.

Buy sesame seeds whole and unbleached; natural food stores sell the best. Wash seeds, rinse and toast in a heavy cast-iron pan. Stir constantly with a wooden spatula for about 10 minutes. The color usually changes to a light brown. To avoid an unpleasant undertaste, be careful not to burn any of the seeds. Remove from the fire and put in a suribachi, a special bowl for grinding. Add salt, place suribachi between your legs, and rotate the pestle with two hands in a counter-clockwise direction. Use a good amount of pressure, but not too much—let your husband prepare it if he does not get enough exercise. Your gomasio is ready when most of the seeds have been crushed. The grinding should not take more than 15 minutes or so.

If you're preparing enough for 2 people for a week, 2 teaspoons of salt and 16 of sesame seeds should suffice.

Sprinkle on rice cream, salads, rice and other grains. Keep closed in an airtight container.

There is no better remedy than gomasio for those prone to seasickness.

Soya Sauce.

In Japan it is considered a crime to pour tamari, or soya sauce, on rice; but it is used liberally in many other preparations such as soups, noodles, salads and tempura. Serve in a small container, perhaps diluted with an equal volume of water. It spoils rapidly this way, so do not prepare much of it in advance.

Pickled Daikon.

We cut pickled daikon very thin and serve it in a tiny dish. Used in Japan for centuries as an aid to digestion, it is quite delicious after a big meal.

Other condiments, sometimes making an appearance at our table, will be found elsewhere in the book, particularly in the chapter devoted to sauces.

Why do we overeat?

It is best to eat sparingly. Thereby a man tends to
lengthen his life. We find among animals and reptiles
that those who eat the least, live the longest.

The Koretzer.

The twenty-year-old boy from Harvard asked the question everybody asks, sooner or later. It was a Monday night, near the end of a
lecture I was giving in my brother's restaurant. The year was drawing to
a close and the boy was undoubtedly preparing himself for Thanksgiving
and the other festive evenings to follow. He didn't want to confront the
delicious and tempting foods of the holiday season uninformed.

It was an easy question for me to answer, for I had suffered through
periods of pathological appetite myself.

"Overeating comes from unbalanced meals. Whenever a meal is not prepared with the proper attention to detail and combination that are necessary to satisfy all the senses of the eater, a desire for more is creat-ed in him. So he goes from dish to pot, taste to gulp and quality to quantity in search of that promised and missing balance. A well-balanc-ed meal leaves you happy. You are not anxious to fill a nervous stomach that has grown alarmed and excited because of wrong proportions or ingredients.

"False hunger is created by constant bombardments of food, which cause chemical stimulation. Too much salt or too many spices can be other sources of trouble. A simple meal has less chance of falsely stim-ulating the stomach than a more complicated one whose ingredients bat-tle tumultuously with one another for first place. It seems as though each kind of food produces its own kind of hunger and desire. And so without end, the blind leading the blind, hunger arises.

"Overeating comes also from inactivity, physical as well as mental. Before discovering fire, Man was a fruitarian whose only work was the collecting of fruits from trees. After the discovery of fire, Man had to become more active to balance the change.

"There is another reason for lack of satisfaction. Imbalance can come from the environment, the ambience of the occasion; when there is no ritual attending the meal, hunger cannot be satisfied. Respect for food is the biggest secret of all.

"When there is no happiness in the hearts of those at the table, overeating results."

The companions
of grains

The curse of confusion
Degrades the victims
And damns the destroyers.
The rice and the water
No longer offered;
The ancestors also
Must fall dishonoured
From home in heaven.

From "The sorrow of Arjuna"
Bhagavad-Gita

"Little somethings" are often a main dish for lazy people who do not find time to chew brown rice. An accompaniment, however, should be a small delight of color at the side of your dish, there to keep your eating measured. Its permanent presence and undisturbed simplicity should be a mirror of your character. You should learn from it how much you are worth.

Pâté en Robe de Chambre. (Clothed pâté)

       Use puff dough for the "robe." (See recipe, page 266.)

       For the pâté prepare the following:

       2 onions, minced

       2 cups cooked lentils, blended

       1 pound bread (yeasted), soaked in water for 1 hour

       ½ cup walnuts, chopped fine

       1 dozen black olives, chopped

       1 tablespoon oil

       Pinch of thyme

       Pinch of coriander

       Pinch of nutmeg

       1 bay leaf

       ¼ teaspoon salt

       2 tablespoons sesame butter

       2 tablespoons miso diluted in 3 tablespoons water

       3 tablespoons parsley, chopped

Saute onions in oil over medium flame until golden. Add moist bread without crust (press it a bit with two hands to remove half the water). Continue stirring mixture, adding water if necessary. Simmer 15 minutes, stirring from time to time. Add thyme, bay leaf, coriander, nutmeg, salt and parsley. Stir. Simmer 5 minutes and add blended lentils. Stir thoroughly and add diluted miso, sesame butter, walnuts and black olives. Simmer 5 minutes while stirring continually. The mixture must be very heavy.

Now roll out dough. Arrange 2/3 of it in an oven-proof mold. Pour in mixture and cover with the remaining sheet of dough. Form flower-petals with pieces of dough. Brush with egg yolk and put in oven (375 degrees) for 30-40 minutes. Allow to cool 1 hour and serve each slice with chopped parsley on top.

This pâté can be made without the robe. If you should make it "en robe de chambre," allow the dough to stand 24 hours—it gives an excellent crust.

Pâté Maison.

> 2 pounds striped bass fillet, chopped
>
> 1 carrot, diced
>
> 1 onion, diced
>
> 2 cloves garlic, crushed
>
> 1 bay leaf
>
> 1 pinch thyme
>
> 2 bars agar agar, soaked in 4 cups water for ½ hour
>
> ½ teaspoon salt
>
> 2 tablespoons parsley, chopped
>
> 2 tablespoons oil

Saute garlic in oil until golden. Add onion and carrot. Simmer 10 minutes. Add thyme, salt and parsley, then simmer 5 minutes more. Stir 2-3 times during the simmering. Add fish, cover and simmer 10 minutes. In a separate pan, bring agar agar to a boil in water, then pour over fish and vegetables. Stir 1 minute. Remove from fire and allow to cool uncovered. After ½ hour, place in large mold or small cups. Chill in refrigerator. Unmold and serve with chopped parsley or any green leaf.

150

Fish roll à la Marocaine.

Prepare a sizable amount of dough. If you should make too much, you can always use it for little individual pies or other specialties. Use puff dough (see recipe, page 266).

For filling prepare the following:

1 ½ pounds striped bass fillet

¼ green pepper, diced

1 carrot, grated

1 small zucchini, diced

1 onion, diced

2 tablespoons parsley, chopped

1/3 cup almonds, chopped

1 tablespoon currants

1 clove garlic, grated

½ teaspoon salt

Saute garlic in oil until golden. Add pepper, stir 2 minutes, then add onions, carrots and zucchini, in that order. Add a few drops of water and simmer covered 10 minutes. Add almonds, raisins, fish and parsley; sprinkle with salt; cover and simmer 10 more minutes, covered. Remove from fire.

Roll out dough. Place mixture on one end and roll up tight. Close ends by pressing with fork. Brush with egg yolk and put in a 400-degree oven for 30-40 minutes. Cut into 1-inch slices and serve hot or cooled.

Carrot Ashamed. (Carrot clothed in puff dough)

Boil 6 carrots in salted water (3 cups). Remove from water when soft (about 7-8 minutes) and sprinkle individually with a *soupcon* of cumin powder.

Roll out dough thinly and cut 6 pieces. Envelop each carrot, but do not close ends; let the carrot section show. Place in baking sheet and put in 400-degree oven for 30 minutes or so. Allow to cool. Slice diagonally and sprinkle with chopped parsley before serving. You may do the same with turnips, but do not use cumin.

Sandwich au gratin.

> 12 slices bread, slightly toasted
>
> Miso spread (see recipe, page 187)
>
> 3 bunches watercress, chopped and sauteed in 1 tablespoon oil
>
> ¼ teaspoon salt

Cover each slice of bread with a thin layer of miso spread. Put watercress on top and cover with the other slice, forming a sandwich. Now make bechamel with the following:

> 1 onion
>
> 3 scallions
>
> 1 carrot, grated
>
> 2 cups water
>
> ½ cup flour, slightly toasted
>
> ½ teaspoon salt (or less)
>
> 1 tablespoon parsley, chopped

(See recipe for bechamel sauce, page 177).

Place sandwiches in baking dish and pour 3-4 tablespoons of bechamel over each sandwich. Put in broiler for 5 minutes. Serve hot, sprinkle with parsley.

Variation:

If watercress is not available you may use broccoli leaves (ask at the vegetable stand, the salesman will get them for you), swiss chard or even spinach.

Hijiki Roll.

¼ cup hijiki

4 carrots, cut into matchsticks

3 onions, minced

4 cabbage leaves, chopped

4 flowerettes of cauliflower, cut into small pieces

1 bunch watercress, chopped

2 tablespoons oil

1 flat teaspoon salt

3 tablespoons tamari

Soak hijiki in water and cook as usual. Saute onions, carrots, cabbage and watercress in oil. Simmer 10 minutes. Add salt and simmer 5 minuetes more. Mix vegetables with hijiki. Wrap in dough and form a roll. Use either puff dough or pie shell (see recipe, page 266).

A second type of covering is formed with flat dough squares, 3" by 3". Place mixture in the center of a square and cover with another. Use a fork to join edges. Deep-fry and serve hot. A sauce made with arrowroot and soya sauce may be poured over the rolls.

Variations:

1- Aduki beans, cooked

2- Carrot pureed

3- Squash pureed

4- Lentil pureed

5- Cooked ground fish, with pieces of olives, chopped parsley

6- Mung-bean threads, grated carrots, onions, scallions

Andalousie pays d'amour.

Use puff dough or pâte sablée (see recipe, page 265).

Roll out dough thinly, cut into circles 5-6 inches in diameter. Oil muffin pan and form cups with dough. Put in preheated 400-degree oven and bake 10-15 minutes.

> 1 ½ pounds striped bass
>
> 1 clove garlic
>
> 1 bay leaf
>
> ¼ red pepper, diced
>
> 1 tablespoon olive oil
>
> ½ cup water
>
> ¼ teaspoon salt
>
> 2 tablespoons parsley, chopped

Saute garlic in oil until golden. Add bay leaf, then pepper and parsley. Simmer 5 minutes. Place fish in skillet, sprinkle with salt, add water and simmer 15-20 minutes. Remove fish and break into small pieces while removing bones.

To serve Andalousies, arrange approximately 1 tablespoon of fish in dough cup. Pour 1 tablespoon sauce with 2-3 pieces red pepper over fish. Serve hot or cool.

Surprised Zucchini.

Peel a large zucchini. Cut into chunks (1 ½ to 2 inches). Cut cleanly so that it will stand vertically. Make a hole (a well) in the upper side, wider at the top, forming a cone. Stuff with filing used for Andalousies and place in a baking dish, covered with fish sauce. Baking dish should have a lid. Bake 30 minutes. Serve one or two per person, hot, and with greens on the side.

Vegetable Zoo. (Aspic)

> 1 cup beets, diced
>
> ½ cup cauliflower flowerettes
>
> 1 cup carrots, diced
>
> 1 cup string beans, diced
>
> ½ cup celery, chopped
>
> 2 bars agar agar, diluted in 4 cups cooled soup stock (use tamari
> broth; see recipe, page 105)
>
> ¼ teaspoon salt
>
> 2 tablespoons oil

Saute string beans and carrots in oil for 2-3 minutes. Add 1 cup water, cover and simmer until tender but firm. In another saucepan do the same with beets. Bring soup stock with agar agar in it to a boil. Remove from fire, wait 10 minutes and add vegetables, including raw celery. Pour mixture in a ring mold and chill for 3 or 4 hours. Unmold over crisp greens such as lettuce, chicory, etc.

Boil n' Roll Festival.

> 1 small Chinese cabbage
>
> 1 bunch watercress, coiled 2 minutes
>
> 2 carrots, boiled whole and cut lengthwise into thin strips
>
> Tamari-grated daikon mixture as a sauce

Separate cabbage leaves and boil 3-5 minutes. Arrange 2 or 3, depending on size, on a bamboo sheet, forming a rectangle 3" by 10". Arrange 3-4 strings of watercress leaves lengthwise; add 1 carrot stick. Roll up bamboo sheet with cabbage inside and squeeze thoroughly to release excess water. Unfold bamboo sheet and cut cabbage roll into 3/4-inch pieces. Serve 3 per person. Dip each piece by hand or with chopsticks in tamari sauce mixture.

Kyoto Lotus Balls.

> 1 piece fresh lotus root (3 inches), grated
>
> 1 fresh burdock root, slivered
>
> 1 onion, chopped
>
> 1 carrot, grated
>
> ½ teaspoon salt
>
> 3 tablespoons w.w. pastry flour

Mix ingredients in a bowl. The consistency obtained should be soft and sticky. Wet hands with water and shape mixture into 3/4-inch balls. Dip and roll in cornmeal and deep-fry in oil. Serve 2 per person with chopped scallions and parsley on the side.

Macrobiotic Marbles.

> 1 cup w.w. pastry flour
>
> 2 teaspoons miso
>
> ½ teaspoon salt
>
> 3/4 cup water
>
> 1 onion, minced

In a bowl mix all ingredients and shape into small balls 3/4 inch in diameter. Deep-fry in oil.

Cha-Gio from Vietnam.

>½ cup carrots, grated
>
>¼ cup turnips, grated
>
>¼ cup onions, chopped
>
>¼ cup Somen noodles, broken into ½-inch pieces and cooked
>
>1 cup chick-peas, cooked and mashed
>
>½ cup corn flour
>
>4 tablespoons parsley, chopped
>
>1 teaspoon salt

Mix all ingredients thoroughly in a bowl and shape into small balls, 1 inch in diameter. Flatten to 1/3 of an inch and deep fry. Serve 2-3 to each person on a lettuce leaf.

Vegetable Patties.

>1 onion, minced
>
>½ cup string beans, boiled 10 minutes and then chopped
>
>½ cup carrots, grated
>
>½ cup w.w. pastry flour
>
>½ cup oatmeal
>
>½ cup water
>
>2 teaspoons salt
>
>¼ teaspoon ginger, grated
>
>1 clove garlic

Mix vegetables, salt, ginger, garlic and water. Stir in flours. Mix and spoon into hot oil to fry until golden brown. Do not use more than ¼ inch oil.

Beignet-croquettes.

> 4 carrots, grated
>
> 1 onion, chopped
>
> 7 medium leeks
>
> 2 celery stalks, chopped finely
>
> 10 tablespoons w.w. pastry flour
>
> 5 tablespoons buckwheat flour
>
> ½ teaspoon salt

Mix vegetables. Add flours and salt and shape into small oblong balls. Fry in ½ inch oil. Serve with bechamel sauce.

Raviolis.

> For the dough use:
>
> 2 cups w.w. pastry flour
>
> 1 egg (or 2 tablespoons oil)
>
> ½ cup water
>
> ½ teaspoon salt

For the filling use cooked spinach, watercress, fish, etc.

Knead dough until smooth and elastic. Cut in two and roll out as thin as possible. Make two rectangular sheets. On one sheet, every 2 to 2 ½ inches place 1 teaspoon of filling. Cover with second sheet, then cut dough between fillings to form raviolis 2 inches square. Pinch edges with fork and, to cook, put in soups, soup stocks, etc. Serve with bechamel sauce or a sauce of your choice. You may fry them after they have been boiled in salted water.

158

Claudia's Pizza.

For yeasted dough use:

2 cups w.w. pastry flour

2 tablespoons olive oil

½ cup water

½ teaspoon yeast diluted in 1/3 cup lukewarm water

½ teaspoon salt

For the filling use:

2 carrots, thinly sliced

3 medium onions, chopped

3 medium zucchini, thinly sliced

¼ red pepper, chopped (optional)

1 tablespoon miso

1 cup bechamel

Pinch oregano

Pinch thyme

1 tablespoon oil

8 black olives

To make the dough, mix all ingredients, knead 5 minutes and allow to stand ½ hour. Knead again. Roll out very thin, 1/8 inch, and form into desired shape. Place on oiled baking sheet, folding in sides to obtain a thicker edge. Put aside and prepare the filling.

Saute onions, zucchini and carrots. Simmer 10 minutes. Add 1/3 cup water. Cover and simmer 10 minutes. Add pinch of salt, miso and bechamel. Mix and pour evenly over dough. Bake in preheated 375-degree oven for 30 minutes. Remove, sprinkle with oregano and thyme. Arrange olives cut in half and bake 5-8 minutes more until edges are slightly browned.

Variation: You may use puff dough instead of yeasted dough.

A Swiss on the Couch.

The Yin-Yang magazine from Paris gives this recipe, in which Swiss cheese is featured. May it not offend you to have some animal food— please enjoy it!

6 slices bread, soaked in the following mixture:

½ cup water

2 tablespoons tamari

1 egg

For the filling use:

6 thin slices Swiss cheese, 3" by 3"

3 butternut squash, cooked and pureed

2 bunches watercress, sauteed in 1 tablespoon oil, chopped

2 cups bechamel, flavored with pinch nutmeg

Oil a skillet and toast bread, 2-3 minutes each side. Place each slice in baking dish. Top with a slice of Swiss cheese, cover with ½-inch layer pureed squash, then with watercress, and finally pour bechamel over the whole (4 tablespoons per portion). Bake at 375 degrees for 15 minutes.

Squash Pie. (Topped with onions)

Use the dough recipe of your choice.

For the filling use:

3 butternut squash, peeled, cooked and pureed

3 onions, diced and sauteed in 1 tablespoon oil

1/3 teaspoon salt

½ cup oatmeal, toasted in 1 teaspoon oil

Roll out dough, place in baking sheet and bake 15 minutes in 400-degree oven. Allow to cool 5 minutes, otherwise it will get soggy. Fill with a layer of squash first, cover with onions and sprinkle oat flakes on top.

Quiche en Fleur.

Use Puff dough. For the filling use:

1 cauliflower boiled in salted water, cut into flowerettes

2 cups bechamel, flavored with pinch of cumin

2 tablespoons tahini

½ cup pumpkin seeds, toasted and chopped

Roll out dough and place in baking sheet. Bake in 400-degree oven for 15 minutes. In a bowl mix bechamel and tahini and add to cauliflower. Pour evenly over crust. Sprinkle with pumpkin seeds. Serve hot.

Variation:

Cut 2 pounds of turnips and saute in 1 tablespoon oil. Add ½ cup water and simmer 25 minutes. Place in crust and pour bechamel over.

The Chimney.

Use dough of your choice. For the filling use:
2 pounds spinach, chopped
1 tablespoon oil
1 cup thick bechamel
½ teaspoon salt

Saute spinach in oil for 2 minutes. Add ½ cup water and simmer uncovered for 10 minutes. Add salt before end. Mix bechamel with spinach.

Separate dough into 2 balls. Roll out each ball into a 9-inch circle. Place one circle in round baking sheet of the same size. Pour in spinach mixture evenly and cover with other sheet of dough. Close edge by pressing with a fork. Poke a hole in center of pie (cut in the upper sheet only) to allow steam to escape. This is the chimney. Bake in 375-degree oven for 40 minutes. Serve hot.

Variation:

Kale
Broccoli, finely chopped
Watercress
Swiss chard

Chaussons Verts.

Use puff dough. For filling use:

1 pound kale, chopped and sauteed in 1 tablespoon oil

2 cups aduki beans, cooked and salted

Roll out dough thinly, cut into 5-6 inch circles. On one half place 2 tablespoons cooked kale. Add 1 tablespoon aduki beans on top. Allow 1 inch between filling and edge of dough. Fold and press with fork to close. Make holes with fork on top and brush with egg yolk. Sprinkle with sesame seeds. Bake at 375 degrees for 20 minutes.

Variation: Pickled cabbage sauteed in oil.

Croque Monsieur.

This sandwich is a delight. It is unusual, so serve it to your friends—it will make them happy.

Cut thinly two slices of bread. For filling prepare finely chopped radish sauteed in miso (diluted in a bit of water). Prepare a tempura batter. Soak bread in water for 2 minutes; drain. Spread with tahini and add a layer of radish. Make a sandwich. Now dip in batter and fry in ¼ inch oil. Serve with a few drops of tamari and a fresh radish.

Variations:

Watercress, sauteed and chopped

Chopped leek, sauteed

Chopped scallions, sauteed

Chip Crowns. (Buckwheat cream)

Serve this delicious, nutritious and tonic accompaniment as a soup. Make buckwheat cream with dark flour. Prepare corn chips and arrange a few of them over the cream. Sprinkle with parsley. Excellent in winter.

Of weak
and strong men

It is better to grow slow and strong than to grow fast and fall. A child fed cereals and vegetables does not grow so rapidly as a child whose meals are principally composed of milk and meat. Considered at the same age, the latter is bigger and heavier than the former.

Yet it is not always size, or speed over the short haul, that is important. The USA usually wins short races in Olympic contests by feeding its athletes milk and meat. Long-distance races are dominated by grain-eaters. Russian athletes, who eat kasha (buckwheat), are clearly superior in such events.

It is better to be a "fragile" man who lives to be ninety than a "strong" man who unexpectedly drops at fifty of a stroke? Those who believe themselves strong, who eat indiscriminately while proclaiming, "Nothing bothers me," are often in danger of sudden death. These heavy meat-eaters, confuse vitality with the false energy delivered by animal food as it decays in the intestines. They are able to endure floods of toxins without alarming symptoms because their nervous systems have deteriorated. They feel nothing more than faint discomfort prior to the onset of serious illness. That is why those who switch suddenly from meat to cereals and suffer a reaction in some kind of illness should be grateful; they should realize that, as the body rids itself of poisons, such discomfort is a sign of returning health. It is also a first and necessary lesson in courage and endurance.

In fact, it is better to be sick more than once. That way a deeper understanding of the methods of adjusting one's food to each day's changing requirements is attained. If we cut our intake of acid and liquid, we are cured of a cold. If not, and if the nervous system is unable to communicate its messages, pneumonia and other complications can develop. Far better to experience numerous difficulties and to know the satisfaction of overcoming them. Better to be a "long-distance runner" in the race toward health and happiness. For quickly-learned knowledge is only a froth on true understanding.

Something fresh
on your dish
(Salads & Pickles)

SALADS

Meat-eaters require large amounts of salad in order to cleanse their systems. On the other hand, those who eat grains and vegetables as a staple can get along with much less, perhaps only a tablespoon—or even a teaspoon if it is a finely-chopped or grated salad made with strong-tasting vegetables such as Japanese radish (daikon). In summer, of course, more salad may be beneficial.

Kemia.

This salad is served in small quantities, ½ teaspoon (1 teaspoon at the most) in the dish accompanying a seaweed.

2 inches daikon, grated

1 inch carrot, grated

Pinch of salt

2 tablespoons umeboshi juice

Put grated carrot and daikon in a strainer and pour 1 cup boiling water over them. Press and place delicately in a small bowl or dish. Add umeboshi juice and salt.

Rendez-vous in May.

1 cup red cabbage, shredded

½ cup carrots, grated

½ cup cauliflower, cut into flowerettes

½ cup apple, thinly sliced

4 lettuce leaves

1 bunch watercress, chopped

1 egg, hard-boiled, chopped

3 tablespoons olive oil

3 tablespoons umeboshi juice

Pinch of salt

2 tablespoons parsley, chopped

Put cabbage and carrots in a strainer and pour boiling water over them. Boil cauliflower in salted water; drain. Soak apples in salted water; drain. In a bowl mix cabbage, watercress, cauliflower, carrot and apple. Add salt, oil and umeboshi juice. Toss and allow to stand in a cool place. Arrange lettuce-leaf on individual dish and set salad mixture atop it. Sprinkle with egg and chopped parsley.

Summertime, early afternoon.

      1 pound Belgian endives

      1 quarter crisp lettuce, chopped

      1 quarter crisp chicory, chopped

      1 quarter crisp romaine, chopped

      ¼ cup scallions, chopped

      ¼ cup cucumber, thinly sliced

      ¼ cup black olives, sliced

      ¼ teaspoon salt

      Mixture of 2 tablespoons tahini, 2 of umeboshi juice and
          2 of tamari

In a large bowl toss together lettuce, chicory, romaine, scallions and cucumber. Sprinkle with salt and chill for 1 hour. Separate and arrange endive leaves on a large serving platter. Form a flower, then arrange salad on top, more towards the center, creating a circle. Pour dressing on top.

Marinated bean salad.

      1 cup aduki beans, cooked. Keep them firm

      1 cup chick-peas, cooked and also kept firm

      1 cup celery, thinly sliced

      ½ cup onions, cut into thin rings

      1/3 cup scallions, chopped

      Dressing:

      3 tablespoons tamari

      2 tablespoons tahini

      1 sprig fresh basil or ¼ teaspoon dried

Toss salad-ingredients together in a large bowl. Pour on dressing 5 minutes prior to serving.

Mung-mung salad.

> 2 ounces mung-bean threads, boiled 5 minutes in salted water
>
> 1 cup flowerettes of cauliflower, boiled 15 minutes in salted water
>
> ½ cup carrots, grated
>
> ½ cup onions, cut into thin rings
>
> ¼ cup scallions, chopped
>
> Dressing:
>
> 1 tablespoon lemon juice
>
> 2 tablespoons corn oil
>
> 1/3 teaspoon salt

Put carrots, onions and scallions in a strainer and pour boiling water over them. Mix ingredients in a large bowl and add dressing 5 minutes before serving.

Variation:

Instead of mung-bean threads you may use 1 cup cooked somen noodles.

Colored lagoon.

> 1 cup wakame, cooked
>
> 1 cup cucumber, finely sliced
>
> 1 orange, peeled, sliced
>
> 1 teaspoon salt

Sprinkle cucumber with salt and let stand 20 minutes. Mix with wakame, add orange and serve each person 1 tablespoon. Try other kinds of seaweeds.

Salade au cresson.

> 1 bunch watercress
>
> 1 tablespoon sesame seeds, toasted
>
> 1 tablespoon miso, diluted in 2 tablespoons water

Boil watercress in 1 cup water for 2 minutes. Place the leaves lengthwise on a bamboo sheet. Roll and press out water, then chop finely. Add miso and sesame seeds and mix.

Variation:

> Instead of miso add 1 teaspoon bonito flakes or
>
> Chopped anchovies (1 tablespoon) or
>
> Spinach, cooked and chopped

Lazy asparagus.

> 1 dozen asparagus
>
> Dressing:
>
> 2 tablespoons tamari
>
> 2 tablespoons tahini
>
> 2 tablespoons umeboshi juice

Boil asparagus in water until soft. Place on serving dish with a small cup containing the dressing on the side. Dip asparagus in dressing and eat with your fingers.

Variation: Leeks.

Swiss chard desiree.

> 1 bunch swiss chard
>
> Dressing:
>
> 2/3 teaspoon salt
>
> 1 tablespoon lemon juice
>
> 1 tablespoon olive oil

Boil swiss chard in water for 10 minutes. Drain and chop. Put in a bowl and add dressing. You may add a pinch of ground cumin. It's excellent!

Variations: Romaine, kale, lettuce, chicory

Cooked salad.

> 1 pound string beans, diced
>
> 1 lettuce, chopped
>
> ½ Chinese cabbage, chopped
>
> 4 celery stalks, chopped
>
> 1 bunch scallions, chopped
>
> 1 onion, chopped
>
> Kernels of 3 ears of corn in season
>
> 2 tablespoons tahini
>
> 3 umeboshi pits
>
> ½ teaspoon salt
>
> 1 tablespoon corn oil
>
> 1 cup water

Saute onions in oil; 2 minutes later add lettuce, Chinese cabbage, string beans, celery and corn kernels. Add water and pits, bring to a boil and simmer 10 minutes. Add tahini and salt and simmer 5 minutes. Add scallions and simmer 3 minutes more. Serve cooled.

Good memories from Tokyo.

>   2 pieces kombu, 3" by 6", soaked and minced
>   1 inch fresh lotus root, sliced and chopped
>   2 celery stalks, finely chopped
>   1 inch fresh daikon, grated
>   2 tablespoons tamari
>   ¼ apple, finely chopped
>   ½ teaspoon salt
>   1 teaspoon oil

Saute kombu and lotus in oil. Cover with water and simmer 1 ½ hours. Add water if necessary. After 1 hour add tamari. Allow to cool and mix all ingredients in a salad bowl. Serve 1 tablespoon with fish or vegetable tempura. Good with soba-tempura recipe (see "The International Chef").

Nato. (Japanese salad)

>   1 ½ cups sour soy-beans, bought in a Japanese store
>   1 ½ inches fresh daikon, grated
>   4 scallions, chopped
>   3 sheets Nori, toasted and broken into small pieces
>   4 tablespoons tamari

Mix ingredients in a salad bowl. Serve 1 tablespoon per person.

Radish salad.

>   1 bunch red radish with leaves
>   2 teaspoons salt

Wash leaves and radish heads thoroughly. Chop leaves finely and slice heads thinly. Sprinkle 1 teaspoon salt on leaves, toss and allow to stand 15 minutes. Press out juice. Do the same with radish heads. Mix the two and serve 1 tablespoon on the side as an accompaniment to fish.

Salade Vinaigrette. (Russian)

> 1 cup beets, boiled, then diced
>
> 1 cup carrots, boiled, then diced
>
> 1 cup turnips, boiled, then diced
>
> 1 cup pinto beans, cooked
>
> 1 cup sauerkraut, shredded, or pickled cabbage
>
> 1 bunch scallions, chopped
>
> Dressing:
>
> ½ cup umeboshi juice
>
> 2 tablespoons tahini
>
> 2 tablespoons parsley, chopped
>
> ¼ teaspoon ginger, grated

Mix all ingredients in a large bowl. Add dressing a few minutes before serving. Toss.

Variation:

Instead of pinto beans you may put chopped smoked- or pickled-herring in this delicious salad.

PICKLES

These tasty little accompaniments go particularly well with fried food, but may be served anytime in small amounts—1 teaspoon or even less, depending on the size of the meal and your appetite. Japanese always include them on their tables.

The best container for making pickles is a wooden keg, but a crock or a glass jar can also be used.

Homemade sauerkraut.

> 6 pounds cabbage
>
> 2 tablespoons salt
>
> 3 umeboshi plums, crushed
>
> 12 small onions

Separate leaves of cabbage; pile leaves atop one another and shred finely. Reserve a few large leaves. Mix shredded cabbage and whole small onions with salt and umeboshi. Put in a large jar and top with reserved leaves. Cover with a piece of cheese cloth. Place a clean garden stone on a plate and set plate atop cheese cloth to weigh down cabbage. A small jar filled with water can be used instead of the stone. Keep in a cool place for 2 weeks. If it is not sufficiently pickled, wash the cheese cloth and replace for a few more days.

Variation:

Boiled water with umeboshi in it can be poured over cabbage, covering it. Then no weight is necessary.

Serve 1 teaspoon as is. Sauerkraut may be sauteed and served as a side dish.

Pickled cucumbers.

     30 small cucumbers, fresh and firm

     1 dozen small onions

     ¼ red pepper, chopped finely

     ½ cup coarse sea salt

     2 quarts water

     2 cloves garlic

     2 bay leaves

     5 sprigs dill

Wash cucumbers, dry and arrange in a big jar with onions. Bring water to a boil in a saucepan; add salt and cool, then add red pepper, garlic and bay leaf. Pour over cucumbers and place dill on top. The liquid should completely cover the cucumbers; if not, boil more water (adding salt). Cover jar with cheese-cloth and keep in a cool place for a week. After 5 days you can serve some if you like them still green and crispy.

Pickled radish.

     1 dozen red radishes

         or

     3 inches daikon

     3 tablespoons tamari

     ½ teaspoon ginger, grated

Wash and slice into thin round pieces. Add tamari and ginger. Allow to stand 2-3 hours before serving.

Variation:

Try lettuce cut into big pieces or celery stalks cut into 1-inch pieces.

Broccoli.

> 1 bunch broccoli
>
> 1 handful salt

Remove tops. Chop stems into ½-inch lengths. Sprinkle with salt. Cover with a weighted plate. Allow to stand overnight.

Turnip and Carrot.

> 6 turnips
>
> 6 carrots
>
> 1 quart boiled water
>
> 4 tablespoons salt

Wash turnips and carrots. Cut into matchsticks and put in jar. Cover with boiled water and salt. Allow to stand 3-5 days in a cool place.

Cauliflower.

> 1 cauliflower
>
> 1 quart boiling water
>
> ¼ cup corn oil
>
> 1 teaspoon ginger, grated
>
> 1 clove garlic, crushed
>
> 1 pinch coriander
>
> 1 tablespoon salt

Separate flowerettes of cauliflower. Put in bottom of jar. Mix all other ingredients and place in jar. Allow to stand 1 week in refrigerator.

Beets in ginger.

> 2 cups beets cooked whole, then sliced
>
> 1 small apple, diced
>
> ¼ teaspoon ginger, grated
>
> 4 tablespoons tamari
>
> 4 tablespoons boiled water

Put beets and apples in jar. Mix other ingredients and pour over beets and apples. Allow to stand 12 hours in refrigerator.

Pickled fish.

> 2 cups cooked fish (mackerel, red snapper, striped bass,etc.)
>
> 1 large red onion, sliced into thin rings
>
> 1 green pepper, thinly sliced
>
> ¼ cup olive oil
>
> 1 teaspoon lemon juice
>
> ½ teaspoon orange peel, grated
>
> 2 bay leaves
>
> ¼ teaspoon oregano
>
> 1 tablespoon parsley, chopped
>
> 1 tablespoon salt
>
> 1 cup juice in which fish has been cooked

When fish is cool, place all mixed ingredients atop it and allow to stand 2-3 hours. Serve with greens (lettuce, watercress, etc.)

Sauces

Sauces are not cover-ups. They might often serve such a purpose in bad restaurants, but in our way of cooking they are the last words of a poem written by an inspired chef!

Sauce Bechamel.

This basic sauce is quickly prepared and can be used almost everywhere, especially on vegetables, grains and gratinees.

   2 tablespoons rice flour

   1 tablespoon tahini

   ½ onion, chopped

   2 scallions, chopped

   ½ teaspoon salt

   2 cups water

   1 teaspoon oil

In a saucepan saute onion and scallions in oil, then add flour, tahini and salt diluted in water. Bring to a boil and simmer for 15 minutes over a low flame, half-covered with lid.

Variation:

Instead of rice flour, use unbleached white flour or toasted wholewheat flour or oat flour. Lightly toasted barley flour can also be used.

A pinch of nutmeg, coriander or basil produces a totally different effect each time.

A cup of mashed chick-peas, lentils or aduki beans can provide countless other variations on this basic theme.

Miso Sauce.

> 1 onion, chopped
>
> 1 carrot, thinly sliced
>
> ½ bunch watercress, chopped
>
> 2 chopped scallions
>
> 2 tablespoons parsley, chopped
>
> 1 tablespoon oil
>
> 1 tablespoon miso, diluted
>
> 1 tablespoon tahini
>
> 2 tablespoons w.w. pastry flour
>
> 2 cups water

Saute onions in oil for 2 minutes, add watercress, then carrots. After 5 minutes of sauteing add miso, then tahini. Sprinkle with flour and cook 5 minutes; keep stirring. Add water and bring to a boil while stirring continuously, then simmer 5 more minutes. Just before serving, add 2 chopped scallions and parsley.

This sauce can be served on rice, noodles, millet or bulghur— but not on kasha.

The Sky Above, Noodles Below.

> 2 leeks, chopped
>
> 1 onion, chopped
>
> ½ carrot, grated
>
> 2 cups water from cooked buckwheat noodles
>
> 1 small teaspoon salt
>
> 1 tablespoon tahini
>
> 1 tablespoon olive oil

Saute onions, then leeks, then carrot in olive oil in a saucepan. After 3 minutes add tahini, water and salt. Bring to a boil, simmer 10 minutes. Serve on noodles, especially soba.

Halo sur les Graines.

> 3 dried mushrooms, soaked in water, then chopped
>
> 2/3 cup broccoli flowerettes
>
> 2 cups water
>
> 2 tablespoons unbleached flour
>
> 2 tablespoons tahini
>
> 2 tablespoons tamari
>
> 1 teaspoon oil

In a saucepan saute mushrooms, then broccoli. Dilute tahini and flour in water, pour over vegetables, add tamari, bring to a boil, then simmer for 15 minutes or so. Serve on cereals.

Sauce Brunette.

>   1 onion, minced
>
>   1 teaspoon olive oil
>
>   3 tablespoons w.w. flour, toasted
>
>   2 cups water
>
>   1 teaspoon lemon juice
>
>   1 pinch oregano
>
>   ½ teaspoon salt

In a saucepan saute onion in oil; dilute toasted flour in water, add spices, then pour over onions. Bring to a boil, then simmer 10-15 minutes, half-covered.

Serve on crêpes or pancakes.

Sauce Chou Fleur.

>   1 cauliflower, cut into flowerettes
>
>   2 carrots, cut into ½-inch slices, diagonally
>
>   2 onions, cut into 1/8-inch pieces
>
>   1 bunch scallions, chopped
>
>   1 quart water
>
>   4 tablespoons arrow-root
>
>   ½ teaspoon fresh ginger, grated
>
>   1 tablespoon dried fish (Chirimen Iriko)
>
>   1 tablespoon olive oil
>
>   1 teaspoon salt

In a saucepan saute scallions for 1 minute; add onions and saute 2 minutes, then add carrots and cauliflower. Five minutes later add dried fish; saute 3 more minutes, continually stirring. Dilute arrowroot and ginger in the water; pour over vegetables and fish, add salt. Bring to a boil, then simmer for 20 minutes.

Variation:

Instead of dried fish, fresh fish cut into small pieces and sauteed lightly can be used.

One Tomato, No Tomato!

      2 beets, cut into thin slices

      2 zucchini, cut into slices

      2 onions, chopped

      3 scallions, chopped

      2 tablespoons brown rice flour

      ½ teaspoon salt

      1 tablespoon olive or corn oil

      1 tablespoon tamari

      1 pinch garlic and another oregano

      3 cups water

      1 tablespoon parsley, chopped

In a saucepan saute scallions and onions in oil for 2 minutes; add zucchini, saute 2 minutes more, then add beets. Simmer 5 minutes while stirring with a wooden spoon. Add 1 cup water, bring to a boil, simmer 20 minutes covered. Allow to cool for a while, then mix in an electric blender. Voila! a vegetable cream. Pour into saucepan. Dilute rice flour in 2 cups water. Pour mixture in saucepan, adding salt and tamari. Bring to a quick boil and simmer 10 minutes. Add garlic, oregano and parsley. Cook 10 more minutes. Serve over noodles, polenta or croquettes.

Variation:

Instead of beets, which give a pink-colored sauce, use 1 butternut squash; you will obtain a sweet and beautifully golden sauce!

Dressings

Dressings are for salads as sauces are for grains. They also make excellent marinates for fish.

Umeboshi Juice.

> 1 large or 2 small umeboshi plums, crushed
>
> 1 cup water

Bring water to a boil with plum in it and simmer 5 minutes. While simmering try to separate flesh from pit to give more taste. Use this juice in dressings.

Ginger-Tamari.

> 3 tablespoons tamari
>
> 1 teaspoon ginger, grated

Mix and pour over salads just before serving. You may also marinate vegetables in it for 2-3 hours if you want a pickled salad.

This little dressing can serve as a sauce for fish when it is baked or broiled.

It can also be used as a dip for fish tempura.

Petite Sauce.

> ½ cup umeboshi juice
>
> 2 tablespoons tahini
>
> 2 tablespoons parsley, chopped

Mix ingredients, beat thoroughly, then pour over salad before serving. You may also serve it with fish fillets of sole or flounder.

Summer Dressing.

> 5 tablespoons olive oil
>
> 3 teaspoons salt
>
> Juice of 1 orange

Mix ingredients and pour over a fresh salad of crisp greens such as lettuce, romaine lettuce, watercress, etc.

Mayonnaise.

This is a classic dressing, excellent with leafy salads or any steamed, boiled or broiled fish.

> 1 egg yolk
>
> 1 tablespoon umeboshi juice
>
> Pinch salt
>
> 3/4 cup olive oil

Put an egg yolk in a bowl, add salt, a few drops of umeboshi juice and a few drops of oil. Beat thoroughly, add a little more juice,then a little more oil. Carefully alternate the ingredients and beat steadily until the consistency becomes light and creamy. Serve with chopped parsley on top.

Marinabelle.

    1 onion, chopped

    1 umeboshi, crushed

    2 tablespoons tamari

    1/3 cup sesame oil

    1 tablespoon parsley, chopped

Put all ingredients in a small *suribachi* and grind thoroughly until the mixture becomes creamy. Pour over salads just before serving.

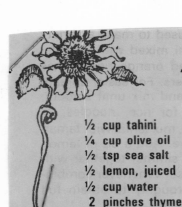

Tahini Salad Dressing

½ cup tahini
¼ cup olive oil
½ tsp sea salt
½ lemon, juiced
½ cup water
2 pinches thyme
  or tarragon

Mix tahini with oil and salt, add lemon juice and mix again. Add water a few spoonfuls at a time at first, mixing thoroughly until smooth. Gradually add remaining water and herb, mixing well. For fuller blending of flavors let dressing stand for 20 minutes or more before serving. Makes about 1¼ cups.

Spreads

Of all the spreads, miso spread is the one we use most. It is extremely useful at a gathering, when you are short of time and ideas. Serve it with thin slices of bread.

Miso Spread.

> 1 tablespoon miso
>
> 4 tablespoons tahini
>
> 3 tablespoons water
>
> ½ teaspoon fresh basil or ¼ teaspoon dried

Pour tahini in a saucepan. Toast it for 3-5 minutes, add miso diluted in water, mix, allow to cook 5 minutes while stirring. At the end add basil and cook 2 minutes more.

Oat-miso Spread.

Instead of tahini you may use oats, which produce an equally delicious spread.

> 1 tablespoon miso
>
> 1 tablespoon sesame seeds, toasted and ground
>
> 1 tablespoon oat flour
>
> ½ cup water
>
> 1 tablespoon scallions, chopped
>
> 1 teaspoon oil

In a saucepan saute scallions for 2 minutes, then add ground sesame seeds (homemade tahini). Add flour and miso diluted in water. Mix, then cook over low flame while stirring for 5 minutes.

Scallion Spread.

> 1 bunch scallions
>
> 2 teaspoons oil
>
> 1 heaping tablespoon miso
>
> 1 tablespoon water

Chop the entire scallion, both roots and leafy parts. Put in a saucepan and saute for 5 minutes, then add diluted miso in water. Cook 10 minutes over a low-to-medium flame while stirring from time to time.

Miso Pâté.

     1 cup cooked and mashed aduki beans

     2 slices bread, soaked in 1 cup water

     2 tablespoons miso, diluted in 1 cup water

     4 tablespoons tahini

     1 onion, chopped

     3 scallions, chopped

     1 tablespoon parsley, chopped

     1 teaspoon oil

     Pinch coriander

In a saucepan saute onions and scallions for 2 minutes. Then add aduki puree, miso mixture, tahini, soaked bread, water and parsley. Mix thoroughly; cook 10 minutes while stirring; add coriander. Pour mixture in a baking pan lined with oiled foil. Bake 35 minutes uncovered at 350 degrees. The top will turn dark brown.

Serve hot or cooled, with lettuce or watercress.

Fish Spread.

- 2 herrings, pickled, cut into small pieces
- 2 pieces dark bread (rye) cut into pieces
- 1 onion, chopped
- ½ apple, cut into pieces
- 1 tablespoon parsley, chopped
- 1 tablespoon sesame oil

In a saucepan saute onions; add apple and saute for 3 more minutes. Add bread, mix and pour in a bowl. Add fish, parsley. Blend ingredients and put through a meat grinder. Serve on toasted bread with black olives.

Variation:

Other pickled or smoked fish can be used, such as anchovies or salmon.

The biochemistry
of violence

May it happen that your days of youth
Have the bitter taste of dandelion
And your death bed be arranged
On the sweet sweet tongue of a nightingale.

"Yes," he said, "I've been eating brown rice for three years. And it works. I'm a new man! Three years ago I was lying in bed, stiff with arthritis, but here, look at my hands now! They *bend*. Brown rice is what did it!"

John Turner, a retired colonel in his late fifties, spoke with understandable enthusiasm. We had just met during this stopover on my tour of the States. Six feet seven or eight inches tall and with clear, direct blue eyes, Turner was nearly a double for John Wayne, although he stood squarely on his feet, not as Wayne does on the outsides of his arches.

"When I was in the army, a career soldier, one of my greatest pleasures was to give new recruits a rough time—especially the doves. I used to enjoy letting them have it. But now I'm a different man in that respect too." Turner was sincere and open. "I read your book, Michel, and I want to tell you it makes sense. I read all the others about Macrobiotics too. I just wish my wife would take a look at one of them. It's hard doing it by myself and I'd enjoy the change of having someone cook for me."

My wife Claude, my children and a friend and travelling-companion were with me in John Turner's livingroom. I couldn't help wondering what might be going through our host's mind with respect to my friend's long hair and beard.

John Turner's wife entered. Her own hair was trimmed as short as a boy's and, while slender at the top, she grew progressively heavier towards the bottom. We shook hands. She hesitated before doing the same with our bearded friend.

"Edna is German," explained John Turner, indicating his wife. "She sure knows how to cook a pork chop. Which is fine for her,—but not exactly the best thing in the world for me."

Edna Turner lifted her chin. "He's been after me for three years to try his brown rice. Well, thanks all the same, I'll stick to meat." Taking a chair, she crossed her legs. Tight jeans betrayed heavy thighs and hips.

"Edna is a good cook," Turner conceded diplomatically, "but it doesn't do me any good. Do you suppose you could teach her a few fundamentals? I really hate to cook for myself."

But the first day we couldn't even get Edna to enter the kitchen, much less to sit down at the table with us to enjoy a cerealian meal.

John Turner said to my wife: "Now this is a treat! You're a real angel, Claude, you don't know how much all this means to me."

The second day Edna joined us and tasted a bit of everything. "This isn't bad at all," she confessed. "If it were all like this I wouldn't mind it once in a while."

"We always eat as well as this," I said.

"But aren't you restricted to just grains and vegetables?" asked Edna.

"Basically, yes, but you can't keep your imagination from running and catching up with what you think is good," answered Claude, groping for words in English. "With simple food we create attractive forms and foreign, beautiful flavors."

The third day Edna was in the kitchen, asking for advice. While the women cooked, John Turner confided, "Michel, your children look like those I've seen in old paintings. They could almost have stepped directly out of a Goya or Reubens."

I nodded, deeply pleased at the compliment.

"You don't see children like them anymore," he went on. "Take my daughter, for example. She can break a horse as well as any man. Break a man too, for that matter, I suppose. She's as tough as a mustang—not very feminine."

That same day Edna and I became fast friends. She had completely lost her first day's animosity. She talked about the ranch, about dogs and horses, and even sang us a song.

The fourth and last day, she was an utterly transformed woman. As we were leaving she promised to cook well for her husband. I felt like kissing her. My wife did. John brought us to the car and I saw tears of joy in his eyes.

"Thanks for everything, Michel. From now on it's going to be like a second honeymoon with Edna."

"Thank you, John. And thank you," I added sentimentally, "for what you are."

I wanted to tell him more but I didn't. I wanted to say he had taught me a deep lesson in perseverence, remaining loyal to his idea through great difficulties. What he had once been was now very far from what he had become—a true man.

A man of war and violence does not eat grain before battle. War demands meat and swords require blood—this is an immutable fact. War is the ultimate effect of self-indulgence.

Soldiers prepare for killing with luxurious nights that dim their sensitivities. They eat, drink and engage in sexual extravaganzas in preparation for the morrow's blind struggle to the death. Such a soldier was John Turner, a man accustomed to war and conflict. By changing his food he changed himself—his blood and his ideas about war.

Violence in the cities, as well as on the battlefields, is but the result of bad blood traceable to food unfit for man. New York, for example, is a city with a sweet tooth. Its sugary ways terminate in crime. Somewhere it has been written, "Whoever eats sweet today suffers a bitter tomorrow, while he who chews well has a life tasting sweeter than wine." Yet ice cream cones and soft drinks in profusion—piles upon piles of them higher than the Empire State Building itself!—feed the youth and foster delinquency.

My own experience with sugar has led me to violent, uncontrollable seizures. I was a miserable young man desperately trying to adjust to his environment. Had I continued on the course I was on, I might eventually have unleashed my anger on the streets the way so many others do; or perhaps I might have developed a psychology that culminated in a rational "philosophy of survival". Millions today are but patients—in the primitive sense of the word—who suffer the strain of maintaining good behavior while anger rages within.

Devoid of memory Man relates to others but mechanically and in darkness, misled by his five senses. Memory is the channel that connects him with the Infinite. Violence begins the instant memory is lost. To remember is to love and to care. To forget is to crush and to hate. Sugar is the sweet fire that consumes man, reduces him to ashes and dark tomorrows. I love because I know who you are, *remember* you; I hate when I am bound to my disturbed and psychological self. Loneliness blankets the soldier and warms his inner determination to kill.

"Remember," my mother said to me once, "don't eat too many olives—you'll have a bad memory and won't be able to work well in school!" That advice came from her grandmother, who had learned it from her ancestors. How profound our ancient wisdom! Too much oil confines the memory, clouds the thought. Even more, clogs both body and mind. Too much meat lowers a heavy curtain between us and the spiritual. Violence arises when Man forgets why he should love. No spirit, no togetherness.

A heavy meat-eater is more active physically than psychologically; he is forced to eliminate excess energy; his violence always takes material forms. The fruit-eater, however, chooses different modes. He is divisive, separatist, expansive and dualistic. He is capable of cruel indifference to human suffering and want. He longs for timelessness and despises the material—even his own blood.

Those who nourish themselves with artificial and chemicalized food are but robots who follow blindly and mechanically the organized routes of the society that manufactures it. Their particular form of violence is wholly unpredictable since their bible is television, and no one knows what *it* might command.

Unfit food produces split, schizophrenic thought that fluctuates between extreme and extreme, between wisdom and violence, hatred and love. Between life and death.

Unfit foods change the history of Man. They are his biochemical determinants. Man cannot help but open and close his mouth according to the expansive and contractive commands of his food. Whoever resists such movement possesses a distorted mouth and utters the speech of a retarded child; for no one can counter his inner will. The polluted currents pouring into the bloodstream already seek to empty into the ocean of death.

Special dishes

If the recipes in this section did not contain grains themselves, they could have been included in the chapter "Companions of Grains." Although not so substantial as a main dish, a special dish may make a complete meal if your hunger is small. You may go through periods during which you will find yourself compelled to try the versatility of this way of cooking, but take care not to neglect that which is most nutritious and fundamental—rice and vegetables.

CROQUETTES

Onigri.

Onigri is the Japanese answer to our sandwich. Oblong-shaped rice-balls, they are made with soft rice and stuffed with a filling of your choice.
To make a soft but not mushy rice proceed as follows:

Put 2 cups washed rice in a good-quality pressure-cooker, cover with 3 ½ cups cold water and add ½ teaspoon salt. Bring up pressure over a high flame. When pressure-regulator jiggles, maintain high flame for 3 more minutes; then on a medium flame allow to cook for an hour and a half. In order to prevent the bottom from scorching place two asbestos pads beneath pressure-cooker. Removing cooker from flame, allow to stand until pressure subsides completely.

To shape onigri, use slightly cooled rice, wet your hands in water and form oblong balls. For stuffing use any of the following:

> Umeboshi—Japanese salted plum
>
> Pickled vegetables
>
> A piece of fish, raw, fried or broiled

Onigri can be served rolled in chopped parsley, or simply fried in a small amount of oil and lightly brushed with soya sauce when done.

Palettes d'adukis.

> 3 cups cooked rice
>
> 1 cup cooked aduki beans
>
> ¼ cup scallions, chopped and sauteed
>
> 2 tablespoons w.w. pastry flour
>
> Cornmeal for coating

Mix all ingredients except cornmeal. Form 2-inch balls and flatten in the palms of your hands. Coat each palette with cornmeal. Fry in a sufficient amount of oil to prevent the burning of either your palettes or your frying pan. Serve with a few drops of soya sauce.

Variation:

Substitute 1 cup rice with 1 cup cooked whole-wheat berries or cooked rye.

Macrobiotic coins.

> 2 cups cooked rice
>
> 2 cups cooked rice cream
>
> ¼ cup oat flour and
>
> 1 egg for coating
>
> ¼ cup scallions, chopped and lightly sauteed
>
> 1/3 teaspoon salt

Blend rice, rice cream, scallions and salt. Form patties. Dip them in flour, then in egg which has been beaten, then in flour again. Fry in a small amount of oil, turning over when one side is done.

Millestones. (The favorites of the house)

> 3 cups cooked millet (soft)
>
> ¼ cup onions, chopped
>
> ½ cup carrots, grated
>
> ¼ cup w.w. pastry flour
>
> ½ teaspoon salt

Mix all ingredients. Form into small balls and deep fry in corn oil. For variation roll in tempura batter before deep frying.

Croquettes de légumes.

> 6 small onions, finely chopped
>
> 6 cabbage leaves, finely chopped
>
> 3 carrots, diced
>
> 5 small pieces seitan
>
> 1 tablespoon oil
>
> ½ teaspoon salt
>
> 3/4 cup wheat berries, cooked
>
> 3/4 cup w.w. pastry flour

Saute vegetables in oil. Add finely chopped seitan and salt. Cover and simmer 20 minutes. Put cooked vegetables in a mixing bowl. Add wheat berries and flour. Mix thoroughly. Form into patties and fry in a slightly oiled pan or grill.

Croquettes de couscous.

> ½ pound steamed or boiled couscous
>
> 1 cup pureed squash
>
> ¼ cup w.w. pastry flour
>
> ¼ cup parsley, chopped
>
> Pinch salt

Mix all ingredients. Form small oblong balls two inches long, then fry in ¼ inch oil until crisp on both sides.

Croquettes bourgeoises.

>   2 cups w.w. pastry flour
>
>   ½ cup carrots, grated
>
>   ¼ cup scallions, chopped
>
>   12 olives, chopped
>
>   1 teaspoon salt
>
>   6 tablespoons olive oil
>
>   12 small onions
>
>   1 clove garlic, crushed (optional)
>
>   1 bunch watercress, chopped

In a mixing bowl combine flour, carrots, olives, scallions and salt. If the mixture is too dry, moisten with water or, better still, soup stock. Form into 1-inch balls, then flatten slightly between the palms of your hands. In a frying pan saute small onions in olive oil. Add balls and simmer covered for 20 minutes. Check every once in a while to prevent balls from burning. Add oil if needed and stir. At the end add chopped watercress and saute for 5 minutes, stirring.

Buckwheat croquettes. (Baked)

a)   3 cups cooked kasha

1/3 cup onions, chopped

¼ green pepper, diced and sauteed

½ cup matzoh meal or oat flakes

½ teaspoon salt

b)   3 large zucchini, sliced

2 tablespoons oil

2 onions, chopped

1 cup water

4 tablespoons tamari

To make the balls blend kasha, onions, green pepper and matzoh meal. Salt. Form small balls. Place on an oiled baking sheet and bake at 375 degrees for ½ hour. In the meantime, saute onions, then zucchini in a heavy pot. After 5 minutes add water and tamari; simmer for 5 minutes covered. Add baked balls; place them over the vegetable mixture and allow to cook covered for 10-15 minutes over a low flame.

Variation:

To make the famous buckwheat croquettes, use the following ingredients:

> 3 cups cooked kasha
>
> 1/3 cup onions, chopped
>
> ½ cup whole-wheat flour
>
> 1 bunch scallions, chopped
>
> ½ teaspoon salt

Mix ingredients, finishing with the flour. Make 2-inch balls, flatten to 1 inch and fry in ¼ inch oil. Serve hot with a few drops of tamari. You may use these with the zucchini-onion mixture in place of the baked variety.

These recipes were included to inspire you to create other combinations of grains and vegetables. All kinds of leftovers, even heavy soups and creams can be used to make delicious croquettes.

LOAVES

Kasha loaf.

> 5 cups cooked kasha
>
> 1 cup cooked rice
>
> 1/3 cup onions, chopped
>
> ¼ cup scallions, chopped
>
> 4 tablespoons parsley, chopped
>
> 1/3 cup pastry flour
>
> 1 small teaspoon salt
>
> Pinch nutmeg
>
> Pinch basil

Combine all ingredients into a loose mixture. If too dry, moisten with water or soup stock. Line a loaf pan with aluminum foil. Place mixture in pan. Press lightly. Bake at 350 degrees for 1 hour or so. Serve with a light bechamel sauce and chopped parsley.

Le Pavé.

  ½ cup toasted raw rice

  ½ cup toasted raw kasha

  ½ cup millet

  1 cup oat flakes

  ½ cup cornmeal

  1/8 cup oil

  2 cups pureed squash

  1 ½ cups water

  1 onion, minced and sauteed

  1 ½ teaspoon salt

Grind millet, kasha and rice in a flour grinder. In a mixing bowl blend water, oil and salt. Add pureed squash and beat thoroughly. Stir in ground grains as well as cornmeal and oat flakes. The mixture should be a heavy liquid batter. Allow to stand 1 hour. Bake at 375 degrees for 1 hour until done.

Sarasina.

> 3 cups cooked kasha
>
> 2 cups cooked bulghur
>
> 1 cup cooked lentils
>
> 1/3 cup onions, chopped
>
> ¼ cup scallions, chopped
>
> 3 tablespoons parsley, chopped
>
> 3 tablespoons miso spread
>
> Pinch basil
>
> 1 teaspoon oil

Saute onions and scallions. In a mixing bowl combine all ingredients. Line 2 loaf pans with aluminum foil. Oil pans, pour bechamel into bottom and arrange grain mixture over it. Bake at 375 degrees for 1 hour covered with a sheet of aluminum foil. Uncover and bake 1 hour more. Wait a while before unmolding the loaves so that they may cool.

Make this special bechamel sauce instead of the classical one:

> 1 cup thick bechamel
>
> 1 tablespoon almonds, toasted and chopped
>
> Pinch of nutmeg

Rye loaf.

     1 cup cooked whole rye

     3 cups bread chunks

     2 cups aduki beans

     2 onions, chopped

     1 leek, chopped

     1 carrot, grated

     3 tablespoons parsley, chopped

     ¼ cup w.w. pastry flour

     Pinch salt

     2 tablespoons miso

     1 cup water or stock to moisten

     1 tablespoon oil

Moisten bread in water or stock. In a frying pan saute onions, scallions, leeks and carrots. Blend all ingredients in a mixing bowl. Pour mixture into a loaf pan and bake at 375 degrees for 45-50 minutes. Before serving glaze with a sauce of arrow-root and tamari.

Leftover loaves may be used for stuffing vegetables. Also combined with additional sauteed vegetables they make delicious fillings for a strudel, a kind of "pâté en croûte." If you make too much of any loaf, you may cut it into slices and fry it in oil. Excellent for croquettes!

STUFFED VEGETABLES

Pauvrettes. (Stuffed cabbage)

      1 medium head of cabbage (curly kind preferable)

      3 cups cooked rice

      1 cup cooked aduki beans

      3 tablespoons w.w. pastry flour

      ½ cup onions, chopped

      ½ cup carrots, grated

      2 tablespoons oil

      2/3 teaspoon salt

      3 tablespoons tamari and

      1 tablespoon tahini diluted in

      1/3 cup water

      Sauce:

2 cups thick bechamel made with aduki bean juice (instead of water) and sauteed scallions.

Parboil cabbage head in salted water. Separate leaves carefully so as not to break them. Allow to cool.

Saute onions and carrots. In a mixing bowl prepare stuffing by blending cooked rice, aduki beans, flour, vegetables and salt. Put 2 tablespoons of this mixture on top of each cabbage leaf. Fold in sides neatly; roll cabbage and close it like an envelope. It may be necessary to fasten it with a toothpick. Place cabbage rolls in a casserole pan, pour tahini-tamari mixture over them. Place in a 375-degree oven for 30 minutes. Remove from oven, cover with bechamel sauce and broil for 10 minutes until top is slightly scorched.

Variation:

> 1 cup onions, chopped
>
> 1 ½ cups carrots, chopped
>
> 1 ½ cup cabbage, shredded
>
> 1 ½ cups bread crumbs
>
> 1 tablespoon olive oil
>
> 2 tablespoons tamari
>
> Pinch nutmeg

To prepare stuffing, saute vegetables, add bread crumbs, tamari and nutmeg. Cook for 5 minutes, stirring. Stuff cabbage leaves in the manner already described. Before baking, sprinkle with water and tamari mixture (4 tablespoons tamari to 1/3 cup water). This type of stuffed cabbage may be served with rice or noodles to make a complete meal.

Colorados.

> 3 acorn squash, cut in half
>
> 3 cups cooked bulghur
>
> 2/3 cup onions, chopped
>
> 2 cups bechamel sauce, flavored with a pinch of allspice
>
> 3 tablespoons almonds, toasted and ground

Prepare squash-halves for baking by scooping out seeds and brushing oil over surface. Bake at 500 degrees for ½ hour. Remove from oven. Saute onions and combine with cooked bulghur. Fill squash with this mixture. Cover with bechamel sauce and put back in oven till squash is done, approximately 20 minutes more. Before serving, sprinkle with almonds.

Onion Mignon.

> 6 large onions, peeled
>
> 2 cups cooked millet
>
> 2/3 cup cooked chick-peas
>
> 1/3 cup scallions, chopped
>
> 1 tablespoon oil
>
> Sauce bechamel, flavored with pinch of cumin

Parboil peeled onions. When cool, cut tops and scoop out insides. In a frying pan saute scallions in oil, add parts of onions you have just cut out, finely chopped. Add chick-peas and millet. Stuff onions with this mixture. Place stuffed onions in an oiled baking pan. Pour on bechamel sauce and bake at 350-375 degrees for 30 minutes or so. Serve topped with chopped parsley.

Zucwhats.

> 6 medium-size zucchini, cut into 1 ½ inch chunks
>
> 3 cups cooked kasha
>
> 3/4 cup onion, chopped
>
> 1 cup fresh corn kernels, cooked
>
> 1/5 green pepper, finely chopped
>
> 1 tablespoon oil
>
> ½ teaspoon salt
>
> 3 tablespoons soya sauce

Scoop out insides of zucchini. Chop what you have scooped out and saute with onions and green pepper in frying pan. Add cooked kasha and corn. Fill zucchini shells with the mixture. Brush surface with oil; place in baking pan and sprinkle with soya sauce. Bake covered in 300-degree oven for 45 minutes. Check occasionally to prevent burning; sprinkle with juice that oozes out of cooking vegetables. If no liquid appears, add ½ cup water with 2 tablespoons soya sauce.

Pissaladière. (Lima's recipe)

This pie makes a delightful party dish. It should serve up to 15 people.

    14 leeks, finely chopped

    3 carrots, cut into matchsticks

    5 eggs (fertilized)

    ½ cup water

    3 slices bread

    5 tablespoons olive oil

    8 olives, chopped

    Puff dough (see recipe, page 266)

In a heavy pan saute leeks in olive oil; add bread chunks, water and carrots. Cover and simmer for 30 minutes. Allow to cool a while. Beat eggs with an electric mixer, then fold into mixture. Bake pie dough for 10 minutes in a 12" by 18" pan. Remove from oven. Pour filling in, sprinkle with olives and bake for 30 minutes at 375 degrees. The *pissaladiere* is a success if the crust is paper-thin.

Komoku. (Another of Lima's special dishes!)

    2 cups uncooked rice, soaked 1 day

    4 cups water

    1 tablespoon oil

    ½ teaspoon salt

    3 carrots, cut into matchsticks

    2 burdock roots, slivered

    1 cup string-beans, chopped

    ½ bunch chopped watercress

    ½ bunch dandelion leaves, boiled, chopped

    12 sardines, rolled in flour and fried

    1 piece tofu 2" by 2", deep-fried and cut into strips

    2 tablespoons oil

    Pinch salt

Toast rice in oil, then cook in water for an hour and a half. In a pan saute stringbeans, carrots and burdock. Cover and simmer for 20 minutes. In a rectangular serving dish arrange in layers: cooked rice, vegetable mixture and boiled dandelion. Over this place fish (fried) and sprinkle with raw watercress leaflets and strips of tofu. Serve carefully, trying not to disarrange the layers.

Cerealian strudel.

> 1½ cups cooked rice
>
> 1½ cups cooked kasha
>
> 1 cup cooked aduki
>
> 1/3 cup onions, minced
>
> 2/3 cup cabbage, shredded
>
> ¼ cup scallions, chopped
>
> 2 tablespoons miso spread, flavored with pinch basil
>
> 1 tablespoon oil
>
> ½ teaspoon salt
>
> Puff dough pie crust

Saute onions, scallions and cabbage. Combine with cooked rice, kasha and aduki beans. Add salt and miso spread. Mix thoroughly. Roll out pie dough as thin as possible. Put mixture at one end and roll up strudel. Bake at 375 degrees for 40 minutes. Serve with chopped parsley. Diced zucchini can be used instead of cabbage. For variation, cut dough into 2-inch squares, stuff with mixture, bake or deep fry. These are the so-called Piroshki, famous in eastern Europe and Russia.

Endwells.

> 1 cup cooked bulghur
>
> 2 cups lentils, cooked and pureed
>
> ½ cup oat flakes
>
> ½ cup sesame seeds, toasted
>
> ½ teaspoon salt

Combine all ingredients in a bowl. Mixture should be soft. Oil a muffin tin; distribute mixture. Bake in a 300-degree oven for 30 minutes. Serve with your favorite sauce on top. Aside, sauteed onions and zucchini.

Summer rice.

> 4 cups cooked rice
>
> 2 thick slices halibut, broiled and flaked
>
> 6 red radishes, sliced thinly
>
> 2 small cucumbers, diced
>
> 3 carrots, grated
>
> 1 bunch watercress, chopped
>
> ¼ teaspoon salt
>
> 1 bar agar agar
>
> Dressing:
>
> 2 cups umeboshi juice
>
> 2 tablespoons tahini

Dilute agar agar in umeboshi juice, then cook. Allow to cool for ½ hour; add tahini and stir in all other ingredients. Pour entire mixture in a ring mold. Chill for 3 hours. Unmold over a salad of greens.

Salada di macaroni.

> 5 cups w.w. macaroni, cooked
>
> 1 cup cooked chick-peas
>
> ¼ cup onions, minced
>
> ½ cup carrots, diced
>
> ½ cup celery, diced
>
> 1 tablespoon olive oil
>
> ½ cup of Marinabelle dressing (see recipe, page 185)

Saute onions, celery and carrots for 10 minutes while stirring. Vegetables should be still crisp. Mix all ingredients in a serving bowl. Pour in dressing and toss lightly. Garnish with chopped parsley.

Levantine. (Bulghur salad)

> 5 cups cooked bulghur
>
> 1 cup celery, diced
>
> 1 teaspoon fresh mint, chopped, or 1/3 dried
>
> 1 tablespoon parsley, chopped
>
> 2 tablespoons tahini, diluted in 3 tablespoons water
>
> 1 teaspoon salt

Combine all ingredients in a large bowl. Toss lightly.

La Japonaise.

> 3 cups aduki beans, cooked until all liquid is gone
>
> 3 cups Udon (Japanese white wheat noodles)
>
> ¼ teaspoon salt

Break noodles into small pieces before putting into boiling water. After noodles are done, cool them for a few minutes. While still warm, combine with cooked creamy aduki beans and salt. Pour mixture into 2 loaf pans. Allow to set. Unmold and cut into squares. Serve with pressed green salad.

La Marronade.

        3 ½ cups rice

        6 ½ cups water

        1 ½ cups chestnuts, presoaked 20 minutes in 4 cups water

        3/4 teaspoon salt

        2 tablespoons oil

Cook chestnuts for ½ hour in water in which they have been presoaked. In a heavy pot saute rice. Add cooked chestnuts. Add water and salt and cook 1 hour. Add a little more water if necessary.

Variation:

        2/3 cup uncooked aduki beans

        4 cups uncooked rice

        6 cups water

        1 teaspoon salt

Pressure-cook 1 hour.

Brazilian rice. (Lima's)

>3 large onions, minced
>
>1 small cabbage-head
>
>3 turnips, cut into matchsticks
>
>2 big leeks, chopped
>
>3 big carrots, cut into matchsticks
>
>2 celery stalks, chopped
>
>5 tablespoons oil
>
>5 cups rice, toasted
>
>15 cups water
>
>2 teaspoons salt

Saute onions and leeks, in a heavy pot. After 2 minutes add turnips, cabbage and carrots, then add toasted rice. Add water, celery and salt. Cover and cook for 1 hour.

O'Sushi.

>6 cups cooked rice
>
>1 ½ cups cooked chick-peas
>
>1 cup dry lotus root, soaked, boiled 3 minutes and chopped
>
>A piece of tofu 3" by 2", deep-fried and cut into strips
>
>½ cup scallions, chopped
>
>4 tablespoons soya sauce
>
>Pinch saffron soaked in 3 tablespoons water
>
>2 tablespoons oil
>
>Pinch salt

In a heavy pan saute scallions for 2 minutes, add lotus root and tofu strips. Saute 5 minutes while stirring. Add rice, chick-peas, soya sauce and saffron. Mix thoroughly and simmer for 10 minutes over a low flame.

Casserole Royale.

> 5 cups cooked rice
>
> 4 carrots, cut diagonally into chunks
>
> 3 turnips, cut diagonally into chunks
>
> 3 celery stalks, cut into large chunks
>
> 6 pieces seitan
>
> 3 cups water
>
> 1 heaping tablespoon arrow-root
>
> 3 tablespoons soya sauce
>
> Pinch ginger
>
> Puff dough for lattice (use ½ amount given in recipe, page 266)

Boil vegetables in water for 15 minutes, covered. Salt and reserve liquid (it should amount to 1 cup). When cool, make an arrowroot sauce with this liquid. Flavor it with soya sauce, ginger and seitan.

Put rice in the bottom of a square casserole dish (9" by 9"). Arrange vegetables on top. Cover with arrow-root sauce. Roll out dough, cut into 8 strips 3/4" wide and equal to the length of your casserole dish. On a baking sheet criss-cross strips to form lattice pattern. Bake lattice at 400 degrees for 15 minutes. Place over vegetables. Heat in oven before serving. Decorate with chopped parsley.

Barley Jardinière.

     5 cups cooked barley

     ½ cup carrots, sliced

     ½ cup parsnips, sliced

     ½ cup onions, minced

     ½ cup dried daikon, washed but not soaked

     2 tablespoons oil

     2 sheets nori, toasted

     1/3 cup bread crumbs

     ½ cup water

     2 tablespoons soya sauce

    Saute onions in a pan for 2 minutes. Add carrots and parsnips. Cook 5 minutes while stirring. Add daikon, then soya sauce and water. Cover and simmer 10-15 minutes. Every once in a while stir to prevent burning. Add a drop of water if necessary. Place barley in the bottom of a casserole pan, cover with vegetables and sprinkle with nori and bread crumbs. Bake at 350 degrees for 15 minutes.

Casserole Belge.

> 5 cups cooked whole oats (1 hour)
>
> 2 cups brussel sprouts (large ones cut into halves)
>
> 2 tablespoons olive oil
>
> 1 ½ cups water
>
> 1 tablespoon arrow-root
>
> 3 tablespoons soya sauce
>
> Pinch salt

Saute brussel sprouts for 5 minutes while stirring, then add water and soya sauce. Cover and cook 15 minutes. Reserve liquid to make an arrow-root sauce (when it is cool). Put whole oats at bottom of casserole dish. Arrange brussel sprouts over them. Cover with sauce and heat in a warm oven for 10 minutes. Sprinkle with chopped parsley or watercress before serving.

Kasha à l'Orientale.

> 6 cups cooked buckwheat groats
>
> 2 cups carrots, cut into matchsticks
>
> ½ cup scallions, chopped
>
> ½ cup onions, minced
>
> 1 ½ cups fresh tofu, cut into pieces
>
> 2 tablespoons corn oil
>
> 2 tablespoons soya sauce
>
> ¼ teaspoon salt

Saute onions, then carrots for 5 minutes. Add tofu, then salt and soya sauce. Simmer 15 minutes, stirring once in a while. Add cooked groats. Mix thoroughly. Saute scallions for 2 minutes and mix into cooked ingredients.

Warsaw 1920's. (Recipe inspired by "The Family Moskat,"
       by I.B. Singer)

       5 cups cooked buckwheat groats

       3 cups cooked macaroni shells (semolina, wheat or unbleached)

       1 cup cooked chick-peas

       ½ cup scallions, chopped

       2 tablespoons oil

       ½ teaspoon salt

    Saute scallions in a frying pan for 3 minutes. Add chick-peas, noodles and kasha. Mix all ingredients thoroughly. Put mixture in a casserole dish and bake for 15 minutes at 350 degrees.

Armenian Pilau.

       2 cups bulghur

       3/4 cup lentils

       2 small onions, minced

       6 ½ cups water

       Sauce aux amandes:

       2 cups bechamel

       ½ cup almonds, toasted and ground

       1 onion, minced and sauteed

    Saute onions in oil in a heavy pot. Add bulghur, then lentils. Allow to cook for 2 minutes. Boil water in separate pot. Pour it over bulghur, lentils and onions and cover pot with heavy lid. Cook for ½ hour over a low flame. Pour into an earthenware pot and cover with sauce aux amandes. Bake in a 375-degree oven for 15 minutes. Before serving place in broiler for 10 minutes.

222

Nori Maki.

> 1 pound boiled soba noodles
>
> 6 nori sheets
>
> 2 boiled carrots
>
> ½ bunch boiled watercress
>
> 1 slivered burdock root
>
> 1 tablespoon oil

Saute burdock in oil for approximately 10 minutes. Stir. Add a bit of water to keep it from sticking to the pan. Toast a sheet of nori on both sides by waving quickly over flame. Prepare all sheets in this manner. Cut carrots lengthwise into thin sticks. Drain boiled watercress. On a Japanese bamboo screen called Maki-Su (designed especially for making nori rolls) lay out toasted nori sheets, one at a time. Spread a handful of noodles over 2/3 of each sheet of nori. At one end place 2 carrot-sticks lengthwise over noodles. Spread approximately 3 leaflets watercress over this and sprinkle burdock shavings entire length. Roll up nori maki inside bamboo screen, squeezing to make more compact. Unfold bamboo screen and remove nori roll. With a sharp damp knife cut rolls into eight sections. Arrange on a plate. Serve with a dish of soya sauce for dipping. This recipe is a variation of Maki Sushi, which is made with rice instead of noodles.

Noodle nook.

> 1 pound Udon (Japanese white wheat noodles)
>
> 1 burdock root, boiled and sliced thinly
>
> 2 onions, chopped
>
> ¼ shredded cabbage
>
> 1/3 cup toasted pumpkin seeds, chopped
>
> ½ teaspoon salt
>
> 2 tablespoons oil

Saute onions in a heavy pan for 2 minutes. Add cabbage. Saute for 5 minutes, cover and simmer for 10 minutes. Add burdock and stir thoroughly. Pour in boiled noodles and finally add pumpkin seeds. Add salt. With a pair of big chopsticks blend all ingredients thoroughly. Cover and allow to cook over a low flame for 5-10 minutes more, stirring every once in a while.

Noodle-croquette.

> 1 pound soba noodles, cooked
>
> 1 cup bechamel sauce
>
> ½ bunch kale (watercress and spinach will do)
>
> 12 deep-fried croquettes (preferably buckwheat croquettes)
>
> 2 tablespoons parsley, chopped
>
> 1 tablespoon oil
>
> ½ cup water
>
> 2 tablespoons soya sauce

Saute kale in a skillet for 5 minutes while stirring. Add water, cover and cook for 15 minutes. Flavor with soya sauce just before end of cooking. Mix noodles with bechamel sauce. Spread noodles in an oiled casserole pan, cover with cooked kale and top with croquettes. Bake covered with aluminum foil at 350 degrees for 10 minutes. Uncover for 5 minutes more. Sprinkle with parsley just before serving.

La Milanaise. (Molded polenta)

> 1 ½ cups polenta (obtained in Italian stores) or cornmeal
>
> 4 ½ cups water
>
> 1 teaspoon salt
>
> 2 cups pureed carrots
>
> 2 cups swiss chard, chopped and cooked
>
> ½ cup oats, toasted

Slowly stir polenta into boiling water. Add salt, cover and simmer for 20 minutes. When polenta is cooked, pour into 2 baking pans (glassware), 14" by 9", which have been previously rinsed with water. Allow to set for 2-3 hours. Spread carrots over the set polenta in one of the baking pans. Unmold other pan over the layer of carrots. Cover second layer of polenta with cooked swiss chard. Sprinkle with toasted oats. Bake for 10 minutes in a moderately warm oven. Cut into large squares.

L'Orleanaise. (Hominy grits, southern style)

   1 cup hominy grits (white polenta)

   4 cups water

   1 teaspoon salt

   Pinto bean sauce:

   1 cup pinto beans

   2 carrots, thinly sliced

   2 parsnips, thinly sliced

   2 onions, chopped

   2 tablespoons oil

   1/3 cup seitan (optional)

   1 teaspoon salt

   5 cups water

For hominy grits, boil water, add salt; slowly stir in grits, cover and cook for 30 minutes. Stir once in a while to make sure it does not burn.

To cook sauce, saute in a pressure-cooker in this order: onions, parsnips and carrots for approximately 5 minutes; add beans and water, and pressure-cook for 2 hours. Bring down pressure, open and add salt. Cook for 10 minutes more.

To serve, place grits in individual dishes, sprinkle with chopped seitan and cover with very hot sauce.

Variation:

Pour cooked grits into a ring mold. Allow to cool. Unmold in a circular baking pan covered with aluminum foil. Pour bean sauce into center of ring. Place croquettes of your choice over it (preferably buckwheat). You may brush surface of mold with an egg yolk to make it appear more festive. Bake at 350 degrees for 15 minutes or so. Sprinkle with finely chopped scallions.

Bi-Cuan. (Vietnamese recipe)

> 2 pieces tofu (2" by 2") deep-fried and cut into strips
>
> 2 turnips, cut into matchsticks
>
> 2 carrots, cut into matchsticks
>
> 1 onion, minced
>
> 2 tablespoons parsley
>
> ½ cup uncooked rice cream
>
> 1 cup cooked somen
>
> ½ bunch watercress, chopped
>
> 1 tablespoon oil
>
> ¼ teaspoon salt
>
> 2 tablespoons soya sauce
>
> 12 thin chapatis, rolled out but uncooked

Saute onions, carrots and turnips for 5 minutes. Add tofu and salt. Cover and cook 15 more minutes, stirring once in a while. Add watercress. Cook for 5 minutes more. Allow to cool, then add rice cream and somen. Put some of this mixture on each chapati. Roll into a cigar shape and close at each end. Deep-fry each roll. Serve with rice and green vegetables on the side.

Gnocci Florentin.

> ¼ pound fine w.w. pastry flour
>
> 4 cups boiling water
>
> 1 teaspoon salt

Bring water to a boil, add salt. Slowly stir in flour. Turn off heat and allow to swell for 10 minutes. Pour hot mixture into platters ½ inch high, rinsed with cold water. Allow to cool, cut into squares and brown in a frying pan. Serve with chopped and sauteed watercress on top or cover with any heavy sauce.

Crêpe Montmartoise.

> 6 w.w. crêpes (see recipe, page 257)
>
> 6 Belgian endives, whole
>
> 1 cup bechamel sauce
>
> 1 tablespoon oil
>
> 2 tablespoons soya sauce
>
> 1/3 cup toasted and chopped almonds

Make crêpes and put them aside. In a frying skillet saute whole endives. Cover and simmer 10 minutes. Add soya sauce. Turn them over and cook for 5 minutes more. Roll one endive in each crêpe. Arrange crêpes in an oiled casserole dish. Cover with bechamel sauce, sprinkle with almonds and bake for 10 minutes at 350 degrees. Broil for 5 minutes before serving.

Variation:

Substitute endives with 6 leeks cut into ½ inch slices. Cream leeks with ½ cup bechamel sauce before stuffing into crêpes. Pour bechamel sauce over neatly arranged crêpes.

Barley Kugel.

1 cup barley

3 cups boiling water

1 teaspoon salt

3 tablespoons bread crumbs

2 onions, minced

6 scallions, chopped

2 carrots, grated

1 burdock root, slivered

Stir barley into boiling water. Bring again to a boil. Add salt, cover and simmer for ½ hour. Saute onions in a skillet for 2 minutes, add scallions, then carrots and burdock. Cook for 10 minutes more while stirring. In a mixing bowl blend barley, vegetables and bread crumbs. Put in an oiled baking dish. Smooth surface of kugel with wet palm. Bake at 350 degrees for 30 minutes until top is brown. Serve with chopped parsley.

Oden.

This is a combination of the well-known Japanese Oden and the Jewish-Moroccan Shkhinah. My wife cooks it this way every Friday afternoon and we eat it reheated on a hot plate.

6 small onions

3 turnips, cut into chunks

4 carrots, cut diagonally into 1-inch slices

4-inch piece daikon, cut into ½-inch slices

6-inch piece jinenjo (Japanese wild potato) cut into 1-inch pieces

3 albi (taro root) cut in half

1 sheet kombu (approximately 6 inches long)

½ pound tofu, deep-fried (cut into pieces before frying)

2 tablespoons oil

1/3 cup soya sauce

1 teaspoon salt

1 cup raw barley

Water to cover

If albi or jinenjo are not available, use ½ cup lima beans or fava beans instead.

In a heavy pot saute onions, burdock, turnips, albi, daikon, carrots and jinenjo. Prepare a cotton bag (11" by 6") by soaking it in cold water. Place barley inside and tie at the top with a thread. Leave enough space for barley to expand. Put bag on top of the vegetables and cover with water. Add salt and soya sauce. Close lid. If pressure-cooking, allow to simmer 2-3 hours. If in a heavy pot, simmer 5-6 hours. Add fried tofu ½ hour before the end of the cooking. To serve, take the barley out of the bag and arrange in a serving dish in one piece. Serve heavy mixture in individual bowls or dishes.

If desired, Oden can be thickened with rice flour. Cooked without barley, Oden can be served as a stew with (or over) noodles.

Whole Wheat Bread

4 to 4½ cups whole-
wheat flour
1 TBS active dry yeast
1½ cups warm water
1 TBS honey
1 TBS safflower oil
1 tsp sea salt

In a large mixing bowl, dissolve yeast in ¼ cup of the warm water, then add remainder. Dissolve honey in this mixture and let sit for a few minutes; then add 2 cups of the flour and beat with a wooden spoon until smooth. Cover and set in a warm place to rise for about 1 hour until light and foamy. Mix salt and oil into batter.

(over)

Add flour a little at a time and mix until stiff and easy to handle. Place dough on a lightly floured board and begin kneading. Knead for 20 minutes or so, adding more flour a little at a time until smooth, elastic, and not sticky. The exact quantity of flour will vary slightly each time; this, as well as the proper consistency of the kneaded dough will be learned with experience. When kneading is complete, dough should be springy enough to almost resume shape when pressed in lightly with finger. Shape into loaf, and place in a lightly oiled standard size bread pan (about 9 x 5 x 3 inches). Cover and set in a warm place to rise until doubled in bulk, about 1 hour. Preheat oven to 350° and bake for about 1 hour until crust is a deep golden brown. Remove from pan at once and cool before slicing.

Baking bread
and other things

Where there is no bread, there is no education;
If there is no education, there is no bread.

Ethics of the fathers

We prepare the bread dough every Thursday night, bake it Friday morning and eat it over the next two days. A loaf of bread makes a table happy and complete. Friday is a special evening for us; our friends come, and by the end of the meal most of the bread is gone. It might be (although perhaps I'm prejudiced!) that my wife makes the finest bread in the world.

In general, flours are not so complete as whole grains, especially when they have been allowed to stand on shelves for weeks after having been ground. Nutritional value is diminished. It is much better to grind grain yourself every time you need to make bread, crepe suzettes, pancakes, chapati, etc. It goes without saying that an electric grinder is easier to use by far; however, a hand-operated mill is sufficient for home use; it is also more economical.

Almost all grains can be used for making breads: whole wheat, rye, corn, oats, millet, rice, buckwheat and barley. Bread made from freshly ground flour should be allowed to stand for at least four hours, preferably overnight, so that the bran particles may soften, thus making the bread more digestible. Mixing different flours can be interesting, but for best results and in order to make the most of each grain, as a general rule use two flours, or three at most. Whole wheat flour is used most frequently. All breads include some of it, often half of it in combination. Its taste blends well with all other grain flours. It can also be used alone. If a fine-textured flour is desired, sift and reserve the bran, which can later be used in casseroles, or loaves of vegetables and whole grains.

Rye flour.

Looks like whole-wheat flour but gives a stickier and less elastic bread. For a lighter rye bread combine rye with whole-wheat flour.

Brown rice flour.

Gives a sweeter and smoother bread. Blends well with other flours and has a high nutritional value.

Buckwheat flour.

Dark. Makes a heavier bread. Is best when used in winter. Needs to be mixed with other flours (e.g. pastry and whole wheat).

Oat flour or rolled oats.

Gives a light and crumbly texture to bread when added to whole wheat or corn flour.

Corn flour or corn meal.

Makes a good bread, but works best when combined with other flours.

Barley flour.

Like rye flour, gives a stickier bread, but with whole wheat flour (half and half) the bread obtained is light and easy to digest.

Millet flour.

Cannot be used alone. It should rather be combined with whole-wheat flour. Proportion: 1/3 millet to 2/3 whole-wheat flour.

Soya bean flour.

When mixed with other flours, adds a sweeter taste to bread. The crust will brown quickly while baking and the bread will stay fresh longer. It is used in small quantities (e.g. 1/5 of the entire flour mixture).

BREAD RECIPES

Batter bread.

The dough of this bread should be wet and slippery, yet stiff and sticky enough to cling to a spoon when mixed. Make sure when making it that the water is evenly distributed and does not rise to the top of the batter, showing at the sides of the bowl.

> 6 cups w.w. flour
>
> 2 cups pastry w.w. flour
>
> 1/3 cup corn oil
>
> 4 cups water
>
> 1 flat tablespoon salt

Blend flours and salt in a large bowl. Add oil. Rub well between the palms of your hands. Make sure that it penetrates the flour mixture completely. Add water gradually and stir with a wooden spoon until you get a heavy, sticky mass. Allow it to stand for at least 4 hours, then pour into 2 oiled bread pans. Bake in a 350 degree oven for an hour. To check if the bread is done, insert a chopstick into a loaf; if it comes out dry, the bread is ready.

Variations:

(1) 4 cups w.w. flour	(2) 5 cups w.w. flour
2 cups rice flour	2 cups corn meal or flour
2 cups oat flour	1 cup buckwheat flour

234

Anne-Marie batter bread.

Anne-Marie, who is from Montreal, made this delicious bread two or three times while my family and I were visiting her. It is light and most digestible.

Great care should be taken in preparing this bread. The batter is very light and watery and could therefore very easily sour. For best results in having the bread rise, very dry atmospheric conditions are required. These are the two methods used:

(1) Put batter in a bowl, cover with a moist towel and expose to sunlight for 6 or 7 hours, then place in an unheated oven for 3 or 4 hours. (Suitable for the summer.) Check regularly to avoid souring.

(2) In winter the batter can be placed in a deep container. Above place a 25-watt light bulb; cover bulb and batter with a dry towel. Allow to stand overnight.

Recipe:

> 3 cups w.w. flour
>
> 2 cups cornmeal or corn flour
>
> 2 tablespoons oil
>
> 1 ¼ teaspoon salt
>
> 3 cups water

Blend dry ingredients in a large bowl. Add oil and patiently rub into flour mixture, a handful at a time. Pour in water slowly and keep stirring in clockwise direction. When all water is mixed, beat thoroughly and forcefully, lifting batter with spoon to allow air to penetrate mixture. The air will help the batter rise. Consistency should be light and sticky with little air bubbles visible on the surface. Let stand in the manner described above. It will rise approximately one inch. Beat it again before pouring into two oiled loaf-pans. Bake in a 350 degree oven for an hour or so. When done, it will appear smooth and shiny on the outside, while the inside will be moist and porous, like a cake.

Casserole batter bread.

This bread is a meal in itself! Cooked grains, rice, buckwheat, cooked beans, adukis, chick-peas and lentils are put into the batter to make delicious combinations. A small amount of sauteed vegetables is a welcome ingredient. You will have to adjust the amount of water with the kind of combination of vegetables you use.

> 4 cups w.w. flour
>
> 2 cups cornmeal or corn flour
>
> 1 cup cooked kasha (presalted)
>
> ½ cup cooked chick-peas
>
> ½ cup sauteed onions
>
> 3 cups water (approximately)
>
> 1 ½ teaspoon salt
>
> ¼ cup oil

Combine flours and salt in a large bowl. Add oil. Rub into flours. Add kasha, mix well with a wooden spatula. Add cooked chick-peas, then the onions and blend thoroughly. Slowly pour in water. If the chick-peas and kasha are soft, you may need less water. The consistency should be like that of regular batter bread. Bake in two oiled bread pans for an hour or more. This bread comes out soft and moist. It will be light and spongy to the touch if you have succeeded.

Variations:

> 4 cups w.w. flour
>
> 2 cups oat flour
>
> 1 cup cooked rice
>
> 1 cup cooked aduki beans

Kneaded bread. (Unyeasted)

This bread has to be kneaded well. It should sit overnight to rise. Two or 3 hours before baking, it should be kneaded again. This way you get a lighter bread. Just before baking, the consistency of the bread should resemble modelling clay, and when rolled it should not stick to the sides of the bowl.

Ohsawa bread.

> 4 cups w.w. flour
>
> 2 cups corn flour or cornmeal
>
> 2 cups buckwheat flour
>
> 2 cups chestnut flour
>
> ¼ cup oil
>
> 1 flat tablespoon salt
>
> 3 1/5 cups water

Blend the dry ingredients. Distribute salt with care. Add oil and rub in well. Break up lumps and work mixture well with your hands. When all ingredients are mixed, knead for about 10 minutes. Touch your ear-lobe to see if it feels about the same as the bread. Allow bread to stand overnight, covered with a wet cloth. In the morning knead it again, and bake two hours later. Just before baking heat 2 loaf pans, then oil; this procedure will make the oil spread more evenly and less will be needed. Smoothe the tops of loaves with your fingers dipped in oil. Cut a simple design on the bread's surface. This is both practical and decorative. Place into loaf-pans and bake in a 350-degree oven for an hour or more. To assure even baking, place a pan of cold water in the oven for moisture.

Variations:

(1) 4 cups w.w. flour

2 cups buckwheat flour

2 cups oat flour

(2) 4 cups w.w. flour

2 cups cornmeal or corn flour

2 cups rice flour

2 cups millet flour

Rye bread.

3 cups w.w. flour

3 cups rye flour

½ cup corn oil

1 ½ cups onion stock

1 teaspoon salt

Prepare onion stock by boiling 2 chopped onions, sauteed beforehand. Strain and reserve the liquid for the bread. Mix oil with the stock and beat with a fork or an electric mixer until it turns white. Combine flours and salt and quickly mix into the oil mixture. This is another method of combining dry and wet ingredients, a satisfactory substitute for the longer method of rubbing oil into the flours between the palms of your hands. It often saves the rye bread from becoming heavy. Leave overnight and, in the morning, knead again. Form two loaves and place each in an oiled bread pan. Bake in a 325 degree oven for 1 ½ hours. This bread is particularly crumbly, its crust very crisp. The secret is the greater amount of oil used.

Cornelia's bread. (Yeasted)

Cornelia Airhara is a tiny Japanese lady who does the job of ten with a smile. Her bread is not even slightly acid. Serve it with miso spread or eat it plain; it is excellent!

4 cups w.w. flour

2 cups rice flour

1 cup buckwheat flour

1 cup white unbleached flour

½ cup oatmeal

½ cup cornmeal

2 ½ teaspoons salt

2 tablespoons oil

½ teaspoon yeast diluted in ½ cup warm water

3 ½ cups water

In a large mixing bowl blend all dry ingredients. Add oil by rubbing it into flours, a handful at a time. Pour diluted yeast into mixture, blend. Slowly add water, mixing it in with your hands. Knead for 5 minutes. The dough should not be too stiff or too dry. It should have the consistency of your ear-lobe. When it no longer sticks to the sides of the bowl and has been well-kneaded, cover with a wet cloth and let stand overnight. In the morning knead for 3 minutes more. Divide the dough and place each half in an oiled loaf pan. Allow to stand for two more hours, then bake in a preheated 350-degree oven for approximately 1 ½ hours. Although many flours have been mixed to make this bread, it still comes out light and springy.

Barley bread. (Yeasted)

This bread is best suited to holidays or special occasions intended to please your guests. Much less yeast is used in this recipe than most bakers employ. However, the dough is allowed to rise overnight, which decreases the amount required. The yeast should be organic, and can be purchased in any natural-food store.

> 3 cups pastry flour
>
> 3 cups barley flour
>
> 3 tablespoons corn oil
>
> 1 ½ teaspoon salt
>
> 2 cups water
>
> 1/3 teaspoon yeast diluted in ½ cup warm water
>
> 1 egg yolk
>
> 1 tablespoon sesame seeds

Blend the flours with salt in a large bowl. Add oil and rub in well to break up lumps. Add yeast diluted in water and blend thoroughly. Slowly mix in water with your hands. Knead for approximately 5 minutes until dough is stiff enough not to stick to the sides of the bowl. Place it on a floured board or table and knead for 5 minutes more. Place in bowl; oil surface to prevent formation of crust, cover with a wet towel and allow to stand overnight. In the morning knead for 5 minutes more. Divide the dough into 3 pieces.

The braid:

Roll each piece into a rope approximately 1 inch in diameter and 18 inches in length. Shape a braid by interweaving the 3 ropes. Oil a single baking sheet; allow bread to rest on it for 2 hours, covered with a damp cloth. Brush top of bread with a beaten egg yolk and sprinkle with sesame seeds. Bake in a preheated 375 degree oven for 1 hour. You'll be proud to serve it!

Spiral bread. Recipe for two spirals

  4 cups w.w. flour

  1 cup cornmeal or corn flour

  ½ cup cooked rice

  ½ cup soya bean flour

  4 tablespoons corn oil

  1 teaspoon salt

  1 ¼ cup water

  1 cup sauteed chopped onions and watercress

In this self-rising bread, rice is used as a starter to begin fermentation. Combine flours, salt and cooked rice. Rub oil into mixture. Add water and mix in well with your hands. Knead thoroughly for about 5 minutes. Cover with a wet cloth and leave overnight. In the morning knead again for a few minutes. Cut dough in half. Roll out each half into a rectangle 8 by 16 inches. On each, spread half the sauteed vegetables (they should be as dry as possible). Make two rolls, folding dough as you would a strudel. Place into two oiled bread pans 8 inches long. Cover with a wet cloth and allow to stand two hours more. Bake in a preheated oven at 350 degrees for an hour or so. This bread, when cut, presents a beautiful green spiral on the soft gold plane of the bread.

Variations:

  4 cups w.w. flour

  1 cup oat flour

  ½ cup cooked kasha

  ½ cup soya bean flour

  1 cup sauteed shredded carrots

Petits pains. (Rolls)

To make rolls use the recipes for kneaded and yeasted bread previously given in this book. Oat flour or oatmeal can be introduced in
larger quantities to make the dough lighter. A larger amount of oil can
be used for the same purpose. Rolls have the advantage of baking faster
than breads.

    3 cups w.w. pastry flour

    1 ½ cups oatmeal

    1 teaspoon salt

    ½ cup oil

    1 ¼ cup water

Blend dry ingredients in a mixing bowl. Carefully rub oil into mixture.
Pour water in slowly and mix with your hands until dough no longer
sticks to sides of container. Knead for approximately 5 minutes. Cover
and let rise overnight in a warm place. In the morning knead well again
and shape into small rolls. On two oiled cookie sheets arrange rolls, cover
and allow to rise for 2 hours more. Put into oven preheated at 350 degrees for 20 minutes, then turn oven up to 400 degrees and bake for 10
minutes more. This recipe makes about 18 rolls. Serve as a sandwich.
Fill with any one of the spreads whose recipes you will find on page 188).

Cloverleaf rolls.

> 3 cups w.w. flour
>
> 1 cup corn meal
>
> 1 cup white unbleached flour
>
> 3 tablespoons oil
>
> 1 ½ teaspoons salt
>
> 2 tablespoons sesame butter
>
> 2 cups water
>
> 2 tablespoons sesame seeds

Beat water and oil in a mixing bowl until it turns milky white. Water is added to the oil gradually. Add sesame butter and beat a bit longer. Then combine flours and salt and slowly mix into oily mixture (emulsion). When it is well-mixed and dough no longer sticks to the bowl, knead thoroughly, cover and allow to stand overnight. In the morning, knead again on an oiled board, then shape into small balls ½ inch in diameter. Oil two muffin pans and place 3 small balls in each well. Brush tops with oil and sprinkle with sesame seeds. Cover with a dry cloth and let rise in a warm place for an hour or two. Bake in a 375-degree oven for 30 minutes. This will produce approximately 2 dozen rolls.

MUFFINS

To obtain best results in taste and texture, it is advisable to use freshly ground flour from whole grains. This recipe is William Dufty's— hence the name "Willies."

Willies.

> ½ cup millet, toasted and ground
>
> ½ cup buckwheat groats, lightly toasted and ground
>
> 1 cup brown rice, toasted and ground
>
> 1 cup cornmeal
>
> 1 cup oatmeal
>
> 3 tablespoons corn oil
>
> 3 ½ cups water
>
> 1 onion, chopped and sauteed

Put ground buckwheat, millet and rice in a mixing bowl. Add cornmeal, oatmeal, onions and salt. Blend thoroughly. Add oil and rub it in with your hands. Slowly pour in water, stirring with a wooden spoon. The mixture is very liquid. Oil 3 muffin tins, place batter in them and bake in 375-degree oven for an hour or so. These muffins are very delicious as well as nutritious.

Squash muffins.

> 4 cups pastry flour
>
> 2 cups cornmeal
>
> 1 cup oatmeal
>
> 3 tablespoons sesame oil
>
> 1 ½ teaspoons salt
>
> 2 cups pureed squash
>
> 2 cups water

Put flours in a bowl, add salt and blend. Rub oil into dry mixture. Slowly mix in water with your hands. When the dough no longer sticks to the sides of the container, knead thoroughly. Oil surface and cover container with a wet towel, letting dough rise overnight. In the morning, pressure-cook squash and mash it. Mix into dough thoroughly until you get a wet mixture. Oil muffin pans and place dough in them. Bake in a 375 degree oven for 45 minutes.

Variation:

Carrots or parsnips can be used instead of squash.
These muffins can be served as a side dish or as dessert.

CRACKERS

The same dough may be used as is used for bread—it needs only a slightly larger amount of flour. A good proportion of oatmeal in the mixture produces the best results. A little more oil and less water will make the crackers lighter and crispier.

    2 cups w.w. flour

    1 ½ cups oatmeal

    3/4 cup water

    1/3 cup oil

    ½ teaspoon salt

    3 tablespoons sesame seeds

Blend water with oil until it turns milky white. Combine flour, salt and sesame seeds. Stir into oily mixture. Knead for 5 minutes. The dough should be stiff. Roll out as thin as a pie crust. Brush with oil, then cut into desired shapes. Place on an oiled cookie sheet. Bake in a 350-degree oven for 15 minutes until golden brown.

How about a drink?

In Morocco, where I come from, we have a tea ceremony that lasts at least fifteen minutes before the first sip is taken. For guests, for show and in Arabic coffee shops, hot tea is poured over fresh mint leaves which are waiting in tall silvered or golden glasses. (On less auspicous occasions both tea and mint are joined together in the pot.)

The mint I speak of is neither alfalfa mint nor peppermint. It's *mint*! I am actually embarrassed when a friend or guest, aware of my sentimental liking for the familiar flavor, arrives for dinner with what *looks* like the real thing. I never know what to do—shall I tell him the truth or serve it and let him believe that this is the precious drink he has heard me talk about for years? Usually I wait until after the meal, when he feels more at home, and then I explain what good mint tastes like.

Drinking tea in Morocco is a ritual which takes place two or three times a day. In a glass five or six inches high one receives an inch-and-a-half of tea. Another half-inch of foam is created by the deft pouring, which is accomplished with the pot held high above the glass and the golden stream arc-ing audibly into its container.

This past summer I enjoyed mint tea perhaps a dozen times, not with Chinese green tea, but with "Bancha Twig," which is a very common tea in Japan. Its flavor is as excellent as the Chinese. At home we always have some ready on the stove.

It is easy to prepare *Bancha Tea*. Slowly toast the twigs until brown, stirring rapidly with a wooden instrument, preferably a flat spatula. Try not to burn it. Remove it from the pan, let it cool and keep it in a tightly covered container. When needed, take a tablespoon for each two cups of boiling water. Allow to simmer ten minutes or so. Serve in small cups. You can use the twigs once or twice more, but each time add another half-tablespoon of twigs to maintain strength and flavor. If for one reason or another you suffer an attack of migraine headache, try it very hot with a tablespoon of soya sauce. It really helps.

Mu Tea is a sixteen-herb mixture, famous for its unusual and rare flavor, which is unsurpassed. It performs the triple function of quenching your thirst while at the same time making you happy and healthy. It also comes from Japan, where it is almost as popular as Bancha. Perhaps its name is traceable to the lost continent of Mu—which lends it dramatic and mysterious overtones. . . . We drink it occasionally, perhaps enjoying it for a day or two and then returning to Bancha for a month. It all depends on the weather, on my wife's mood, or on a guest's perference.

To prepare it, boil four to five cups of water—best in a Pyrex kettle. Drop in a bog of Mu tea and let simmer ten minutes. The same leaves can be used again. This time simmer twenty minutes.

Dandelion Coffee is a drink we sometimes have after a slice of apple pie. It is now sold in all health-food stores. I was still sick when I tasted it the first time, so I didn't make the usual attempt to compare it with regular coffee. I can't really say if you'll like it. There are other coffees of the same family, some sweeter and some more bitter. *Bardan coffee* is made of burdock root and chicory. *Yannoh* is made of toasted rice, wheat, aduki beans, chick-peas and chicory—it's excellent with dessert. There are other teas which we sometimes use such as *Barley tea* and *Rice tea.*

When the stomach or intestines are upset we drink *Kuzu*, which is a white powder resembling arrow-root in texture. The powder is extracted from a very deep-growing root, three to four feet long, which is cultivated in Japan. When our children develop runny noses, we give them a little Kuzu, and that takes care of it. It is perfect for colds, excess acidity, stomach cramps, etc. To prepare it, dilute a teaspoon of Kuzu in a small cup of cold water—never warm. When diluted, place over fire and keep stirring. The muted white water turns into a clear gelatinous mixture when heated. When bubbles appear, add soya sauce, one teaspoon to one tablespoon, and keep stirring for a few moments. Serve piping hot.

For disturbances of a gastric nature, a salted plum may be added to the above drink. If in addition a teaspoon of grated ginger and two tablespoons of grated white radish are supplemented, you have the equivalent of an occidental Grog. It will make you perspire under heavy blankets and will quickly knock out the most tenacious cold.

In our house we don't serve teas such as Jasmin, Anis, Mugwort, Thyme, Sage, Rosemary, Gentian and Camomile, all of which I consider good. I would have included them if I needed their particular benefits, but as a matter of fact, what we eat very seldom gives us any trouble. Nevertheless, I wouldn't hesitate to drink any one of them at any time.

Tempura

The electric deep-fryers in which American cooks make French-fries are not what the Japanese use for preparing tempura. Even if a Japanese restaurant has more customers than it can handle, it will still not use any modern-day deep-fryer. This repugnance is not due to the stubbornness of the cook who prefers to cling to the old-fashioned; it is rather that the quality and taste of this dish can be obtained only by using traditional methods.

Preparing tempura is a simple process. All pieces are first dipped in batter (a mixture of flour and water) and then deep-fried in oil—usually corn or sunflower oil. Here are a few things you should know if you want to succeed in making tempura:

Use between 3/4 and 1 inch of oil. The same oil can be filtered and re-used in several batches. If the oil becomes cloudy, it can always be cleared once you are finished by tossing in a single umeboshi plum, which will act as a precipitant.

The oil temperature must remain around 350 degrees; it may go to 375, or even as high as 400, but that is the limit. Beyond 400 degrees the oil may begin to burn, giving an unpleasant, bitter taste to the tempura.

Preparing the batter is a breeze. There are many and varied combinations, and once you get into this business you'll be constantly running into people who will tell you that *they* have found the *best* batter mixture. However, the best proportion usually is:

> 1 cup w.w. flour
>
> 1 ¼ cups cold water
>
> 1/3 teaspoon salt

You'll have to find the proportions that work best for you. For example, if you're a beginner, you may find it easier to work with a heavier batter. Just add a little more flour.

And never forget to use *cold* water. You can even put the batter in the refrigerator an hour or so before making tempura.

How to prepare a batter of the abovementioned flour, water and salt? Just mix the three ingredients in a bowl, stirring gently with chopsticks. Do not over-mix.

Variations:

For a tempura that stays crisp for a long time use:

> 1 cup unbleached flour or w.w. pastry
>
> ¼ cup brown rice flour
>
> ¼ cup corn flour
>
> 1/3 teaspoon salt
>
> 1 ¼ cups water

Or try this combination:

3/4 cup unbleached or w.w. pastry flour

¼ cup brown rice flour

1/3 teaspoon salt

1 ¼ cups water

Always roll shellfish and unskinned fish in flour before dipping in batter; otherwise, the coating may not adhere. Use this method with anything slippery or difficult to cover with batter.

If you run out of vegetables, fish, or shellfish and have left-over batter, drop it by the spoonful into hot oil; it gives miniature popovers.

If you know the proper way to cut it, you can dip in batter and deep-fry just about anything. Just remember that your core material cannot be so thick that its covering cooks faster than it does. In fact, the batter may burn while the central ingredients remain raw.

For a light tempura use celery leaves, carrot tops, spinach, parsley, watercress, swiss chard, kale, fennel springs, etc. The complexity of a leaf can give your tempura-pieces unexpected and surprisingly beautiful forms. For tempura, cut as thin as possible the following vegetables: carrots, turnips, lotus root, parsnips, jinenjo, onion (rings), cauliflower and broccoli (in flowerettes), etc.

You can even deep-fry large pieces of kombu. First dampen them with a wet cloth. You'll notice that when kombu is covered with batter and deep-fried, it becomes chewy. Some people like it this way. However, if you fry it without batter, it turns crisp and tastes as though it were flavored with the finest Oriental spices.

Cut fish filets into squares and rectangles before deep-frying. One-quarter inch thichness gives the best results.

Serve tempura as hot as you can. If a vegetable tempura, serve on the side in a basket along with a tiny saucer containing soya sauce. For fish tempura, prepare a special sauce (see recipe, page 183). For a delicious way to fry vegetables and fish together (Fish Kebbab) see the recipe on page 274).

Why do we cook our foods?

"Why do we have to cook our foods?" asked a young man in his twenties who, as one could see, had been a vegetarian for several years.

It was a hot summer evening. The windows were wide open to provide ventilation for the crowd of young people. It was perhaps the fifteenth lecture among sixty delivered during a tour that took us to every major city in America; ten thousand miles in ten weeks with a lecture almost every night.

Outside, nature displayed herself in the movements of trees and faint showers of light, as if warning me to answer to accord with her laws.

"Monkeys and all raw-food eaters are fragile beings difficult to approach. Their phobias make them fluctuate between likes and dislikes of people and things. They are suspicious of foods and friends, and are on this earth like ghosts on bail, awaiting trial for the crime of refusing to become Man.

"The right home of Man is Nature, which not only gives him grass roots and trees, but also fire with which to adjust to his world. Nature gives to Man what Man requires. She is not an unconscious giver whose desire is to see Man grow like an animal, or the trees. Man is a king in Nature; out of Nature he builds thoughts, ideas and societies. From stones he creates fire, and with fire he creates or destroys life. In him is the profound will to become Man; from this will comes the discovery of fire that enabled him to elevate himself to higher stages. That great discovery was not mere coincidence; it was interwoven with his destiny the way the husband is wedded to the wife, enabling her to grow at his side. One transmutes, and the other transcends.

"Cooking food is to go one step ahead toward Manhood. To eat only raw food is an act of regression, which makes its consumer resemble a plant rather than a man."

Flours
make
wonderful
things

Crêpe Suzettes.

Crêpe houses in New York City serve you a Crêpe Suzette as thin as a handkerchief, filled with a "soupcon" of nothing, and charge you from one dollar to three-and-a-half. You can finish it off in thirty seconds—in fact, in one single bite—but to be polite, you cut it into small parts and pretend to chew, biting down on nothing but airy dough which slides uselessly down your throat. It's a game dapper gentlemen from uptown frequently play with their elegant ladies on concert nights.

We cook crêpes the way people from Brittany do, half the thickness of a pancake. It's an exquisite side dish, the best-looking dessert imaginable. Here are some important points you should remember.

The batter, a combination of flour and water, can be made with different grains. There are various methods and styles.

Generally, use 3 parts water to 1 part flour. Add a pinch of salt. If you wish to begin cooking the crêpes at once, whip the batter by hand or even beat it in an electric mixer. Otherwise, allow it to stand for at least 2 hours.

Use a smooth and even cast-iron frying pan. You may also use enameled cast-iron. The pan edge must be low so that you can operate easily with a spatula.

Heat the pan well. Oil it with a brush or a piece of cloth. Before adding batter, lower the flame to 1/3 of its maximum. The quantity of the batter depends upon the dimension of the pan. For a pan with a 9-inch diameter, use 7 ounces of batter. For a thin crêpe use 5 ounces, or even less.

As you pour the batter with your left hand, turn the pan clockwise to spread the batter evenly. Cook 5 minutes for the first side, 3 to 5 minutes for the second. Exact timing depends on the thickness of the crêpe. Before turning, detach the crêpe carefully with a very flat stainless steel spatula.

Variation 1

1 cup corn flour

2 cups w. w. flour

Variation 2

2 cups w. w. pastry flour

1 cup unbleached flour

9 cups water

1 tablespoon oil

2 flat teaspoons salt

Mix ingredients. Let stand or use mixer. In this recipe, the oil will prevent the crêpe from drying up when kept a few hours.

Buckwheat crêpe.

> 2 cups fine buckwheat flour
>
> 1 cup pastry flour
>
> 9 cups water
>
> 2 flat teaspoons salt

Stuffings.

You can stuff a crêpe with many things. It all depends on when and where you serve it. Always fill it with smooth vegetables, never with starchy or hard ones. For the best presentation, cut or mash stuffing into tiny pieces, so that you may roll up the crêpe easily. Zucchini makes a perfect filling; so do onions, or zucchini combined with onions, watercress, squash puree, endives, etc. Also see the dessert chapter for sweet fillings

Pancakes.

A pancake looks very much like a crêpe, but is a bit thicker. Its batter is heavier, and it is cooked in a covered pan. If the batter is allowed to stand overnight, the pancake will rise and will be fluffier.

    2 cups brown rice flour

    2 cups water

    3/4 teaspoon salt

    1/2 teaspoon oil

Blend flour, salt and oil in a bowl. Add water and beat with an electric mixer or whisk. Allow to stand for at least 1 hour. Brush oil over the surface of a cast-iron skillet. Heat skillet and pour in about 1/4 inch of batter. Cover and cook over a low flame for about 5 minutes. Turn over and cook 5 minutes more.

Variation:

    1 cup w. w. pastry flour

    1/2 cup cornmeal

    1/2 cup oat flakes

Waffles.

Children like hot waffles for breakfast along with their cereal cream. You can make good desserts or snacks with them, if you wish, by putting a layer of filling between two waffles. Try squash puree, applesauce, or chestnut cream softened with coffee-kuzu.

    Use:

    2 1/2 cups w. w. flour

    2 cups water

    1 tablespoon corn oil

    1 teaspoon salt

In a bowl blend flour and salt. Rub oil into mixture, then add water. Beat thoroughly with an electric mixer for 3 minutes. This allows air to penetrate the batter, and is a good substitute for the usual baking powder. It is not necessary for the batter to stand for any length of time. Heat up a waffle iron. Oil top and bottom griddles with a brush. Wait until temperature needle points to "bake," then pour in batter with a ladle. Bake for approximately 5 minutes until golden brown. This recipe gives about four waffles. If lighter waffles are desired, simply increase the water by half a cup.

Variation:

    1 1/2 cups w. w. pastry flour

    1 cup buckwheat flour

Chapati.

Chapati is still one of the staple foods of India. In Mexico a similarly popular preparation is called a tortilla. Chapati comes from far back in Biblical times, when it was the daily bread of our ancestors. This simple bread has numerous advantages; it is quickly prepared and is very useful for travelling and picnics.

> 3 cups w. w. pastry flour
>
> 1 tablespoon oil
>
> 3/4 teaspoon salt
>
> 1 cup water

Blend flour and salt, add oil and blend thoroughly. Add and mix in water. Knead well. The dough should have the consistency of your ear lobe and be slightly sticky. Let dough rest for 1/2 hour. Separate into small balls 1 1/2 inches in diameter, roll into flat rounds on a floured board. The thinner you make them, the crisper they will be. Heat a heavy cast-iron frying pan. Oil each chapati on both sides, but do not oil pan. Cook each side for a minute or two until it turns lightly brown. The chapati will puff; to help it along, take a napkin and gently press around each bubble; this will provoke larger bubbles. Cook the first side a bit longer. Fold cooked chapati in half to keep it soft until served.

Variation:

> 1 1/2 cups unbleached flour
>
> 1 1/2 cups buckwheat flour
>
> 1 cup water
>
> 3/4 teaspoon salt

Variation: Tortilla

> 3 cups corn flour
>
> 1 tablespoon oil
>
> 3/4 teaspoon salt
>
> 1 cup water

The tortilla can be rolled out like chapati, or a special tortilla press can be purchased.

Baked chapati.

Chapati can also be baked. Use one of the recipes mentioned above, then place several chapati on an oiled cookie sheet and bake in a 350-degree oven for 15 minutes until golden brown.

Chapati cooked in a pan and baked in the oven can be served plain or with a spread.

Deep-fried chapati.

Use the regular chapati recipe; simply omit oil in making dough. Roll out thinly and deep-fry in corn oil.

Variation:

> 1 cup w. w. pastry flour
>
> 1 cup rice cream
>
> 1 cup barley flour

This chapati puffs up and is very crisp.

Corn chips.

> 2 cups unbleached white flour
>
> 1 cup cornmeal
>
> 1/4 teaspoon salt
>
> 1 cup water

Blend all ingredients. Knead until you obtain a dough of earlobe consistency. Roll out on a floured board. Cut into small diamond shapes and deep fry. Place the fried corn chips in a dish lined with paper towels. Sprinkle with salt while still very hot. Serve with any grain for a bit of bright cheer

Beignets Marocains.

Serve a Moroccan beignet to a sad friend and save him a few visits to his psychoanalyst! The form and taste appeal not only to the lower senses, they also fulfill our deepest desires to eat simply and satisfyingly.

In Morocco at 6 o'clock in the morning, you can see people standing in line, waiting to buy a dozen or two "shfenz" which the merchant cook skewers on a strip of straw as though they were giant beads. Many people come out from the Medina, the Arabic quarter, with necklaces of shfenz in their hands. They walk home rapidly, before the beignets get cold, then eat them accompanied by a glass of green tea flavored with fresh mint.

Yeast makes the beignet puff up in the hot pan of oil, doubling or even tripling its volume. To obtain the proper lightness, the beignet batter has to be made of unbleached white flour or a very fine pastry flour.

Make them for the children—but not too often, since they contain yeast. You will find that they are similar to doughnuts.

    4 cups pastry flour

    1 teaspoon salt

    1/2 teaspoon yeast diluted in 1/2 cup warm water

    2 cups water

Put the flour in a deep container (the dough will rise three or four times). Add salt and blend well. Add diluted yeast and water, mix thoroughly with your hands. The dough should be very soft and elastic, and should stick to the sides of the container and to your fingers. Shape into a ball and cover the top of the container with a wet cloth. Allow to stand overnight in a warm place. In the morning, heat oil in a deep frying pan. By then the dough should have risen a great deal, and bubbles should be seen on its surface.

Place a bowl of cold water near the frying pan, wet your hands, and take a handful of batter. Form a ball, then make a hole in its center, pinching it between your thumb and middle finger. Aim for a shape resembling a doughnut. Act quickly because the batter can drop from your fingers. Place gently in hot oil. It will puff up almost immediately. Allow each side to fry until golden. Serve plain.

It is a joyful Friday morning meal. Serve it with a glass of very hot tea, preferably the traditional bancha tea brewed with mint leaves.

Pie crust.

There are several ways to make a successful pie crust. The following recipes are intended for a pie dish 9 inches in diameter. They generally serve 6 people.

The most popular method for making crust is to use ice-cold water in the dough.

Pâte sablée. (Sandy crust)

> 1 1/2 cups w. w. pastry flour
>
> 1/2 cup w. w. flour
>
> 4 tablespoons oil
>
> 1/2 teaspoon salt
>
> about 1/3 cup ice-cold water

In a mixing bowl combine flour and salt. Rub in oil with your hands. Mix in water, form dough and knead a little. The less it is kneaded, the better the crust. Put the dough in a freezer for half an hour. Roll out between two sheets of waxed paper to prevent dough from sticking to the rolling pin or board; shape into the form you want, place in baking dish. The more oil you add, the flakier the pie crust will be. Don't over-do it!

Variation:

> 1 1/4 cups w. w. pastry flour
>
> 3/4 cup oat flakes
>
> A flaky crust like this one is excellent for an uncovered pie.

Note:

If the filling used for the pie is wet, the crust has to be baked
alone for about 15 minutes in an oven preheated to 400 degrees. Then
fill the crust and bake for 30 minutes more at 350 degrees until crust is
golden brown.

If the filling is dry, the crust can be filled right away, then baked for
about 40 minutes in an oven preheated to 375 degrees. The rim of the
pie can be oiled 10 minutes before baking, to keep it from burning.

Pâte feuilletée. (Puff-dough)

This specific pie crust has the advantage of being very digestible. It is
easy to roll and stays crisp after it is baked.

> 2 cups w.w pastry flour
>
> ¼ cup sesame oil
>
> ½ teaspoon salt
>
> 2/3 cup boiling water

Boil water, then pour it into a bowl. Add oil and beat thoroughly with
a fork. An electric mixer is even better. When the mixture becomes
milky white, add flour and salt. Mix with a spoon first until the dough
cools slightly, then knead for approximately two minutes. Put in the
refrigerator for ½ hour, then roll it out on a floured pastry board. It can
be rolled very thin if desired. Bake for 15 minutes in a 400-degree oven.
To prevent burning, place a pan of cold water in the oven. This provides
moisture and insures even baking.

Variation:

> 1 ¼ cups w.w. pastry flour
>
> 3/4 cup rice flour
>
> ¼ cup sesame oil
>
> ½ teaspoon salt
>
> 2/3 cup boiling water

This kind of crust is best-suited to a covered pie or a strudel. Use the same amount of oil, salt and boiling water.

Note:

For covered pies and strudels, prick tiny holes in the pie or strudel top; this will allow excess moisture to evaporate, and some of the juice will escape during baking.

Pie shell.

This very crumbly kind of pie is prepared very quickly.

> 3/4 cup oat flakes
>
> ¼ cup w.w. pastry flour
>
> ¼ cup wheatena
>
> ¼ teaspoon salt
>
> 1/3 cup oil

Blend all ingredients together in a bowl. Line a 9-inch pie dish with the mixture. Press it in firmly with a slightly smaller plate for an even spread. Put into the refrigerator for ½ hour, then bake in a 375-degree oven for 8 minutes.

Variation:

> ¾ cup oat flakes
>
> ¼ cup cornmeal
>
> ¼ cup chestnut flour
>
> ¼ teaspoon salt
>
> 1/3 cup oil

Pie shell is most suitable for custard pies or creamy pies made with vegetables and fruit.

268

Croissants. (Crescent rolls)

This is not the croissant you know, which is sold in fine pastry shops and served with coffee and milk in French cafes. This one is crustier and less puffy—but it's healthier!

> 3 cups w.w. pastry flour
>
> ¼ cup oil
>
> ¾ teaspoon salt
>
> 1 cup boiling water
>
> 2 tablespoons sesame seeds

Proceed in the same way as for *pâte feuilletée;* however, allow dough to rise overnight in a warm place. In the morning, roll it out on a floured board into a circle 12 inches in diameter. Cut out 8 triangular wedges. Roll up each one, working from the outer edge toward the inner. Place on an oiled cookie sheet. Brush top of crescent rolls with oil, and sprinkle on sesame seeds. Set rolls in a warm place for an hour or two. Bake in a 375-degree oven for 20 minutes until golden brown.

Pie crust left overnight can be used to make these delicate crescent rolls.

The acid
and
the alkaline

> The well-being of the soul can only
> be obtained after that of the body
> has been secured.
>
> Maimonides (Guide of the Perplexed)

The balance between acid and alkaline is so important that a failure to maintain it can be extremely harmful to the body. Biochemists have discovered that death always occurs when there is positive acidity in the organism. We must maintain alkalinity to survive!

The movement that sustains life in our organism is just this change in our cells, from potassium, which is acid and Yin, to sodium, which is alkaline and Yang. By a process of transmutation, sodium changes to potassium by taking an atom from oxygen. In an experiment by the French scholar Louis Kervran, a fish was put into heavily salted water. After eight days the fish died. Autopsy showed that death occured at the moment of positive acidity in the organism. The salted water, combined with oxygen, created an overdose of potassium and killed the fish.

Acid forming substances rob the body of minerals such as calcium. This is one of the causes of tooth decay and other bone defects. Eating grains and vegetables is not the instant answer to all problems, especially if they are not chewed well. Acid-forming substances will result from *anything that is not chewed properly.* Carbohydrates are digested primarily in the mouth; if they are not thoroughly chewed they will cause an acid condition.

Eating any grain mixed with oil (i.e. fried rice, rice with sesame butter, etc.) causes acidity in the stomach. Oil covers the grains, making them harder to digest.

Bread and fruits are a poor combination. Bread alone, chewed well, does not produce acidity. Mixing it with fruits, however, is more likely to produce acidity, resulting often in a cold in winter. This is why some fruitarians do not like whole-wheat bread. They are "swallowers" rather than "chewers". They treat bread as though it were fruit, unaware of any change in substance. Swallowing unchewed carbohydrates produces acidity, which in turn forms mucus, which results in colds and most other sicknesses. Chewing makes food more alkaline, but there should also be a good balance between acid and alkaline in what we eat.

It is not only advisable to avoid eating bread and fruits together, but bread with any kind of liquid capable of disturbing proper digestion of the grain. Most people make the mistake of eating whole-wheat bread with soup or tea. They fail to chew the bread; instead, they swallow it, softened by liquid. This practice hampers proper digestion.

With food we can control our balance between sodium and potassium, as well as between red and white blood cells. Too much sugar turns red blood cells into white cells, while salt helps build red blood cells. This does not mean, however, that a great intake of salt is advisable. Salt is almost a medicine and should be used carefully, according to physiological and not pathological needs.

Cooking fish

To eat merely to satisfy a
craving is a form of transgression.

The Mikolayever.

Fish is scarce here in upper New York State. We wouldn't mind having some once in a while, but with no fish market in the vicinity, we have discovered once again that we can live without it, and be perfectly content.

In New York City, only the presence of so much striped bass, red snapper and other elegant fish tempted us on occasion.

Certain questionable practices such as the dipping of fish in an antibiotic solution before selling represent potentially serious hazards to health. A truly fresh fish is also hard to find. It is rare to see a tail still moving—or even red gills, a sign of good condition.

Here are a few things you should know before buying and cooking fish:

Always look for a fish with bright bulging eyes and shiny scales so tight against the skin they are almost impossible to remove; a harsh sound should result when a scaling-knife scrapes the fish. The flesh should be firm: press with your thumb to see if it springs back.

We do not eat shellfish. If you do, buy only those with a tightly shut shell. Better still, try to find ones kept alive in a tank of water—they will be fresher and cleaner.

Do not wash fish under water; this removes some of its nutritive value. It is better to soak it in cold salted water for a few minutes.

There are many ways to cook fish, all equally good. Broiling is perfect for certain kinds of fish; poaching, steaming and baking are good for others. Here are a few recipes which may inspire you to develop your own creations. It is not my intention to spoil you with too many rules and regulations, thereby possibly limiting your imagination.

Broiling fish is as easy as going to the fish market, buying the proper fish, and lighting your broiler. Place the fish under the flame, covered with a simple mixture such as tamari-and-ginger sauce.

Steaming is done by placing the fish in the upper pot of a steamer. Wrap it in cheesecloth to prevent its breaking while being cooked. The most interesting possibility in this method is putting spices in the lower pot: their flavors penetrate the fish above and impart a fine taste to it. Try herbs such as thyme, bay leaf, celery, garlic, cumin, etc. When the fish is cooked you may dress it with a sauce or, more simply, with umeboshi juice, lemon juice, soya sauce, etc. You may also use liquid from the lower pot for your sauce.

Baking fish is accomplished in a large covered platter. If left uncovered, baste with juices to prevent drying. A cover helps to retain color and shape. Always keep the head, not only for esthetic reasons, but most of all for the flavor it transmits to the whole fish.

Poaching is simmering fish in a covered casserole, using any kind of sauce. Bake in a 350-degree oven.

To broil halibut, sword fish, flounder, sole or any fish fillet, use this very practical and simple sauce:

3 tablespoons soya sauce

1 teaspoon ginger, grated

Double or triple the amount for more fish.

Mix soya sauce and ginger, then soak both sides of the fish. Place fish in a 450-degree broiler, wait 5 minutes, turn fish over, pour 1 tablespoon of sauce over it, then broil 5 minutes more. You may even allow it to broil 7 minutes on the first side, depending on the thickness of the fish and on whether you want it soft and juicy or dry.

Try this little sauce:

½ cup umeboshi juice

3 tablespoons tamari

1 tablespoon lemon juice

Broiled Snapper à la Provençale

1 red snapper, cleaned (keep head)

1 handful fennel leaves

1 tablespoon parsley, chopped

2 tablespoons corn oil

2 tablespoons lemon juice

1 pinch salt

½ cup water

Oil a baking dish. Stuff fish with fennel and parsley. Put in broiler for 5 minutes, then remove. Prepare a mixture with water, lemon juice and salt and pour half of it over fish. Return to broiler for another 5-7 minutes. Every 2 minutes pour part of the remaining mixture over it. Serve sliced with juice.

Instead of red snapper you may use striped bass.

You may also use ginger-tamari sauce instead of the lemon-juice mixture.

274

Broiled Fish Kebbab.

> 1 pound flounder, cut into 1 ½ by 3-inch pieces
>
> 2 tablespoons oil
>
> ½ lemon
>
> ½ green pepper, cut into ¾ by 1-inch pieces
>
> 1 large onion, cut into 1 by 1 ½-inch pieces (use 2 layers at a time)
>
> 3 tablespoons parsley, chopped
>
> 1 cup umeboshi juice

Marinate fish for ½ hour in mixture made with umeboshi juice, parsley, oil and lemon juice. Roll up fish and skewer it, alternating with vegetables on a bamboo skewer purchasable in most Japanese stores. First skewer onion, pepper, then fish. Repeat the procedure 4 times, but use no more than 2 pieces of pepper. Brush abundantly with the juice in which it has been marinated and place in a 400-degree broiler for 5 minutes. Turn over, brush again with juice and return to broiler for another 5 minutes. Serves 4.

Fish Kebbab Tempura.

Prepare fish kebbab as above adding a thin slice of carrot skewered after each piece of onion. Dip in tempura batter and deep-fry in oil.

Fried fish from Brooklyn.

> 6 filets of flounder or sole, or even slices of sword fish
>
> 3 tablespoons cornmeal
>
> 3 tablespoons pastry flour or w.w. flour
>
> 1 tablespoon corn oil to saute onions
>
> 2 onions, diced
>
> 2 tablespoons corn oil to fry fish

In a skillet saute onions in oil until golden brown. Put onions aside. Mix flour and salt. Heat skillet, add 2 tablespoons oil; when oil is hot roll fish in flour mixture and fry in oil. After 2 minutes add sauteed onions. Simmer 5 minutes. Serve hot or cold.

Salmon Casserole.

> 3 pounds salmon, fresh and cut into slices (remove bones)
>
> 2 onions, diced
>
> 2 carrots, diced
>
> 1 tablespoon oil
>
> 4 tablespoons soya sauce mixed with 2 tablespoons water
>
> ½ teaspoon ginger, grated
>
> 1 cup water
>
> 2 tablespoons w.w. pastry flour

In a large saucepan saute onions in oil; 2 minutes later add carrots. Simmer 5 minutes, add salt. Mix soya sauce and ginger, dip pieces of fish in it and place them over simmering vegetables. Add ½ cup water and simmer 15 minutes. Remove fish from pan and add to vegetables flour diluted in ½ cup water for thickening. Simmer 5 minutes. To serve, place fish in individual dish and pour thick sauce over it.

Truite à la menthe. (Trout flavored with mint)

        4 trouts

        8 - 12 anchovies (filets)

        2 tablespoons oil

        2 tablespoons parsley, chopped

        1 teaspoon mint leaves (or 1 handful fresh)

        1 teaspoon lemon juice

Saute trout in skillet until almost done. Add chopped parsley, mint leaves, lemon juice, anchovies and a few drops of water. Cook covered 10 minutes over a low flame.

Coquille St. Jacques.
Serves 6 people

        1 medium carrot, diced

        1 onion, diced

        1 handful string beans, diced

        2 mushrooms, diced, or 1 burdock root

        2 slices halibut, diced

        2 slices salmon, diced

        2 tablespoons oil

        Bread crumbs

        3 cups bechamel (see recipe, page 177)

In a skillet saute onion 2 - 3 minutes, add carrots, mushrooms and string beans, then simmer for 5 minutes. Add diced halibut and salmon. Cover and simmer 10 more minutes. Place this mixture in shells, pour bechamel over it, add bread crumbs, put in oven 10 minutes, then in broiler a few minutes, just long enough to brown the top.

The original recipe, which is Yvette DeLangre's, included scallops instead of halibut. Try it!

Salmon Rice Patties.

> 3 slices salmon, ½ inch thick, diced
>
> 3 cups cooked rice
>
> 1 egg
>
> 1 teaspoon fresh ginger, grated
>
> 2 tablespoons scallions, chopped
>
> 2 tablespoons parsley, chopped
>
> 3 tablespoons w.w. pastry flour or w.w. flour
>
> 1 teaspoon salt

Mix all ingredients. Form 6 patties, round and flat. Roll in bread crumbs or cornmeal and fry in oil. Use ¼ inch oil and a medium flame. Fry each side until light brown. Serve with chopped parsley on top.

Fish pancakes.

> 2 cups w.w. flour
>
> 2 cups water
>
> ½ teaspoon salt
>
> ½ cup scallions, finely chopped
>
> 1 cup sole or flounder, ground
>
> ½ cup carrot, grated

Mix ingredients and cook covered in oiled skillet 9 inches in diameter. Fry first side 8 minutes or so and other side 3 - 5 minutes, until brown.

Sardine Wedding.

Cut off heads of sardines, open bellies and cut lengthwise delicately to the tail. Gently remove the back-bone and cut inside a bit more, being careful not to go through the fish with your knife. Flatten the sardine; repeat the process with another. Join them, keeping the skin side out. Hold with a toothpick as if sewing them together. Place in a broiler for a few minutes. Serve hot with a few drops of lemon juice.

Ridiculous Smelt.

Remove heads. Open smelt at the belly as you did the sardines. Once flattened, sprinkle insides with a bit of salt, lemon rind, some flour and chopped watercress. Roll from head to tail, tail out. Use toothpick to keep roll tight, sprinkle with flour, then fry in ¼ inch oil.

Striped Bass Maison.

> 1 striped bass (3 - 4 pounds) cut into ½-inch slices
>
> 3 tablespoons olive oil
>
> 6 celery stalks with leaves, sliced
>
> 2 carrots, finely sliced
>
> 2 cloves garlic, crushed
>
> 2 bay leaves
>
> 2 tablespoons parsley, chopped
>
> Pinch saffron diluted in 1 cup warm water
>
> ½ teaspoon salt

Clean bass, retaining head and tail, which will give a good consistency and taste to the dish. Heat oil in a large saucepan, add garlic, and saute until golden. Add bay leaves and parsley, simmer 2 minutes, then add saffron-water. Bring to a boil, then simmer 2 minutes. Add carrots, celery and simmer 10 minutes, covered. Place slices of fish in saucepan, sprinkle with salt, cover and simmer 20 - 25 minutes.

Serve a slice of fish with vegetables on the side. Pour 2 tablespoons of the remaining sauce over the fish.

Mackerel in Umeboshi Juice.

> 6 mackerel, cleaned (keep head and tail)
>
> 1 cup umeboshi juice
>
> 2 tablespoons parsley
>
> 3 tablespoon soya sauce
>
> 1 tablespoon lemon juice

Fry mackerel in oil 3 - 5 minutes on each side. If the skillet is too small, use shallow platter and place in oven. Mix umeboshi juice, parsley, soya sauce and lemon juice, then pour over fish. Simmer 10 minutes in skillet, or bake 20 minutes in 375-degree oven.

Sashimi. (Raw fish)
Serves 6

> 1 ½ pounds striped bass filet, cut into 1 ½ by 2-inch pieces,
>   ¼ inch thick
>
> 1 cup parsley, chopped
>
> 1 carrot, grated
>
> 1 cup daikon, grated
>
> 12 tablespoons soya sauce
>
> 1 teaspoon ginger, grated

Display pieces of fish flat atop one another as if spreading a deck of cards. Serve 6 for each guest. Delicately arrange daikon, carrot and parsley on the side. Everyone will dip fish in a ginger-tamari mixture before eating. Serve sauce in tiny individual dishes. Instead of parsley, you may use sprigs of fennel.

Turbo. (Raw fish)

> 12 ounces turbo
>
> 1 apple, sliced
>
> 1 beet, boiled and sliced
>
> ½ cup water
>
> ¼ teaspoon salt
>
> Ice cubes
>
> ½ teaspoon lemon juice
>
> 1 ½ tablespoons soya sauce

Wash and clean fish. Dice and place in individual bowls with slices of apple and beet. Mix salt with water and pour some in every bowl. Serve with 2 or 3 ice cubes, a few drops of lemon juice and soya sauce.

Don't call a doctor,
I need a cook!

It is changes that are chiefly responsible for diseases, especially the greatest changes, the violent alternations both in the seasons and in other things. But seasons which come on gradually are the safest, as are gradual changes of regimen and temperature, and gradual changes from one period of life to another.

Hippocrates

Overeating is the unfortunate other side of the coin of ignorance. What cannot be absorbed in the way of knowledge or wisdom is too often compensated for in the consumption of large volumes of food. The over-eater is not a philosopher; nor is he a scientist. He is but a taut bag pathologically crammed with nervous urges and permanent sorrows. His only philosophy is forgetfulness. He builds around himself a shell of grime and fatty tissue that insulates him from the world of understanding, which he associates with the bugaboos of "asceticism and continence." He believes that science ought to serve his needs, excitements and curiosity alone. Along with so many others, he is totally unaware of the causes of his troubles. He does not even suspect that over-eating, the source of almost all sicknesses, may be at the root of his own problems.

Overdoing anything is dangerous, and over-enlarging ourselves actually makes us less than what we could be. Our pathological misbehaviors are the prophetic yesterdays of our very pathetic tomorrows. This awareness, grown to a certainty over the past ten years, has enabled me to become my own healer.

My mornings are illuminating friends who lead my day. A little pain here or there tells better than any theorizing what my exact situation is. I adjust by eating less and learning more, and I am a better doctor next day. I have gone through difficult moments, baffled by incongruous pains. Approaching the problem from various points of view, quite often I could find nothing but my own ignorance.

Since then I have learned that it is not so all-fired important to know the absolute, ultimate cause of every sickness. Other things must be learned, too, such as how to eat at one's own discretion, at one's desire and will, without worrying about getting sick; how to be flexible and free of fears and rigidities; and not least of all, how to pass through a morning without being excessively watchful of one's own internal mechanisms. To achieve such independence and happiness is really no more difficult than it is to prepare a good meal every day. Eventually our desires will be satisfied as we achieve the status of true men.

A well-balanced meal is the solution of pathological relapses and uncontrollable hungers and thirsts. Good cooking over a long period of time gives to body and mind an opportunity to become acquainted with companions other than the five senses. A good cook, even if she is only a humble, unassuming wife who cannot distinguish the liver from the stomach, is a better doctor than all the great and learned physicians and even mother Nature.

* * *

On days when my wife suffered because of misbehaving children or a guest with atrocious manners, my stomach was an accurate barometer of the miseries she endured. My cramps and pains were an orchestral accompaniment to the tumultuous percussion of spoons, pots and pans. I felt internally the angers and plots born among casseroles and colanders. As I swallowed, I could taste the bad temper like curry in cooking.

Sickness comes from such unfaithful, nervous, unsympathetic arrangements of a meal.

But there is no one to blame except ourselves in whatever we do. A cook has ample time to rid herself of anger before entering her kitchen.

To be sick is to swear by the teachings of others. But to be healthy is to have concluded that what one learns, believes and talks about, one is.

The first act of freedom is to accept the pain of our long sicknesses. The rest depends upon one's willingness to grow.

* * *

I learned from various schools of medicine (mostly from the Chinese) and from tussling with my own defects, some tricks, which can help in case of minor illnesses. In a sense, it is from my faults and defects that this book is being born, because it was in the kitchen they were cured. Their presence ought to be considered as "blessings in disguise," inasmuch as they are guide posts to health. Getting rid of them quickly because of fear is unwise. The slower they go, the better.

If your urine is more brown than yellow, your liquid intake is not excessive. Very dark brown, however, is not a healthy color—it may be the result of too much salt and not enough liquid. A clear yellow urine is caused by too much liquid or too little activity. In general, it is an indication that the body is no longer able to assimilate its food properly. There is more quantity than quality.

Fecal matter is better when it floats in the water than when it sinks. Buogancy means that food has been chewed and mixed well. Drinking and eating were appropriate, too, in that they were taken at a proper time, not together. Sinking fecal matter means that you should eat better, chew better, find better companions to visit for dinner, or get another wife.

There are two kinds of constipation, one associated with dilation of the intestines, the other with constriction. Dilation occurs when the intestines are overly full of food and liquid. Having lost elasticity, their natural contractive-expansive movements diminish or cease altogether.

What most people attempt by way of remedy is to drink enormous a-
mounts of water as though flushing a toilet, trying to accomplish mechanically what should properly be done physiologically. They swallow
a quart of liquid, then two and three, then pills and syrups, creating
waves and tides in their intestines. Their bowels are as lazy as their
constipation is evidenced in the mouth and eyes.

Constrictive constipation is as rare as people who drink little with a
meal. Only one in ten thousand may suffer from it, the intestines forming a narrow tube through which almost nothing can pass.

For the more common constipation (dilated) there are no better
cures than (1) buckwheat groats and brown rice, (2) greater activity
and less water and (3) a few sauteed Yang vegetables and a small bowl
of miso soup every day.

Diarrhea comes from failure to keep the intestines warm. The source
of cold can be external or internal—such as too much icewater; or perhaps there may be too much water in the intestines along with food
which has not been thoroughly digested. Stools are glutinous because
of too much mucus. Over-acid conditions in the body come from sweets
or meats. When the intestines hurt badly, it means they are inflamed.

Pain in the area from the base of the neck to the shoulder is an indication of bad intestines. Tension in the muscles in that region is caused
by too much liquid. The muscles should be soft when at rest. Experiment by eating and drinking less for a while—your pain will disappear.
Massage helps because it brings heat to muscles which require it for re-
laxation. However, massage provides only symptomatic relief similar to
the application of cream or a hot compress. Such fast solutions do not
really go to the root of the problem. First unburden your intestines and
your shoulders will be automatically eased.

Pain in the knee is often caused by a bad liver, overtaxed or actually
intoxicated. Sometimes bad kidneys are the source. I understand now
why, when I played basketball years ago, I was forced to wear band-
ages on my knees.

Pain in the articulations (or joints) comes from bad kidneys and intestines. Sugar and too much liquid are the main causes; especially soft
drinks.

Dandruff has one most fundamental cause: too much food. Overloaded organs, our natural storage-houses of protein, fat, etc., do the best they can to get rid of surplus when it accumulates. Sometimes tired and incapable of fully performing their functions, they expel excess in any way they can. The result is dandruff or hard skin.

* * *

For more than twenty years I suffered from hemophelia. I kept a tube of yellow cotton with which to stuff my nose whenever I bled. More than a few hours were required to stop a simple nosebleed. I remember on some nights awaking with a sensation of dampness under my cheek. Flicking on a light I would see a fantastic mirror-image, red from head to shoulder. I had bled all night and hadn't known it.

It happened more than once that, while dancing or simply talking or walking with a friend, I would have to excuse myself, run to the closest men's room and lie on the floor until the bleeding stopped. I considered myself fortunate if I happened to have some of the miraculous yellow cotton in a pocket.

I know today where all this came from. My blood was too thin, too Yin. My food was too rich. I was taking in too much potassium and not enough sodium. As soon as I introduced salt into my diet and cut out fruits and sugars, the bleeding immediately ceased. According to Chinese medicine I was too Yin. I had to make myself Yang. To become Yang is to eliminate all Yin food and to become more active. I did so and was cured.

The same thing applies to people who bleed easily when they shave. Just a few days on a balanced diet, avoiding too much liquid, fruit and all very Yin food, and shaving is changed into a pleasurable morning ritual.

If you have pimples, consider what you eat. Pimples are like dandruff; they are signs that things have gone too far; the organs are giving up.

Blood-shot eyes can mean many things such as bad digestion, acid stomach, or loss of vitamin B due to too much liquid, food or insufficient chewing.

Bags under the eyes indicate bad kidneys. Other deep circles around the eyes can be a result of either bad liver or intestines.

Headaches follow a chaotic life. High acidity often produces small hemorrages, which then produce pain.

A swollen lower lip is a sign of bad intestines. Such a person is prone to constipation. Crossing the arms indicates an ill-functioning stomach, and crossing the legs when sitting is another sign of bad intestines.

People whose mouths, swollen and red-lipped, remain open all the time can produce an unconscious closing of it by creating a physiological constriction of their stomach and intestines.

My grandmother taught me how to get rid of hiccoughs in a few seconds. Although symptomatic, it is an effective and harmless method: take seven small sips of tea or water while ceasing to breathe. After the seventh sip hold your breath as long as possible. Inhale rapidly two or three times through the nose, bringing the air to the stomach. It never misses. Incidentally, only people with Yin conditions suffer from hiccoughs, owing to a dilated glottis.

Stomach cramps result from either eating too fast or too far on the acid side. In any event, eating too fast produces acidity. Good chewers never have stomach-problems, unless they overeat. A bad mixture of food and liquid can also be a contributing cause.

Everyone knows that heartburn is caused by acidity, which often results from chatoic eating. Bread, especially when it is whole-wheat and is eaten with soup or some other liquid, can cause heartburn; bread must be chewed alone and thoroughly, so much so that you can almost drink it. Only if you have a sensitive stomach can you drink something afterwards.

Insomnia is caused by bad kidneys, lungs or liver, or sometimes by a great accumulation of food in the stomach.

Sores in the mouth stem from a constant intake of rich food.

Tooth decay is caused by over-acidity, which robs the body of minerals such as calcium.

Sore throat comes from eating rich food in excess and drinking cold liquids—especially beer.

Deafness is caused by bad kidneys or gall bladder.

Irregular menstruation comes from chaotic eating. Dairy foods are the primary culprits. Menstruation occurs naturally at the time of the new moon. Moon-time is Yin and blood is Yang. Yin attracts Yang outside!

The flu is not caused by a virus! Flu results from internal weakness. A cold is the accumulation of mucus formed by an over-acid condition. People usually attempt to cure themselves by taking lots of liquids. That's the "Yin" way, the symptomatic way; it consists of "covering up" the acidity with fluid—and more fluid. The "Yang" way is to let the mucus dry up by eating and drinking less. It takes longer than the symptomatic way the first time, but there are hardly ever any re-occurrences. If there are, recovery does not take more than one or two days because so little mucus is present in the system.

What we enjoyed last week

The best thing I can think of to help beginning-adventurers in this new way of cooking is to have my wife herself present what we enjoyed during one week in December at our own table. We know it is difficult, especially for newcomers, to put ingredients together in a manner that will create well-balanced meals.

If wintertime menus don't agree with your habits or schedules, by all means adapt them to your own convenience. You may also want to eat in lesser or greater quantities. My wife developed her menus both for the family and for guests, and I must say, after reviewing the week's output, that we don't ordinarily eat so widely or in such great amounts.

You will notice that our first meal is more of a lunch than a breakfast. We usually skip breakfast altogether and, instead, take a more substantial meal at noon. At times, when we rise very early, we enjoy a a grain in cream form, such as rice, barley, oats or buckwheat.

But let my wife speak for herself:

This is what I always keep in mind before I start cooking:

Miso soup once a day, either morning or evening.

Rice at every meal.

Bread once a week, enough for two days.

Every day a different grain, whole and plain.

A portion of seaweed every day, in miso soup or served in a dish beside the vegetables.

A portion of beans, preferably aduki, every other day.

In winter, a small portion of pickled vegetables two to three times a week.

In summer, a small portion of salad.

At every evening meal, at least two different vegetables.

I am always careful not to include much salt in my cooking. I prefer to let my husband, children or guests add it in the form of soya sauce or sesame salt if they wish to.

Always and above all I keep in mind the paramount importance of making everyone at the table happy. For that I suffer moments of doubt and stage-fright. But the result is worth all the trouble.

SUNDAY

(Noon)

Miso Soup
Rice
Buckwheat Waffles

(Evening)

Rice
Soba in hot bouillon
Vegetable Tempura on stick
Baked squash & carrots
Aduki beans

I cooked enough Miso soup to have some left over for the next day. Because I had little time, I made waffles by blending the ingredients in an electric mixer. Whipped water and flour give the same result as adding eggs or baking powder. I didn't even have to let the mixture sit a while.

Unexpected guests dropped in at the last minute. Nonetheless I decided to prepare a full, complete dinner, and concluded that soba-tempura was best-suited to the occasion. I also baked vegetables since they do not require much attention. I pressure-cooked aduki beans and spent most of my time preparing tempura. In order to avoid running between the pan of oil and the diningroom, I skewered the vegetables on sticks in the form of shishkebbab. I dipped them in batter, deep-fried them in corn oil and served two of each to every guest.

MONDAY

(Noon)

Miso Soup
Rice

(Evening)

Oat Soup
Pinto beans on Polenta
Rice
Sauteed Broccoli
Hijiki Seaweed

In the morning I cooked rice with 10% whole-wheat berries, which makes it more chewy. The oat soup at the evening meal had the advantage of being both light and nourishing. I planned the main dish the way I imagine an artist must compose his painting. I always give great care to the associations of colors. For stronger, although harmonious contrast, I placed snowy-white polenta alongside black seaweed. To develop the picture, I poured creamy baked beans over the polenta. The broccoli, cut into flowerettes and sauteed, completed the landscape with its beautiful green.

TUESDAY

(Noon)

Barley Cream
Pickled Cabbage
Fried Rice Croquettes

(Evening)

Miso Soup flavored with
Iriko
Kasha Glace, broiled &
covered with bechamel
Lentils in Kombu
Rice
Half baked squash with
bechamel

I have a sentimental liking for barley cream. It was the first course of the first meal I ever had at a cerealian restaurant, Guen Mai, in Paris, a delightful introduction. The barley cream came with croutons and chopped parsley. Delicious!

To prepare the rice croquettes I simply moisten my hands with salted water, shaped a handful of cooked rice into triangles with two-inch bases, then fried both sides until crisp. A tablespoon or two of pickled salad was a perfect complement.

At dinner we entertained a charming lady who was just beginning the diet. I knew her to be a gourmet, so I prepared our miso soup from a stock base made with a handful of small fish and a piece of kombu boiled together for 10 minutes. I later served the small fish on the side with fresh-grated ginger and a few drops of soya sauce. The kasha was prepared in a special way. The previous night I toasted the groats, blended them into a meal, then cooked them in water. This produced a thick cream which I poured into small bowls. The next day, slipping the molded kasha out of the bowls, I placed the individual portions under a broiler for 15 minutes. They were served covered with bechamel. The dish also included rice and lentils cooked together with small pieces of kombu. A halved acorn squash stuffed with creamed onions provided the final touch.

WEDNESDAY

(Noon)

Miso Soup
Rice

(Evening)

Rice
Bulghur Bechamel
Sauteed carrots with seitan
Hijiki seaweed
Sauteed string beans

There wasn't much work to do with miso soup and rice left over from last night and only our own little family to cook for. I prepared everything in a little more than an hour.

THURSDAY

(Noon)
Miso Soup
Rice

(Evening)

Millet Soup
Aduki & Celery & Onion in
Casserole flavored and
seasoned with sesame butter
and soya sauce
Rice
Crepe Suzettes filled with
sauteed zucchini

I prepared a new miso soup this morning, using kombu instead of wakame. As usual, I steamed the rice and served it hot in bowls.

For dinner, just our own little family again. It was a holiday for the children. I made crêpe Suzettes. The millet soup was a rich one suited to a cold winter night. I prepared the aduki beans in a different way, mixing them with sauteed onions and celery after cooking, adding soya sauce and sesame butter and then putting the mixture in the oven. For a change I used corn flour in the crêpe batter, which I mixed with whole-wheat pastry flour. As with the waffle recipe, the batter was whipped instead of letting it sit one or two hours. It made a smooth liquid batter, not too thin and not too heavy. I used two frying pans to save time. The crepes can be cooked a little ahead of schedule and reheated in the oven.

The dinner took me two hours to prepare—perhaps a little bit more.

FRIDAY

(Noon)

Miso Soup
Millet Croquettes
Rice

(Evening)

Bread and Spread
Couscous
Cabbage Strudel
Baked Apple
Pressed Salad

Some miso soup was left from the day before. I served it with croquettes, made from last night millet soup cooked. The soup resembled a custard. I added some whole-wheat flour and a chopped onion to it and formed small balls which I then deep-fried. They were delicious with rice.

Friday is usually a busy day. The evening is long and full of friends.

I always bake bread for the occasion. To enjoy a relaxed Saturday, I prepare Oden in advance. It is our regular Saturday meal.

Dough for the bread was prepared Thursday night and baked Friday at noon—it must rise, but not turn sour. If I fail at making a good bread, I feel ashamed and guilty for at least two days.

The spread is always different; sometimes it looks like a firm pate, sometimes it is very smooth. For every Friday night I cook the traditional Moroccan dish, couscous. Although a meal by itself, I like to present a little specialty as "entree." That Friday we had a cabbage strudel. The cabbage used had been pickled for several days. I kept it in a big jar in the refrigerator for two weeks, then simply sauteed it for the strudel. A pressed salad of greens was a light and colorful note in the dish."

SATURDAY

(Noon)

Oden & Barley

(Evening)

Pizza Pie
Rice
Burdock in plum juice
Corn kernels baked with scallions

I prepare oden stew inspired by two traditions, Japanese and Moroccan. I place a cotton bag filled with raw barley or any other grain in a deep, heavy pot. All sorts of other ingredients are added such as beans, carrots, turnips, white radish, onions, etc. I let it simmer for a few hours in a rich liquid made with soya sauce. I serve the stew as a soup in bowls, with the barley as the only grain.

Friday's couscous and Saturday's oden are a ritual that family and friends enjoy so much in our home.

The pie I served that night as entree could also have doubled as dessert. Its sweet taste came from sauteed carrots, onions and cabbage that were crushed with a fork, mixed with bechamel and poured into a pie crust rolled out very thinly and already half-baked. It could have duplicated the exact taste of pizza if prepared with a different dough, a pinch of oregano and thyme, and a few black olives finely chopped.

Fresh burdock, cut into half-inch pieces and pressure-cooked with one or two salted plums, lends a totally different taste to the roots. I served them cooled alongside rice.

Corn kernels, soaked overnight, were pressure-cooked for more than two hours. When cooked, I put them in the oven for 30 minutes with slightly sauteed scallions. The dish looked beautiful.

SUNDAY

(Noon)

Rice Cream
Bread and Spread

(Evening)

Miso Soup
Rice
Kasha Loaf
Sauteed Carrots
Sauteed Daikon
Corn Chips

I served miso soup in the evening after a day without it. The kasha loaf was a composite of leftover grains and vegetables—the best I ever made!

I combined rice, barley and vegetables from the oden, a sauteed onion or two, and four or five chopped and sauteed scallions. To the mixture I added five tablespoons of whole-wheat flour, then formed a firm loaf which I put in the oven for thirty minutes or so. To have something crisp for the teeth, I deep-fried small thin squares of dough made of meal and pastry flour. The result was delicious corn chips. They remain fresh for several days.

The ceremony

When you eat and take pleasure in the taste
and sweetness of the food, bear in mind that
it is the Lord who has placed into the food its
taste and sweetness. You will, then, truly serve
Him by your eating.

Baal Shem Tov.

In our family what was presented at the table was always held to be
sacred. We approached an evening meal in a serious and joyful mood
that prepared us for a holy ceremony. We never spoke till my father
distributed bread he had broken with his own hands. We respected this
solemn act which gave us dignity. When later we were caused to be
separated from our parents for many years, upon our return we always
happily resumed our age-old ritual which sanctified the relationship between Man and his daily bread.

Grandmother told us the simple act of offering a prayer made one eat less with greater satisfaction. Thirty years later I had only to open my eyes to observe an almost universal abuse of this principle. People came from the streets with improper thoughts—nervous, hateful and sick—came directly to their tables without first composing themselves with a prayer, without even pausing in a brief meditation perhaps measurable only in the gleam of an eye. I saw customers in coffee shops hastily ordering, hurrying to the toilet, and upon their return, briskly installing themselves before a meal which was then gulped down with an absentmindedness no different from the inattention given to urination: an identical carelessness for opposite acts.

The Japanese, whose civilization is as old as the memory of Man, possessed customs similar to those observed in my own family. For them the kitchen was a sacred enclave. Only those entered whose high judgment merited such distinction. In the kitchen the health of the man of tomorrow was determined. Each gesture was executed with a most profound respect for the nutriments. It was in the kitchen that the first life-giving movement occurred which would later differentiate into the varied forms and forces of human nature.

The plants of the field were thought of as young blood which would be subsumed into Man, thus continuing the original course of creation. Care was mandatory in the handling of a vegetable, for no one must savagely decapitate the anthropological form of the person who was about to be born.

All ritual reminded Man of what was within him, reinforced each day the memory of his long history. Yesterday he had been a plant; today—human. Let him therefore be humble and happy in the awareness of his magnificent journey.

The kitchen was the embryo of both joy and unhappiness. Those who were aware of this fact and who sacrificed a plant with proper respect, created a kingdom of heaven on earth. By honoring as they consumed, alert to the eternal, they brought about a paradise which remained invisible to those who were oblivious to their secret.

Man has been left with only pathological and degraded remnants of his former attitudes toward food. Olden rituals have been replaced by a shoddy *savoir-faire* which only pallidly imitates the manners of ancient, sacred feasts. Everything is now only a function of comfort and taste. A pig is served upon a silver platter which will hopefully lend it dignity; it is hidden under succulent, colorful sauces intended to mask its true color and pork taste. Chefs, so-called masters of *haute-cuisine*, knowing next-to-nothing about man's health and even less about his thought, decide what customers will eat without having once ever seen them, unaware if they be sad, fat, thin, diabetic, nervous or ulcerous. The ritual progression from kitchen to table is the condensed story of life, but the modern cook is completely ignorant of this movement; he is a remorseless man dedicated to the twin tasks of execution and embalming.

In oriental homes reverent hostesses presented treasured bowls in gracious hands; nowadays in their places stand elegant hotel managers who bow deeply for shallow reasons. Those ceremonies which were long ago respected and honored as representing life's deepest essence, tracing its development from a humble biological inception to the highest spiritual expansion, have given way to cynical, degenerate attitudes that mean nothing.

Which is only justice, only harmony. For man is what he eats, each dish creates a point of view, and the plate that lacks "soul" deserves its unappreciative customer.

But the good and holy ceremony is a natural accompaniment of good and holy food.

The
international
chef

Even if you know that the man who is
knocking at your door came to kill you,
and you know that he is hungry, open your
door and feed him.

Jewish-Moroccan saying

Here are some recipes inspired by the countries from which they
came. They differ slightly from the originals for I've manipulated them
a bit to adapt them to our way of cooking.

JAPAN

One night a friend, just back from Japan, dined with us. We hadn't seen him for three years while he had been studying the language and various arts of Japan, including its martial art, Aikido. He described to us the excellent quality of Japanese cooking, which he had sampled in various regions of the country, expressing regret at having been compelled to leave because of obligations in the U.S. "I'd have stayed there just for the food," he declared. But that was before my wife and Ella, a girl who is staying with us, brought in the pots, dishes, bowls and baskets of—soba-tempura.

Our friend, Martin, couldn't believe it; his eyes widened in astonishment. Only a movie camera could have done justice to his expression.

"What do you think about that, Martin?" I asked.

Martin tasted the noodles, bit experimentally at a piece of tempura, "It's unbelievable, he exclaimed, I'm back there!"

After two more mouthfuls, nearly embarrassing my wife with compliments, he declared, "It's even finer than the best I ever had in Japan!"

Of all the dishes, this is the one I recommend most if you're short of time or if a very dear friend is visiting with whom you might wish to talk through dinner (and for that rice is not recommended). Soba-tempura is always light, hot, tasty and nourishing.

Preparation of Soba-Tempura and side dishes.

For 6 - 8 people

Cook 12 ounces of noodles. (Use light buckwheat noodles, not the dark ones).

Prepare 1 ½ quarts of bouillon (soup stock; see recipe, page 105).

Chop 3 scallions very finely.

Toast 2 nori sheets and break them into small pieces.

Soya sauce should be poured in tiny dishes, 1 tablespoon per person

Pickled daikon or any other vegetable of the same consistency

Make a salad with the following ingredients:

1 celery stalk, finely chopped

1 ½-inch slice of raw daikon or white radish, grated

1 handful of Mung bean threads, cooked 5 minutes in 1 cup water

1 scallion, chopped finely

2 tablespoons soya sauce

1 pinch of salt

Mix ingredients together and put in a bowl.

For the vegetable tempura which you will make at the very end, do the following:

Wash and cut 1 carrot into long matchsticks

Cut 1 parsnip into very thin and longitudinal slices

Mince 1 large onion into thin rings

Trim a broccoli into 12 flowerettes

Wash and cut celery leaves, parsley, watercress, etc., into 2-3 inch pieces

Prepare batter, dip vegetables into it and deep fry in oil. (See tempura recipe, page 251).

This is what you should now have on your table:

Noodles in a pot

Hot bouillon in a pot with a ladle

Vegetable tempura, leaves and roots in individual baskets. (You may add to this a large piece of deep-fried kombu)

Chopped scallions in a bowl

Shredded, toasted nori in a bowl

Tiny individual dishes with soya sauce

Pickled daikon in a small dish

Finely chopped salad in a bowl

To serve:

Place noodles in a large individual bowl. Don't go overboard; the level of the noodles must be ½ inch below the edge of the bowl.

Place 3 - 4 pieces of vegetable tempura (leafy variety) on the noodles and pour in 2 ladles of very hot bouillon. Sprinkle on some shredded nori and add a dusting of chopped scallions.

In each individual straw basket gently place the different forms of tempura—celery leaves, carrot-matchsticks, etc.—arranging them with good taste. Each guest will use chopsticks or fingers to dip the tempura into soya sauce. Salad can be served during the meal, but the pickled daikon is saved for a final touch of elegance.

FRANCE

Ruisseau de Provence.

Choosing a recipe out of hundreds of French specialties is no easy matter. But Provence had been for me the most pleasing part of France. There, in my ailing days, I had felt happiest.

"Ruisseau de Provence," not entirely a recipe from Provence, is instead a mixed concoction inspired by my remembrance of the charm and happiness of the south of France. To what might have been "only another soup," I have added a few ingredients that transform it into a dish elegant enough to be served alone and sufficient in itself for an entire day's sustenance. I expressly made it equal to a couscous or a soba-tempura so that southern France would not be slighted on this social and international table.

For 6-8 people

1-   1 striped bass, scaled, cleaned (keep tail and head) and cut into
        1-inch pieces

      1 red snapper

      1 mackerel

2-   3 onions, minced

      2 bay leaves

      2-3 garlic cloves, finely chopped

      3 tablespoons parsley, chopped

      2 tablespoons olive oil

      2 quarts water

3-   2 cups brown rice

      4 carrots, cut into chunks

      4 turnips, cut into chunks

      6 celery stalks, cut into chunks

      1 pound brussel sprouts

      6-8 slices of bread, toasted

1-   Put the pieces of fish in a bag of thin cloth (preferably cheese-
cloth) which can be tied with a thread. Do the same with the rice.

2-   Make the following sauce:

Heat a large pan, put olive oil in it, wait a few seconds, lower the flame,
then add chopped garlic. Be careful not to burn it; it must simmer 2-3
minutes until golden. Add onions, bay leaves, parsley and ½ cup of water.
Simmer 10 minutes.

3-   Place the rice bag in the pan in which the sauce is simmering.
Add carrots, turnips, celery and brussel sprouts, then add the 2 quarts
of water, cover, bring to a boil and simmer 45 minutes. Place the fish

bag in the pan, raise the flame and bring to a boil for 2 minutes. Simmer another 25 minutes. Bring the cooking pan to the table and let everyone help himself.

How to serve it:

Place a toasted slice of bread, which you can rub with a garlic clove, in the middle of a soup dish. Pour hot bouillon over it and sprinkle with chopped parsley. Voila! the soup. In another dish serve one or two pieces of each vegetable. Open the rice bag and serve 2 tablespoons or more; open the other bag and serve 1 piece of each kind of fish.

In the middle of the table place 1 small dish of red radish, 1 bowl of salad, 1 dish of black olives and, perhaps, in a straw basket, a few slices of yeasted bread.

ITALY

Mimosa de Venise. (Polenta)

In all of Italy, search as you might, you will never find this recipe. While the polenta and sardines are genuinely Italian, much has been changed in order to make the dish an international equal it its "compadres" in this chapter.

For 6-8 people

1- 3 cups yellow polenta

9 cups water

1 ½ teaspoons salt

See page 60 for directions for cooking polenta.

2- 1 ½ cups chick-peas

See page 66 for directions for cooking chick-peas and beans.

3-   For the sauce use:

3 scallions, finely chopped

1 onion, chopped

Half green pepper, chopped

2 carrots, diced

2 garlic cloves, finely chopped

3 tablespoons arrow-root diluted in ½ cup water

5 cups water

2 tablespoons olive oil

1 teaspoon salt

Heat a large saucepan, put in olive oil and, using a very low flame, saute garlic for 2 minutes until golden. Add green pepper; 2 minutes later add onions and carrots. Simmer covered for 10 minutes. Boil 5 cups of water and pour into simmering mixture. Add salt. Simmer 10 minutes and add diluted arrow-root. Mix immediately to prevent lumps from forming. Add scallions, stir and remove from fire.

4-   For fish use:

12-16 fresh sardines, cleaned and rolled in corn flour. Dip sardines in corn flour and deep fry in corn oil (use tempura method). Serve hot with a few drops of lemon juice.

This is what you should have on your table when everything is ready:

Cooked polenta, hot and placed in the center of a large wooden board. Encircling the board will be 1 large bowl of cooked chick-peas, 1 porcelain or earthenware pot with the sauce, 1 large platter containing the dried fish, and a salad.

Everyone helps himself to a large square of polenta, which he places in the center of his dish. On top he will add 2-3 tablespoons of chick-peas, then pour on a ladle or two of sauce. Sardines and salad will be placed on the side.

MIDDLE EAST

Falafel.

This dish is best when served on a hot summer's day. It has its place here because it possesses all the drama of a social occasion. For some who are used to having rice with every meal this might not seem substantial; for my part it is quite enough; the happiness it brings makes up for what it lacks.

In Israel falafels are sold on the streets like pretzels in Philadelphia or roasted chestnuts in Paris. They are cheap and hot and come wrapped in a paper napkin. You can re-create a middle-eastern ambience in your home by serving it to a dozen guests—who, I guarantee, will never forget the event!

A falafel is a sandwich composed of flat Syrian bread, chick-peas croquettes, salad and a sauce made of chick-peas and Tahini. You can buy the Syrian bread in Armenian stores or, if you prefer something more organic, bake it yourself—it's easy!

For the pitah (flat bread) use:

6 cups w.w. pastry flour or unbleached flour

2 cups water

1 teaspoon yeast (granulated) diluted in ½ cup lukewarm water

1 tablespoon salt

3 tablespoons oil

Mix water, oil and diluted yeast in a bowl. Gradually blend in flour and salt. Knead on a slightly floured board for 5 minutes until smooth and elastic. Place in a bowl, oil top of the dough to prevent the formation of a crust, and set in a warm place. Let rise overnight. In the morning knead again for 3 minutes, shape into balls 3 inches in diameter, and flatten with palm and fingers or roll out on a floured board until you obtain a 7-8 inch circle. Place on an oiled baking sheet and allow to stand 1 hour. Bake in preheated 375 degree oven for 20-25 minutes.

Note:

Because you are going to use chick-peas for 2 different preparations, you will have to cook enough of these for both. Cook 3 cups chick-peas in 10 cups water (do not forget to soak them overnight). Keep the water in which they have been cooked.

For the croquettes use:

2/3 of the cooked chick-peas

1 cup onions, finely chopped, almost grated

1 tablespoon parsley, very finely chopped

4 tablespoons w.w. flour

After you have poured off some water, crush the chick-peas with a fork. They should be wet enough to crush easily. Add flour, parsley and onions. Mix well. The mixture should have a consistency which enables you to form little balls whose diameter will not exceed ¾ inch. Fry balls in hot oil until brown. Place on a paper towel.

For the heavy sauce prepare:

1/3 of the cooked chick-peas

½ cup of tahini

2 garlic cloves, crushed

1 or 1 ½ cups liquid from cooked chick-peas

If the chick-peas are not salted, add 1 small teaspoon salt; if previously salted, add only ½ teaspoon.

Blend chick-peas with water. You should obtain the consistency of a fine cream. In a bowl add crushed garlic, stir in tahini and salt. If too thick, add more water.

For the salad prepare:

1 small lettuce, chopped

4 scallions, chopped

4 celery stalks, chopped

½ cup umeboshi juice (see recipe, page 183)

2 cups of any kind of pickled vegetable; try cucumber, cauliflower, etc.

1 pinch salt

Mix ingredients together and put in a large bowl.

When everything is cooked and ready, this is what you will have on
your table.:

Pitah in a basket, croquettes in a large dish, heavy sauce in a bowl,
olives (black) in a small dish, and the salad in its bowl.

Serve heavy sauce in individual dishes or saucers. Take pitah, break
open, and stuff with croquettes, salad and 2 or 3 tablespoons heavy
sauce. You can also break the bread into pieces and dip into sauce.

INDONESIA

Nasi Goreng.

On the island of Bali they serve you hot Nasi Goreng on a large
platter along with various small bowls filled with exotic delicacies.
People ask for it the way American tourists in Chinese restaurants always demand Chow Mein—as though there were nothing else on the
menu.

I have changed the recipe to some extent, adding a trifle here or sub-
tracting a tidbit there, so that it might be properly included in our
international table.

Prepare:

2 cups brown rice, soaked in water for 5 minutes and toasted
   until golden

4 cups water

½ teaspoon salt

4 small onions, diced

6 scallions, chopped

1 clove garlic, crushed

2 tablespoons oil

1 ½ pounds tuna fish or 3 slices cut into ¾ inch squares

3 tablespoons soya sauce

1 pound tofu cut into ¾ inch squares and presoaked 1 hour in
   soya sauce

2 cups bechamel sauce

Put toasted rice in water and salt, in a heavy pot. Cover and bring to
a boil, then simmer for 1 hour and 15 minutes or so (the rice should not
be sticky or soggy).

In a large pan saute garlic in oil until golden, being careful not to burn
it. Add onions, simmer 5 minutes, then add tuna fish. Simmer uncovered
5 minutes, stirring 2 or 3 times. Cover and simmer another 5 minutes.
Raise the flame, wait 30 seconds and add soya sauce. Immediately afterwards add cooked rice. Put the mixture in oven-proof individual dishes,
place 3 pieces of tofu on top, and cover gently with 4 tablespoons bechamel. Put in broiler for 5-10 minutes until golden brown.

Serve hot with various salads and accompaniments. Serves 6-8.

CHINA

The Gardens of Hong Kong.

We saw the gardens of Hong Kong in New York city!

It was no dream. China came within reach of our chopsticks, and America faded to a distant memory. We were tourists, and my wife was a gardener who, on a lovely Saturday evening, displayed for us the finest flowers of the Orient. . . .

This dish is unique. Its presentation can be extremely theatrical, and its taste can give the most discerning gourmet enough to gossip about for a week. It is as vain as a peacock, completely dissimilar to a humble bowl of brown rice. Yet a man of simple tastes may partake of it, for vanity has never been contagious.

Nothing is easier to cook. It is composed of:

Buckwheat noodles (the slender variety)

1 heavy sauce

Fried home-made noodles and

Pickles on the side

Prepare:

12 ounces buckwheat noodles

When cooked, drain through a strainer and keep in pot.

For sauce use:

3 onions, minced

4 carrots, thinly sliced

1 Chinese cabbage, shredded

6 scallions, chopped

6 slices halibut, cut into 1-inch squares, soaked in ginger and tamari sauce and broiled (see page 273 for broiling)

1 ¼ quarts water

3 tablespoons arrow-root diluted in 1 cup water

1 teaspoon ginger, grated

4 tablespoons soya sauce

½ teaspoon salt

2 tablespoons oil

Saute onions in oil; 2 minutes later add carrots and Chinese cabbage. Simmer 5 minutes. Add water and bring to a boil. Simmer 10 minutes. Stir in diluted arrow-root; add salt, ginger and soya sauce. Then add pieces of broiled fish and scallions. Simmer 2 minutes.

For the fried noodles make the following dough (prepare in advance):

1 ½ cups white unbleached flour or pastry

1 egg, slightly beaten

¼ teaspoon salt

½ cup water (perhaps less)

Mix water and egg and stir in rest of ingredients. Knead 5 minutes. The dough must be smooth and elastic. Allow to stand 1 hour. Roll out thin on flour board and cut into fine strips which should look like matchsticks. Deep fry in oil.

Serve in a large bowl or in a deep dish. Gently place noodles in center of individual dish. With a ladle, pour heavy sauce on top, then sprinkle on a handful of fried noodles. On the side serve salad and a small accompaniment.

Serves 6 to 8.

UNITED STATES

America-America.

Corn was the staple of the American Indian. Among various ways of cooking it, there must have been a recipe similar to this one. America, unlike most countries, has no national dish which includes cereals, I thought it about time such a contribution was offered.

Prepare the following:

Grain.

Kernels of 15 corn cobs

Sauce.
3 onions, diced
4 tablespoons parsley, chopped
1 bunch scallions, chopped
2 cloves garlic
3 tablespoons corn oil
¼ teaspoon salt
3 slices bread, diced
4 tablespoons tamari
½ teaspoon ginger, grated
1 cup water

Vegetables.
12 small onions, whole
3 carrots, cut into chunks
3 turnips, cut into chunks
1 pound brussel sprouts
1 teaspoon salt
and enough water to boil vegetables

Fish.

2 ½ pounds fresh tuna (keep it uncut)

and

12 slices of bread, toasted

Precook vegetables by boiling in water. While they are cooking, do the following:

For the sauce, saute garlic in saucepan until golden. Add parsley while stirring; 1 minute later add scallions and onions. Simmer 5 minutes, adding salt near the end. Place fish in saucepan with the sauce. Arrange diced bread around fish. Add a few drops of water, cover and simmer 5 minutes. Mix ginger and tamari and pour over fish. Cover and simmer 4-5 minutes. Pour cup of water over fish, cover and simmer 3 minutes. Remove fish. Now place boiled vegetables in saucepan. Simmer 10 minutes, covered.

For 30 seconds soak the 12 slices of bread in water in which vegetables have been cooked.

This is what you should have on your table:

Hot kernels in a bowl,

Fish in a serving platter, with watercress or lettuce

Sauce in a saucer,

Vegetables in a large dish and

12 slices of bread in a dish

Serve in the following way:

Place one slice of bread in individual dish, spread with sauce and top with a second slice. Cover abundantly with corn kernels and surround with vegetables. Leave some room for a slice of tuna fish.

Variation:

Instead of corn you may use barley. For holidays tuna fish can be re-placed with chicken, which should first be boiled in salted water for approximately 10 minutes, then cut into large pieces and put in the saucepan with simmering sauce. Although I've never cooked it, I remember the recipe from my mother's repertoire.

SPAIN

Feria de Sevilla.

The inspired cooks of Andalusia are silent poets whose dishes teach the tourist more about the south of Spain than could be learned from the finest guides. Soul is served in a simple bowl, character is displayed in the manner of presentation, and in the pouring of wine the true story of the country is laid bare. This is not history from books; it flows from the heart. Horses and soldiers and kings, the equipage of violence and struggle, burden it; death more than life shadows the telling; and yet speech is always accompanied by a smile.

"Feria de Sevilla," dedicated to my memories of Spain, is in fact a paella which I have converted into a more digestible dish.

Prepare rice in the following way:

2 cups rice

4 cups water

½ teaspoon salt

2 tablespoons olive oil

Wash rice until water is clear; toast it until golden over a low flame. Keep stirring to prevent burning. Put all ingredients in a heavy pan, bring to a boil covered, and simmer 1 hour or so until rice is soft. Add a few drops of water if still uncooked. If you prepare rice in a pressure cooker, use only 3 cups water. Cook 45 minutes after the pressure gage begins jiggling.

While rice is cooking prepare the following:

4 onions, diced

4 medium carrots, diced

6 scallions, chopped

½ green pepper, diced

¼ teaspoon salt

1 tablespoon olive oil

Saute garlic in oil until golden. Add onions, carrots and green pepper. Stir for 2 minutes or so, cover and simmer for 10 minutes. Add scallions, stir 1 minute and remove from fire. Do not cover.

Now prepare this:

1 tablespoon olive oil

2 cloves garlic

2 scallions

1 bayleaf

1 pinch saffron presoaked in 1 cup warm water for 1 hour

1 pinch salt

3 small mackerels cut in half

1 striped bass, cut into 1-inch slices

6 celery stalks cut in half

1 handful parsley, chopped

Saute garlic until golden. Add bay leaf and the cup of water in which it was presoaked and simmer 5 minutes. Gently place mackerel, striped bass, celery stalks and parsley in pan. Cover and simmer 20-25 minutes.

To serve, mix rice thoroughly with vegetables. Arrange in a dish and place fish and celery over it. Serve salad, olives, etc., on the side.

Serves 6 to 8.

INDIA

The Nights of Benares.

India is the country of mystics and spices. All that a guru can teach of sweetness can be transformed into fire in one curry-laden mouthful. Although I spent a long time in search of a recipe which would perfectly represent India, I never found it. What you can expect from the Yoga-country, then, is spice—and *more* spice! But why not? Once every blue moon or so . . . .

Soak, toast and cook 2 cups rice in a pressure cooker for 45 minutes, using 3 cups water. Then prepare the following:

> 2 tablespoons oil
>
> 3 onions, sliced
>
> 2 pounds swordfish, sliced
>
> A mixture of 3 tablespoons soya sauce and 1 cup umeboshi juice
>
> 2 garlic cloves
>
> 2 tablespoons almonds, boiled and peeled
>
> 2 tablespoons currant raisins
>
> ½ teaspoon cinnamon
>
> 1 pinch nutmeg
>
> 1 pinch saffron
>
> 1 teaspoon salt
>
> 2 tablespoons parsley, finely chopped
>
> 1 teaspoon ginger, grated

Heat a large saucepan and saute the onions in oil. Simmer until golden and add 6 slices of fish. Sprinkle on diced onions and parsley. Simmer 2 minutes; add mixture of umeboshi juice and soya sauce. Add grated ginger and stir. Bring to a boil, simmer and add garlic, almonds, currant, saffron, salt, cinnamon and nutmeg. Let cook 2 minutes, then add the cooked rice. Cover and simmer 10 minutes. Stir 2 or 3 times.

Serve in the following manner:

Remove rice delicately and put in an earthenware pot. With a spatula place fish in center of individual dish and cover with rice. Gather nuts and raisins that may have remained in the bottom of the saucepan and place over rice. Serve hot with 1 stalk celery cut into chunks and perhaps a small accompaniment on the side.

RUSSIA

Piroshki Sailing on the Volga.

In St. Petersburg, before the revolution, elegant ladies sipped Schtchi with wooden spoons in the Old Town and chatted in French whenever they gossiped about Parisian cabarets, theaters or social goings-on in the "City of Light." They preferred old French wine to vodka, which was in those days looked upon as a vulgar drink. To please their rich male customers, cooks would pour a few drops of white or red wine on their Schtchi, and this was enough to create awe and admiration among the snobbish women.

"Piroshki Sailing on the Volga" is a mixture of two Russian recipes. Piroshki is anything enveloped in dough and fried or baked. Schtchi is the Bouillabaisse of the Ukraine. Together they comprise an excellent meal, especially when accompanied by buckwheat croquettes.

> 2 tablespoons oil
>
> 1 cup umeboshi juice
>
> 3 tablespoons parsley, chopped
>
> 1 onion, diced
>
> 1 bay leaf
>
> 1 bunch kale or swiss chard, chopped
>
> 6 herrings
>
> 1 ½ quart water
>
> ½ teaspoon salt

Saute minced onion for 2 minutes, then cabbage. Simmer 3 minutes, then add umeboshi juice with its plums. Bring to a boil and add carrots, parsley, diced onion and bay leaf. Cover and simmer 10 minutes. Add water. Bring to a boil and allow to simmer while you prepare the following:

Roll herrings in pastry flour and fry in oil. You will later put them in the soup and simmer 10 minutes before serving.

For Piroshki use:

3 cups unbleached or pastry flour

1 egg (optional—makes a lighter dough)

1 cup water

1/3 teaspoon salt

1 teaspoon oil

1 pound herring fillet, ground (try the pickled variety)

2 tablespoons parsley, finely chopped

Stir egg and oil in water. Add other ingredients. Knead 5 minutes. The dough must be smooth and elastic. Allow to stand ½ hour to 1 hour. Roll out thin and cut into pieces 2 by 5 inches. Place mixture of ground fillet and parsley on dough and roll into small cigar-shapes approximately 2 inches long and 1 inch in diameter.

Make buckwheat croquettes (see recipe, page 202).

Serve in the following way:

First place fried herrings in the simmering soup, then add piroshki. To prevent the piroshki from opening in the soup, pinch ends with a fork or place in a colander and dip in soup. Fish and piroshki must stay in soup 10 minutes before removing.

In a dish place 2 or 3 piroshkis

1 buckwheat croquette

1 herring and

some vegetables.

Pour one ladle of juice over the ingredients. As a soup, serve on the side a bowl of the same juice.

MEXICO

Seis Cigarillos Para Seis Amigos.

Cigars stuffed with fish sold as tortillas in Mexico?

Friends who know the country well all replied, "Certainly," while confessing they had never seen such a dish. Not knowing anyone who might further enlighten me, I took the liberty of "inventing" something that looks Mexican. The cigarillos and flat tortillas layered with vegetables (called "tostados") are cousins at least of the Mexican variety.

For the tostado-filling use:

2 cups pinto beans, pressure-cooked in

6 cups water for 1 hour

½ teaspoon salt

The beans should be almost mushy when cooked.

1 cabbage, shredded

1 lettuce, shredded

1 onion, diced

½ cup sesame butter mixed with

1 cup water

¼ teaspoon salt

Boil water (2 quarts) and put in cabbage; 3 minutes later add lettuce. Leave 1 minute or so. Remove cabbage and lettuce and place in a large bowl. Add sesame mixture, 1 diced onion and salt. Mix well. Allow to cool.

Now prepare enough dough for tostados and cigarillos. (See recipe, page 262).

Use 12 cups of corn flour. You should obtain 30 tortillas, 7-8 inches in diameter. Reserve 18 for the tostados and 12 for the cigarillos.

To make tostados, place 1 tortilla in center of dish, smooth on layer of beans, top with another tortilla, add a layer of cabbage and lettuce and top with a third tortilla. It is ready to eat.

For the cigarillos use:

1 pound striped bass fillet, ground

1 clove garlic

1 tablespoon olive oil

2 tablespoons parsley, finely chopped

¼ cup water

¼ teaspoon salt

Saute garlic in oil until golden. Add parsley, simmer 1 minute, and add fish. Keep stirring over medium-high flame. Add water and salt and simmer 5 minutes.

On the uncooked tortilla place fish and form a cigar. Fry in 1/8-inch oil until brown. Serve individually wrapped in a lettuce leaf. Eat with fingers.

MOROCCO

Couscous.

Ideally, couscous should be cooked in a primitive earthenware steamer, but these no longer exist today. We use a square-shaped steamer from Japan, which I believe is best for the purpose. There are different sizes of couscous. Buy the medium; it is the size most commonly used in Morocco. Sold by weight or in boxes, you can find it in natural or gourmet food stores or in Armenian, Italian and Arabic shops. A one-pound box serves 5 - 6 people. Couscous is a meal in itself. Learn to enjoy it alone . . . without rice on the side. Serve it with a pickled salad and a light dessert.

For 6 - 8 people

1. 2 cups chickpeas presoaked overnight in lukewarm water

    4 quarts water to cook the chickpeas

2. 1 1/2 pound couscous

    2 tablespoons olive oil

    1 teaspoon salt

    1 cup lukewarm water

3. 6 carrots, cut into chunks

    2/3 butternut squash, cut into chunks

    2 turnips cut into chunks

    6 small onions, whole

    1/2 cabbage, shredded

    2 tablespoons oil

    2 1/2 teaspoons salt

Boil water with the presoaked chickpeas in a large enough pot that could hold all the vegetables enumerated above. We start with the chickpeas since they take the longest to cook. In the meantime, pour couscous into a large deep platter. Rinse it three times under running water as you would do for the rice:

Hold the platter with your left hand giving it a slant position, keeping the grains from falling with your right hand. After the third time, when all the water is out, allow the couscous to stand for 10 minutes in the platter, the grains will absorb the humidity that enrobs them. They will look bigger and fluffier. Add for every pound of couscous from 1 to 1 1/2 teaspoons of olive oil and roll the grains between the palms of your hands until each grain becomes separated. After the chick-peas have boiled for about 40 minutes, pour in the vegetables, add 2 tablespoons of olive oil and 2 1/2 teaspoons of salt. Put the couscous into the upper pot. Place the latter on top of the lower pot (3/4 full of water) and cook over a medium flame. The steam from the lower pot will penetrate the quarters of the upstairs tenants, thus cooking them. When the steam has heated the couscous, remove it to a large receptable and let it stand 10 to 15 minutes. Once again roll the couscous between the palms of your hands (ifyou can stand the heat), otherwise bruise with a wooden spoon. Keep stirring while you add slowly 2/3 cup lukewarm water and 1 flat teaspoon salt. Fluff with your fingers the couscous for a few minutes in an upward movement. When grains begin to fall like rain, add 1 teaspoon olive oil and roll in with your hands.

Return the couscous to the upper pot and resteam it for an additional 20 minutes. It is now ready, but it can be steamed over and over each time before serving.

Serve in this way:

Place the couscous in the middle of each individual dish. The grains should form a circle 7 inches in diameter and approximately 1/2 inch high. With a big serving spoon poke a large hole in the middle of the little mountain to form a crater. Now carefully place the vegetables in the heart of the volcano — 1 or 2 pieces of each vegetable and a scoop or two of chick-peas. Pour 1/2 cup of very hot juice over the couscous and vegetables.

Desserts

On Christmas no man shall partake a dinner
of more than three courses. . . . Nor shall the
olde habit of eating and making plumme
puddings and pies be followed, for these
heathenish things are abominable.

Parliament Law,
London, 1644

A few years ago, when young people used to visit our house to taste the food my wife had prepared, sentiments of friendship caused us to eat more desserts than we should have. I don't remember sitting down very often at a table set for only a few; there were usually half-a-dozen or more. I wish you such happy and plentiful meals.

I advise you to eat the foods in this section only occasionally. If you are a beginner and are in relatively good health—especially if you are an adventurer—enjoy them as often as you wish. Later you will be amazed at the increasing simplicity of your desires. Desserts will then be a "moment of moments," not just a mechanical punctuation at the end of a meal.

Summer delight.

3 apples, cut into 1/8-inch pieces

3 peaches, cut into medium pieces

2 cups strawberries

½ cup raisins

3 tablespoons arrow-root diluted in ½ cup water

½ cup apple juice

½ cup water

½ teaspoon salt

Lemon peel (grate 1 lemon)

Mix apple juice and water in a pot. Add salt and raisins, bring to a boil. Put in apples, allow to simmer 5 minutes, then add peaches and simmer for another 5 minutes. Sprinkle grated lemon peel over fruit and pour in diluted arrow-root. Cook for 5 more minutes. Put in strawberries. Turn off heat so that strawberries remain whole. Allow to cool before serving. Serves 6 to 12.

Variation.

3 apples

6 fresh plums with skins, cut in a cross at the top

2 cups cherries

Both of these recipes may be used as filling in pies. To thicken consistency, increase the amount of arrow-root.

Crêpe Fourrée à la Bechamel. (Stuffed crêpe)

> 6 crêpes
>
> 3 tablespoons raisins
>
> 2 cups apples, minced and sauteed in sesame oil (1 teaspoon)
>
> 2 tablespoons almonds, toasted and chopped
>
> For bechamel use:
>
> 3 tablespoons sweet rice flour or pastry
>
> 3 cups water
>
> 2 tablespoons apple spread
>
> 1 tablespoon sesame butter
>
> 1 small piece vanilla bean
>
> ¼ teaspoon salt

Mix all ingredients in a saucepan, bring to a boil and simmer 10 minutes.

To serve, line a few raisins, apples and toasted almonds on each crêpe. Roll up crêpe and place it in an individual dish. Cover with hot bechamel and eat with a little spoon. You may also serve the crêpes on a larger platter with the bechamel already crowning them.

Winter Compote.

> 6 apples, quartered
>
> ¼ cup raisins
>
> ¼ cup prunes
>
> 3/4 cup apple juice
>
> 1 tablespoon arrow-root
>
> Peel of half an orange, grated
>
> 1/3 teaspoon salt
>
> 3 tablespoons sesame seeds

Soak raisins and prunes overnight in ¼ cup salted apple juice. Oil a casserole pan and put the mixture in it. Arrange quartered apples over the mixture, sprinkle with orange peel and glaze with arrow-root diluted in some apple juice. Cover and bake in 350-degree oven for 30 minutes. Serve hot, garnished with toasted sesame seeds. Serves 6 to 12.

Variation:

> 3 apples, cut in quarters
>
> 3 pears, cut in quarters (small variety)

Apple Crisp.

> 6 large apples, sliced
>
> ½ cup oatmeal
>
> ½ cup w.w. flour
>
> ¼ cup sesame seeds
>
> ¼ cup ground nuts
>
> ¼ cup oil
>
> ½ teaspoon salt
>
> ¼ cup apple juice with pinch of salt and ¼ teaspoon cinnamon

In a bowl combine oatmeal, flour, sesame seeds, nuts, oil and salt to make a crumbly mixture. Arrange half the amount of apples in an oiled casserole pan and pour apple juice over them. Sprinkle half the crumbly mixture over the apples. Make a second layer out of the remaining apples and cover with the rest of the crumbly mixture. Bake in a 350-degree oven for 40 minutes. Serve hot or cooled.

Not recommended for a delicate stomach!

California Crisp.

>   4 large apples, chopped
>
>   ½ cup oatmeal
>
>   ½ cup brown rice flour
>
>   1 cup cooked barley (soft consistency)
>
>   ¼ cup raisins
>
>   ¼ cup ground nuts
>
>   1/3 cup oil
>
>   ½ teaspoon salt

Combine oatmeal, rice flour, barley, nuts, oil and salt. Mix into a dry but fluffy mixture. Arrange half the dry mixture in an oiled casserole pan and cover with apples and raisins. With the remaining mixture cover apples and raisins. Bake at 350 degrees for 40 minutes. Serve cooled, lightly covered with Sauce Moka (see recipe, page 349).

Blueberry Caught in Agar Agar. (Kanten)

>   ½ cup chopped raisins
>
>   ¾ cup blueberries
>
>   1 cup water
>
>   2 bars agar agar dissolved in
>
>   1 ½ cups apple juice
>
>   ¼ teaspoon salt

Put raisins and blueberries in water and bring to a boil. Simmer for 5 minutes. Add agar agar diluted in salted apple juice and, after a quick boil, simmer for 5 minutes. Pour into a square pan approximately 9 by 13. Cool. It will turn into a soft gelatine. Cut into squares.

Variation:

You may substitute blueberries with strawberries, cherries, blackberries, scoops of watermelon or melon. These fruits need not be cooked; as soon as the water boils, put them in and turn off the flame.

Aduki Kanten.

>   1 cup aduki beans
>
>   1 cup chestnuts
>
>   3 cups water
>
>   ¾ teaspoon salt
>
>   2 bars agar agar soaked in 1 ½ cups water

Pressure-cook adukis and chestnuts in 3 cups water for 1 ½ hours. Cook agar agar in its water. Mash aduki beans and chestnuts, add salt. Pour into agar agar. Simmer for 5 minutes. Pour into 6 individual bowls (or more). Allow to set in a cool place.

Chizuko's Custard. (Served at a dinner party in her house)

>   6 apples, peeled and cut into small pieces
>
>   2 cups strawberries
>
>   2 tablespoons kuzu or arrow-root
>
>   1 bar agar agar
>
>   2 cups apple juice
>
>   1 small piece vanilla bean
>
>   2 tablespoons tahini
>
>   ¼ teaspoon salt

Cook apples, strawberries, vanilla and salt in 1 cup apple juice. Simmer covered for 10 minutes. Blend with tahini in electric blender. Pour back into pot, add agar agar and kuzu dissolved in 1 cup apple juice. Cook for 5 minutes. Pour into a square dish. When cooled, put it into the freezer. After 1 hour beat the custard with an electric or hand mixer. Put back into freezer for 1 hour. Beat again before serving.

Kagetsu Ice Cream.

The Kagetsu is a beautiful restaurant in Seattle which serves excellent food. This ice-cream recipe was given to my wife by the cook.

> ½ cup Kohkoh (mixture of flours, available in natural-food stores)
>
> ¼ cup fine soya powder
>
> ½ cup dried apricots, chopped
>
> ½ cup raisins, chopped
>
> 2 bars agar agar
>
> 1 ½ cup apple juice
>
> ½ teaspoon salt

Soak raisins and apricots in 1 cup water for 1 hour. Cook for 10 minutes in the soaking water. Blend in an electric blender. In a bowl mix kohkoh, soya flour, salt and 2 cups water. Add agar agar soaked in apple juice. Blend with fruit mixture. Bring to a boil. Allow to simmer for 15 minutes over a low flame; it should be covered. Cool in a dish rinsed with cold water. Allow to set. Put in freezer. Remove after 1 hour and beat with an electric mixer. Put back into freezer for 1 more hour. Beat again before serving. It may be served in an ice-cream cone which recipe is given below.

Variation:

> ½ cup kohkoh
>
> 2 tablespoons soya powder
>
> 2 tablespoons brown rice flour
>
> 2 bars agar agar
>
> 1 cup apples, chopped
>
> ¼ cup raisins
>
> ¼ cup almonds, chopped
>
> 1 ½ cups chicory coffee

Follow the preceding recipe. Serve in individual dessert bowls or inside homemade ice-cream cones.

Ice-cream cones.

Roll out *puff dough* and cut into strips ¼ inch wide. Roll each strip around a metal cone obtained in a store that specializes in pastry supplies. Deep-fry the cones. Remove them from the metal forms and fill with an ice-cream of your choice.

Cherry Clafoutis.

> 1 cup cherries, cut in half
>
> ½ cup barley flour, slightly toasted
>
> 2 cups water
>
> 2 tablespoons tahini
>
> ¼ teaspoon salt
>
> A piece of vanilla bean
>
> Pinch of cinnamon
>
> 9 inch pie crust, already baked

In a pan blend flour, water, tahini, cherries, salt, vanilla and cinnamon. Cook for 20 minutes over a medium flame. Cool. Pour into the pie crust.

Variation:

Kohkoh may be used instead of barley flour.

Mister Scrooge. (Corn Pudding)

    1 cup cornmeal

    ½ cup brown rice flour

    6 apples, peeled and cooked in 1 cup water, then pureed

    ½ teaspoon salt

    2 cups water

    2 teaspoons tahini

    ½ cup raisins

    Pinch cinnamon

Mix all ingredients in a pan. Bring to a boil. Cover. Simmer for 20 minutes, stirring every once in a while, adding more water if mixture is too thick. When thoroughly cooked, pour into individual bowls or cups. Allow to set, unmold and serve with apple sauce or a sauce made with 2 glasses of apple juice and 1 tablespoon of arrow-root to thicken it. Pour apple sauce or this simple sauce over the pudding.

Yellow Pompidou.

    1 cup cooked brown rice

    1 tablespoon soya bean powder

    2 cups pureed squash

    1 bar agar agar

    1/3 teaspoon salt

    ½ cup toasted filbert nuts

    1 cup apple juice

Dissolve agar agar in apple juice. In a pan mix all ingredients. Bring to a boil. Cover and simmer for 15 minutes. Allow to cool. When it begins to thicken, turn into your favorite mold shape. Chill until firm. Serve topped with toasted nuts.

Variation:

Use 2 cups of pureed chestnut instead of squash.

The Fat Diplomat. (English plum pudding)

½ cup uncooked barley

¼ cup raisins

¼ cup prunes

½ cup currants

½ cup bread crumbs

2 tablespoons tahini

½ cup mixed nuts, chopped

1 cup carrots, grated

1 pinch cinnamon

1 pinch nutmeg

1/3 teaspoon salt

For the juice use:

2/3 cup water

1/3 cup apple juice

Peel of 1 orange

1 leaf of umeboshi plum (if there is no leaf in your jar, use 1 pit)

For the pudding, mix all ingredients in a large bowl, then place in the bottom of a 6" by 10" white cotton bag. The bag should be spacious enough to allow the barley to expand to 3 times its volume. Tie it at the top. Place the bag in a pressure cooker. Submerge in a mixture ot 2/3 water and 1/3 apple juice. To enhance the flavor introduce into the juice the grated peel of one orange, and to make it more alkaline add 1 leaf or 1 pit of umeboshi plum. Pressure cook for 1 hour. Can be served hot or cold, plain or with a sauce on top.

One Potato, Two Potato.

>2 cups sweet rice, pressure-cooked
>
>1 cup aduki beans, pressure-cooked with
>
>1 cup chestnuts, mashed together
>
>1/3 cup almonds, toasted and ground
>
>1/3 cup raisins, chopped fine
>
>¼ teaspoon cinnamon

All ingredients should be cooked. Take a small handful of rice, roll and form into cylinders rounded at the ends. Cover each one with the puree of chestnuts and aduki beans. Finally roll in the mixture of almonds, sesame seeds, raisins and cinnamon.

COOKIES

Oatmeal cookies.

>2 cups oatmeal (put through a blender to make it finer)
>
>½ cup walnuts, ground
>
>1/3 cup apple juice
>
>2 tablespoons oil
>
>½ teaspoon salt

Mix apple juice, oil and salt. Stir in the rest of the ingredients. The dough should be quite stiff. Separate into small balls. Flatten them on an oiled cookie sheet. Bake in 375-degree oven for 10 minutes or so.

Variation:

Use ½ cup of pureed squash, carrot, or parsnip instead of apple juice.

Oatmeal Cookies

3 cups rolled oats
1 cup wholewheat flour
¼ cup oil
¼ tsp cinnamon
½ cup raisins
¼ cup honey
1 tsp sea salt
½ tsp vanilla
2 cups warm water

Mix oats, flour, and oil in large mixing bowl, first with a spoon and then by rubbing mixture between hands until lumps are gone. Mix in cinnamon and raisins. Dissolve honey, salt and vanilla in warm water and add to dry ingredients, mixing thoroughly. Let mixture stand for 15-20 minutes and preheat oven to 350°.

(over)

Cookies Cheri.

      1 cup rice flour

      ½ cup almonds, chopped

      ½ cup sesame seeds, toasted

      4 tablespoons oil

      1 egg, slightly beaten

      2 tablespoons raisins soaked in 2 cups water and blended in an
          electric blender

      ¼ teaspoon salt

  Blend all ingredients. Make a stiff dough. Chill in the refrigerator (preferably overnight). Shape into very small balls. Flatten on an oiled cookie sheet. You may use the bottom of a glass for this purpose. Bake in a 350-degree oven for 10 minutes or until the cookies turn golden brown.

Petit Malin.

      1 cup oatmeal

      1 cup buckwheat flour

      ¼ cup raisins

      ½ cup sesame seeds

      4 tablespoons oil

      2/3 cup water

      ½ teaspoon salt

  In a bowl mix water, oil and salt. Stir in oatmeal and buckwheat flour. Add raisins and sesame seeds. Form into a ball which is then rolled out to a ¼-inch thickness. Cut into squares or diamonds. Place on an oiled cookie sheet; oil the surface of the cookies. Bake in a 375-degree oven for 15 minutes.

Willie Bars. (William Dufty's recipe)

> 1 cup cornmeal
>
> 1 cup w.w. pastry flour
>
> 1 cup wheatena (purchased in any grocery store)
>
> 1 cup oatflakes
>
> 2 tablespoons soya powder
>
> ¼ cup oil
>
> 1 cup sesame seeds, toasted
>
> ½ cup raisins, chopped and boiled in 3 ½ cups water and ½ teaspoon salt
>
> Grated lemon peel

Soak oatflakes and soya powder in raisin mixture for ½ hour. Add oil. Mix thoroughly, then stir in flours with rest of the ingredients. A heavy batter should be obtained. Allow to stand ½ hour. Pour batter into baking pans (thickness of the bars should not exceed 3/4 inch). Bake in a 375-degree oven for 15 minutes, then cut into squares and put back into oven for 15-20 minutes. When ready, they are very crumbly.

Biscuit d'Anne.

> 1 cup w.w. pastry flour
>
> ½ cup soya flour
>
> 3 apples, peeled, cut into small pieces and sauteed in 1 teaspoon oil
>
> Pinch cinnamon
>
> ¼ cup walnuts, chopped
>
> 2 tablespoons tahini
>
> 2 eggs, slightly beaten
>
> 1 cup apple juice
>
> ½ teaspoon salt
>
> ½ pound dried chestnuts, pressure-cooked in 3 cups water and pureed

In a bowl mix all ingredients except chestnut puree. Pour batter into the bottom of an oiled pan, 8" by 12". Place a layer of chestnut puree over the mixture and bake in a 375-degree oven for 30-40 minutes.

Biscuit d'Yvette.

> 4 cups brown rice flour
>
> 2 cups w.w. pastry flour
>
> 3 eggs
>
> ½ cup carrots, chopped
>
> ½ cup apples, chopped
>
> Handful currants
>
> ¼ cup almonds, chopped
>
> ½ cup sesame seeds, toasted
>
> ½ cup oil
>
> 1 ½ teaspoons salt

Mix all ingredients into a heavy batter, adjusting the amount of water accordingly. Pour into a cake pan and bake in a 375-degree oven for 1 hour.

Variation:

Eggs are used in the batter to lighten the consistency of your cake. If you would rather avoid them, substitute 1/3 teaspoon dried yeast diluted in a small amount of warm water. Allow to rise overnight.

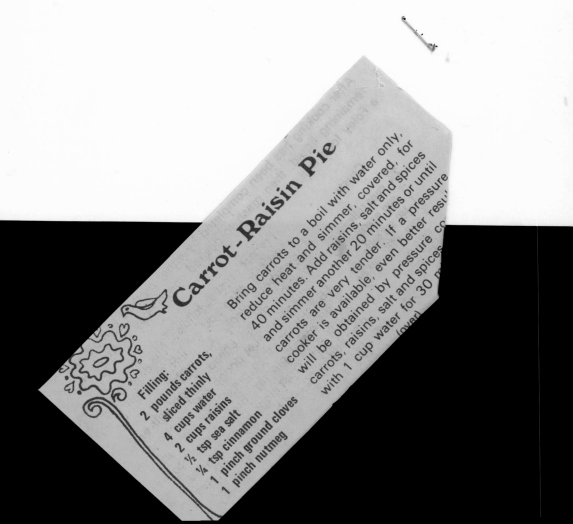

Carrot-Raisin Pie

Bring carrots to a boil with water only, reduce heat and simmer, covered, for 40 minutes. Add raisins, salt and spices and simmer another 20 minutes or until carrots are very tender. If a pressure cooker is available, even better results will be obtained by pressure cooking carrots, raisins, salt and spices with 1 cup water for 30 p
(over)

Filling:
2 pounds carrots, sliced thinly
4 cups water
2 cups raisins
2 tsp sea salt
½ tsp cinnamon
¼ tsp ground cloves
1 pinch nutmeg

Chestnut Muffins.

> 1 ½ cups chestnut flour
>
> 1 ½ cups oatmeal
>
> 1 cup w.w. pastry flour
>
> 2 tablespoons soya flour
>
> ¼ cup oil
>
> ½ cup raisins, chopped
>
> ½ cup toasted sesame seeds
>
> 2 cups water
>
> ½ teaspoon salt
>
> 1 teaspoon Pero Coffee
>
> ½ teaspoon orange peel, grated

In a bowl mix water, oil and salt. Beat thoroughly. Stir in all other ingredients. The dough should be soft and sticky. If too dry, add ½ cup apple juice. Cover with a wet cloth. Allow to stand overnight. In the morning work the batter well again. Pour into oiled muffin tins. Bake in a 350-degree oven for 50 minutes or 1 hour.

Bûche de Noel. (Yule Log)

The preparation of this dessert may take some time. Nevertheless, it is worth it.

> 3 w.w. pastry flour waffles kept whole, measuring approximately 5" by 9"
>
> 6 large apples, peeled, cooked and pureed
>
> 1 pound chestnuts, pressure-cooked in 3 cups water, pureed
>
> 1 cup almonds, toasted and chopped
>
> 1 cup of coffee jello *(moka sauce:* see recipe, page 349)
>
> 3 cups water, boiled with orange peel in it

Soak waffles in orange-flavored water for ½ hour. Place one waffle at the bottom of a serving platter. Pour over it ½ of the pureed apples. If consistency is too thin, thicken with arrow-root and chill before using. Place another waffle above the apple puree. Spread chestnut puree over this second waffle; sprinkle with ½ cup toasted almonds. Cover a third waffle and spread abundantly with the remaining apple sauce. Set aside ½ hour, then spread with the left-over chestnut puree. Place the *bûche* in the refrigerator to chill for approximately 3 hours, or put in the freezer ½ hour. Just before serving, glaze with sauce moka and decorate with remaining nuts. Cut into squares.

Apple Dumplings.

> 2 ¼ cups w.w. pastry flour or unbleached flour
>
> ½ teaspoon salt
>
> 2/3 cup oil, chilled
>
> 6-8 tablespoons water
>
> 6 medium-size apples
>
> 6 teaspoons tahini
>
> 3 teaspoons raisins

Core the apples, fill each one with 1 teaspoon tahini, ½ teaspoon raisins and a pinch of salt. In a bowl, rapidly mix flour, salt, oil and water. Form a dough. Knead it for a little while and roll it out. Cut into 8 inch squares. Place an apple on each dough square. Moisten the edges of dough. Pinch the corners together, pressing at the top to enclose the apple completely. Press all edges as well. If you wish, you may glaze the top of the dumplings with egg yolk. Bake in a 450-degree oven for 15 minutes. Reduce the heat to 350 and cook for 30 minutes more. The dumpling may be served hot, as is, or with your favorite dessert sauce.

PIES

For pie crusts refer to the chapter entitled "Flours Make Wonderful Things."

For fillings try the following:
> Pureed squash topped with toasted oat flakes
>
> Pureed chestnuts and adukis topped with chopped, toasted al-
> monds
>
> Pureed carrots, glazed with raisins, blended and thickened with
> arrow-root
>
> Apple-sauce sprinkled with raw rice cream and placed in oven
> for a few extra minutes to let the rice cream cook

50 Tuxedo. (Mrs. Semark's recipe)

For this pie use the puff dough.

½ cup aduki beans, half-cooked, still hard but edible

1 cup fresh plums, pitted and cut in half

3 apples, peeled, sliced and sauteed in 1 teaspoon oil

1/3 cup raisins

¼ teaspoon salt

Prepare dough for a double crust. Roll out the bottom crust, a circle 9 inches in diameter. Place it at the bottom of the pie dish. Spread the aduki beans. Cover with plums, then with slices of apples and raisins mixed. Cover with top crust. Press edges with a fork. Prick small holes in the surface. Bake in a 375-degree oven for ½ hour.

Strawberry Royale.

Use *pie shell* recipe for crust.

1/3 cup oat flakes, soaked and cooked in 1 cup water

3 cups strawberries, soaked in salted water

2 tablespoons arrow-root

1 cup water

½ cup apple juice

Peel of one lemon, grated

¼ teaspoon salt

Bake the pie shell. When cooled, spread oat cream over it. Arrange 1 ½ cups uncooked strawberries in the shell. In a saucepan mix the remaining soaked strawberries, water, apple juice, salt, lemon peel and arrow-root. Cook and keep stirring, or cook the mixture without arrow-root; when it boils, add diluted arrow-root in water. Allow to cool. Chill. Glaze the pie with this mixture.

Apple Strudel.

Use puff dough.

3 cups apples, peeled and cut into small pieces

¼ teaspoon salt

3/4 cup ground almonds

½ cup raisins, soaked in ½ cup water

½ cup bread crumbs

1 teaspoon grated lemon rind

1 tablespoon tahini

1/3 teaspoon cinnamon

1 teaspoon sesame oil

In a pan saute apples in sesame oil for approximately 3 minutes, then add raisins, nuts and salt. Saute for 2 minutes. On a floured piece of cloth, roll out pie dough as thin as possible. The shape should be rectangular. At one end, covering approximately 1/3 of the surface of this pie dough, spread apple mixture, over which you can sprinkle lemon rind and cinnamon. Spread tahini over the remaining 2/3 of the surface, using an oil brush. Top tahini paste with bread crumbs. Raise cloth and roll up strudel, beginning with the filled side and guiding it with the other hand. Place strudel in an oiled baking pan. Brush its top with oil or egg yolk. Bake at 400 for 30-40 minutes until brown and crisp.

Variation:

Replace the apple filling with the following:

1- 3 cups cherries, pitted

2- 2 cups apples and 1 cup raspberries

3- 3 cups blueberries

Introducing tahini and bread crumbs into a strudel is of great advantage, because these two ingredients help the layers of rolled dough separate from each other and therefore make the strudel lighter, flakier and crisper. You may also roll into small individual strudels.

Dufties.

      1 ½ cups chestnut flour

      ½ cup w.w. pastry flour

      2 tablespoons arrow-root

      ½ cup raisins, soaked in 2/3 cup water, then blended

      1/3 teaspoon salt

In a bowl mix flours, salt, raisins, and raisin-juice, then make a soft dough. Knead for 5 minutes. Cover and let stand overnight. Before using, knead again, then roll out into a sheet 1/8-inch thick. With a glass cut out rounds. In the center of each round cut out a thimble-sized hole. The result is a doughnut shape. Deep-fry each Dufty in oil. They will puff up. Serve hot, alone or with a custard.

Chestnut Aura. (Japanese recipe)

      3 medium butternut squash, peeled and cut into pieces

      12 whole chestnuts

      1 cup aduki beans, pressure-cooked and mashed

      2 cups w.w. flour

      ½ teaspoon salt

      1 teaspoon oil

      ½ teaspoon lemon rind, grated.

Boil the chestnuts in water until tender, but still firm.

Saute pieces of squash in oil, add ½ cup water, cover and cook until tender. Then mash into puree. When cool, add flour, lemon rind and salt. Mix to ear-lobe consistency. Form balls of 1 ½ inches, then flatten into patties. Make smaller balls with aduki puree. Put 1 chestnut inside the aduki balls, then wrap the squash patty around the aduki ball. Deep fry. Serve hot.

Marmelade.

> 2 pounds apples, unpeeled and cut into pieces
>
> 1 cup water
>
> Orange peel from one orange, cut into thin matchsticks
>
> ¼ teaspoon salt

Mix all ingredients in a saucepan, cover and cook for 2/3 hours, then pass mixture through a vegetable mill. Put back in the saucepan to cook 1 hour more, until a thick consistency is obtained. Use marmelade as a spread on crackers or as filling for crepes. Use a very low flame; otherwise, it will burn!

Quick Filling.

> 1 cup apple juice
>
> 1 tablespoon arrow-root
>
> 1/3 teaspoon lemon rind, grated (or orange rind)

Mix ingredients in pan, bring to a boil and simmer 3 minutes. Allow to cool. Serve on puddings, pies, pancakes, etc.

Sauce Moka.

> 1 cup water
>
> 2 tablespoons apple spread
>
> 2 teaspoons Pero Coffee (or chicory, dandelion, etc.)
>
> 1/3 teaspoon salt
>
> Handful of currants
>
> A piece of vanilla bean
>
> 1 tablespoon arrow-root

Mix all ingredients in a saucepan, bring to a boil and simmer for 3 minutes. Allow to cool. Serve over custards, pancakes, pies and cakes. Sprinkle with toasted nuts.

The Nutty Orange. (Sauce Orientale)

  2 cups almonds

  1 tablespoon orange rind

  2 tablespoons tahini

  1 ½ cups apple juice

  Pinch of salt

Mix all ingredients in a blender. When mixture is smooth, it is ready to be served on puddings, baked apples, individual pies, etc.

The traveller's pack

"When travelling, what should I eat and where? I am an actor, a carpenter, a mechanic, a salesman, constantly on the road. How can I find the time and wherewithal to fix myself lunch or dinner in a hotel room?"

In the case of my own family, solving such problems was a fun-filled adventure. At the outset we used to worry a bit before moving even a few hundred miles; now we have developed techniques of avoiding any kind of trouble at all. For Americans, used to immediate, automatic service wherever they go, I imagine the problems might seem insurmountable at first. However, I have met many who manage even better than we do, perhaps because they travel more and have therefore had to create revolutionary "techniques of the road." In any event, there are now so many restaurants in America serving brown rice and vegetables, you may not find it difficult at all to eat well while on the road.

Let us begin with a simple trip of a few hundred miles. If the journey is to last one day, the following is what you should carry with you:

Chapati
Nori sandwich (rice balls)
Sauteed carrots and onions
Bancha tea in a thermos

Bring bowls, chopsticks, knife and paper cups. See recipe for chapati, page 262. For nori sandwich, see page 48. For miso spread recipe (in case you prefer bread to chapati), see page 236.

If you should be taking a longer trip, prepare similar food for the second day; it won't spoil. For succeeding days, however, you'll have to find a motel with a kitchen (the management may allow you to use its personal facilities). Here is what you can prepare quickly:

Soba noodles
Rice for two days
Sauteed vegetables
Bancha tea
Perhaps more chapati, if you wish something chewy

Soba can be sauteed in oil with scallions. Don't expect it to keep long without spoiling. Preferably, eat it in the motel or in the few hours immediately following departure. Soba is excellent as a change-of-pace.

If you have children, bring along rice crackers made by Spiral Foods; they're especially good with miso spread.

Carry the following utensils with you:

Pressure-cooker
Skillet
Medium-sized saucepan
Wooden spoon or spatula
Giant chopsticks for cooking

Don't forget rice, noodles (always practical), miso, sesame butter, soya sauce and sesame salt. Remember oil for sauteing vegetables, or for creating a delicious journeyman's tempura.

If you should decide not to cook in a motel, or even prepare a little something in advance of your trip, this is what you can do:

In a natural-food store buy whole-wheat bread, sesame butter or tahini, miso and two or three bags of rice crackers. Consider these items your staples. Whatever else you need may be found in a restaurant, where you can order sword-fish, flounder with vegetables or a simple plate of noodles. If the menu contains none of these, choose whatever suits you best. An upset stomach can be remedied by taking a salted plum (umeboshi). In the beginning, all this may seem a bit complicated but, after a while, it will be rewarding, especially in terms of better health.

If you are travelling by plane and are headed for a hot climate, you will have an opportunity to test your brand-new knowledge relating to foods and change of locale. Be careful not to eat locally-grown fruits immediately. Your body is still cold. If you have come for a vacation, try to adapt yourself by boiling the fruits. Eat them raw later, and sparingly. If you have moved permanently to Florida or Southern California, take your time. Let your body acclimatize itself gradually. Eat almost as you did before in, say, New York. Introduce a smidgeon of fresh salad. Eat more vegetables but continue enjoying rice at least once a day. Your body will tell you when it's time to change your diet. It may be next month, or even next year.

The most important thing about doing your own cooking while travelling is that you will develop great self-confidence. Succeeding in the creation of a well-balanced meal between your arrival on a bus and your departure on a plane, is an ultimate act of respect for your body and mind. What you thus give to yourself is a finer blessing than any teacher could ever impart.

The Ten Commandments of Health

Doctor Kenzo Futagil M.D., used to give his patients and disciples these commandments for health:

Eat less and chew well,
Ride less and walk often,
Have fewer clothes and launder often,
Worry less and work harder,
Waste less time and continue to learn,
Talk less and listen more,
Frown less and laugh often,
Speak less and act more,
Blame less and praise others,
Take less and give a hundred times over.

He lived a hundred years.

Epilogue

Why, since we so rarely use them in our home, have I included so many spices and eggs in my recipes? The answer is simply this: I like to tell and to be told good stories, and in every story there comes a moment when you need to add a little spice to make it more dramatic, more real. A storyteller may not require spices to live by, but he cannot spin exhilarating tales, without them. Anyway, it isn't that we *never* use spices in our home; we do, but only occasionally.

Some of Lima Ohsawa's recipes, in which she uses eggs, have been included in this book. This has been done so that you may more deeply understand what I hope you already know—namely, that there are two ways to teach; one by saying, "Do not," and the other by saying, "Do."

* * *

358

Years ago I couldn't help worrying about the young people whose concepts and creations were built upon terribly weak foundations. Their constructs seemed to spring from fear. They resembled the modern novelist who often displays his inhibitions on paper, seeking verbally a fuller expression of his life. Instead of creating a real existence, he invents a fiction in which he identifies himself with a lifeless ideal.

And so with the young, who grow without roots, their minds a clutter of frightful dreams. Any door that opens is eagerly entered, be it that of a new religion, a new movement, or a current political ideal. For lack of sane and homogeneous thought they grasp at whatever catches the eye—like crows gathering bits of shiny glass—their judgments utterly superficial. Gradually losing their human qualities, they are assuming the characteristics of a generation of robots.

In New York City new movements and even newer ideas have proliferated to such an extent, and have enmeshed so many souls in their dogmas, that it is becoming increasingly difficult to find a free man anywhere. As I write these lines, young people by the hundreds are committing themselves to "masters" who provide "answers" to all questions. The young are afraid, desperately afraid. Schools are vestibules in which tomorrow's androids twiddle their thumbs in boredom; the professions are adjusted only to the sensorial needs of the nation; and Man is nowadays worn out after thirty years of drudgery. He is a horse who plods along faithfully for a rider who cares nothing about his fatigue, his fear, his larger quests. Is it any wonder that he sometimes bucks with rage, or takes the bit in his teeth and runs wild?

Women are fearful, too. They are being held responsible for the mentally retarded children to whom they are giving birth. The contraceptives, tranquilizers, soft drinks and thousands of chemical compounds they swallow daily are, in a diabolical cadence, producing strange creatures who terrify them. Their judgments are so twisted that they forbid their children to follow a natural diet. They believe, poor creatures, that the pills and products of modern-day laboratories are an equivalent of tradition; it is as though America, unable to possess what is old, were in reaction clinging fanatically to what is new, adopting it as its most reliable and trustworthy ancestor.

* * *

I was a Don Quixote, born a bit late into a "psychological era," who took for Dulcinea the first girl who could tell him a good story. And years ago America did tell me that story. But once here on this continent I found that my first whispers of love had changed into reprimands—as often happens with a most cherished person or ideal. In place of sweet words and blandishments prepared with affection over the years, I uttered instead cruel criticisms. It was *her* fault! *She* had asked for it! *She* wouldn't slacken her unceasing demands for material and moral comfort! Ah, America. . . .

But I don't know if I worry so much anymore about what is happening. Perhaps it's that I am growing used to the pain, or that things after all are proceeding fairly well.

At any rate, today my tool is food. About tomorrow I can't say because I don't know what Man will be eating. But if I write another book (and already I am thinking about it), what will it be like? Will it be a third cookbook? I wouldn't mind! In these times of chaos and ill-health, a recipe is as beneficial an offering to Man as the most profound or poetic words.

Recipe Index

Tamari = soya sauce